REGENT'S UNIVERSITY LIBRARY

17028285

REGENT'S
UNIVERSITY LONDON

**Park Campus
Library**

D1612035

REGENT'S
UNIVERSITY LONDON
WITHDRAWN

Superbrands®

Annual 2016

REGENT'S
UNIVERSITY LONDON

Superbrands.uk.com

SCIENCE MUSEUM
ACC No:
CLASS

REGENT'S UNIVERSITY LONDON
ACC No. 1702 8285
CLASS 658.827 SuP

Chief Executive
Ben Hudson

Brand Liaison Directors
Liz Silvester
Daren Thomas

Brand Liaison Manager
Amanda Gilbert

Social Media Manager
Jessica Riches

Head of Accounts
Will Carnochan

Editor
Jennifer Brough

Copywriter
Karen Dugdale

Proofreader
Angela Cooper

Designer
Ami Sunners

Also available from Superbrands UK:
CoolBrands® 2015/16
ISBN: 978-0-9932998-0-3

To order further books, email
brands@superbrands.uk.com
or call 020 7079 3310.

Published by
Superbrands (UK) Ltd
4 Great Portland Street
London
W1W 8QJ

© 2016 Superbrands (UK) Ltd

All rights reserved.

No part of this publication may be reproduced
or transmitted in any form by any means,
electronic, digital or mechanical, including
scanning, photocopying, recording or any
information storage and retrieval system relating
to all or part of the text, photographs, logotypes
without first obtaining permission in writing
from the publisher of the book together with the
copyright owners as featured.

Printed in Italy

ISBN: 978-0-9932998-1-0

MIX
Paper from
responsible sources
FSC® C015829

Contents

CONTENTS

KEY
Ⓑ Business Superbrands
Ⓒ Consumer Superbrands

Endorsements

Martin Glenn

CEO
The Football Association

For all we read about how digital media has wrought a sea of change in marketing and how the increasingly savvy consumer can see through and decode brands, I always look forward to the certainty of the Superbrands Annual. I love the fact that it's called an 'annual', which for marketeers of a certain age are things that were a staple of Christmas past that have slowly and steadily disappeared from the stockings of today's Christmas present. But it's not the title that is cause for celebration, but the fact that in this over-communicated and shrinking world, good brands have a big role to play in terms of providing points of certainty and trust. All the brands represented in the annual make people's lives easier and more pleasant; each brand would be sorely missed if it weren't there. When you think about it, there probably isn't a better accolade for a brand than that, but let's hear it for the annual whose certain and predicable perennial appearance makes for some welcome certainty in what is, for sure, a more chaotic world.

Scott Knoxx

Managing Director
Marketing Agencies Association

Securing a place in the Superbrands annual is a true accolade because it's a publication that recognises the brands that are the most dynamic, exciting and entrepreneurial in the market.

Due to the twin transforming forces of technology and globalisation, Superbrands aren't necessarily those that adapt and evolve more swiftly than others. They understand that building strong connections with real people, with the public, are vital in today's business culture.

Representing a trade body that operates under the banner '#DoDifferent', I recognise that Superbrands have the motivation to behave differently within their organisations and embrace change rather than fearing it.

From my perspective, talking to marketing agencies and advertisers on a daily basis, it's become apparent that to achieve and maintain this spirit requires collaboration with both business partners and customers on a constant basis. This open-minded approach is now the only true route to Superbrands status.

John Noble

Director
British Brands Group

This collection of Superbrands reminds us how brands permeate so many aspects of our lives, but also how we have our favourites while some barely touch us at all. We may be familiar with them and be confident they deliver, but somehow they are just 'not for me'.

This reinforces how brands are deeply personal, built in each of our minds over time in response to our specific personal needs, individual preferences – and no doubt prejudices – as well as a lifetime of experiences. It is remarkable to consider that we connect with some at both a rational and emotional level and have been doing so for decades. Those really are the Superbrands.

Consistency of brand promise and continuous behaviour in line with brand values must be two forces that, in particular, forge these long-term connections. The companies that achieve them deserve our applause.

We are delighted to support this edition of Superbrands and be reminded just how important our role is in striving to shape a policy climate in the UK where they can be sustained and thrive.

Sherilyn Shackell

Founder
The Marketing Academy

One of the things that unites all of the Superbrands featured in this annual is their ability to connect with the customer on a level that goes far beyond the traditional supply and demand model. In today's market, the customer demands much more from the companies they engage with and want to see evidence that the brands they are buying from have a strong sense of purpose and values.

The organisations that do more than pay lip service to 'doing good' and authentically demonstrate how much they care about their impact on the world are the ones succeeding in today's competitive market place. The most successful brands are those who show they are listening to what the customer cares about and a desire to communicate transparently about brands, products, values and their purpose, makes the difference.

Brands need to connect with their customers on a deep and personal level, through their advertising, delivering of the brand promise and providing flawless customer experience. Brands that get this right, as evidenced by the companies featured here, deserve to be elevated to Superbrand status.

About
Superbrands

First published in 1995, the Superbrands books showcase some of the strongest consumer and B2B brands in Britain and establish how they have managed to achieve such phenomenal success. The 2016 Annual explores the history, development and achievements of some of these much-loved brands, with each case study providing valuable insights into their branding strategy and resulting work.

Brands do not apply or pay to be considered for Superbrands status. Rather, the accolade is awarded to the country's strongest brands following a rigorous and independent selection process; full details are provided in the Appendix.

Superbrands was launched in London in 1995 and is now a global business operating in more than 50 countries worldwide. Further details can be found at Superbrands.uk.com.

Travel with confidence

abta.com

ABTA is the UK's largest travel association representing around 1,200 travel agents and tour operators that sell £32 billion of holidays and other travel arrangements each year. ABTA's purpose is to support and promote a thriving and sustainable travel and tourism industry. The ABTA brand stands for support, protection and expertise. These qualities are core, as they help ensure that ABTA Members' customers travel with confidence.

Market
The products ABTA Members offer reflect the diversity of the UK travel market from overseas and domestic package holidays to independent and business travel arrangements. Over 90 per cent of package holidays sold in the UK are provided by ABTA Members, along with millions of other types of bookings, from hotels and villas to flights and business travel. UK holidaymakers were estimated to have taken more than 38 million foreign holidays in 2015, with package holidays representing approximately half of these.

Product
ABTA helps its Members and their customers navigate their way through today's travel landscape by raising standards in the industry; offering schemes of financial protection; providing an independent complaints resolution service should something go wrong; giving guidance on issues from sustainability to health and safety, as well as presenting a united voice to the Government to ensure the industry and the public get a fair deal.

Achievements
During its 65-year history, ABTA has a track record of leading the travel industry in improving standards and shaping its response to developing regulatory change.

Through proactive policy and lobbying work in the UK and Europe over a number of years, ABTA has led the call for the creation of a simplified, proportionate, and deliverable system of consumer protection for holidays within the UK, to benefit both consumers and the industry.

In 2011, ABTA was a founding member of the Fair Tax on Flying Campaign whose work helped to raise awareness of levels of Air Passenger Duty in the UK, resulting in Government action to reduce overall levels of the Duty.

DID YOU KNOW?
Over 74 per cent of people expect their holiday company to be a Member of ABTA.

ABTA recently restructured its customer support services to improve complaint-handling capability, and became the first travel industry body to be approved by the Trading Standards Institute for its Alternative Dispute Resolution scheme.

Recent Developments
The last five years have seen very considerable changes in the structure of the industry, which bring new challenges and opportunities for the organisation. ABTA's strategic goal is to strengthen its position and reach within the UK and to become a premium supplier to the international travel industry of the future and its consumers.

Given the level of regulatory change impacting the industry, ABTA's goal is to ensure it remains at the heart of financial protection for holiday arrangements, following the Package Travel Directive and Air Travel Organisers' Licensing review by European and UK government.

ABTA is further developing its 'Travel with confidence' brand, for holidaymakers and business travellers and extending the scope of consumer services offered.

The ABTA strategy is to strengthen its position at the international forefront of travel and tourism sustainability. At the heart of its sustainability strategy will be the continued rollout of Travelife as the preferred management tool and accreditation system for travel organisers and their supply chains.

Promotion

At the end of 2014, ABTA overhauled its messaging and brand position for consumers under the new banner of 'Travel with confidence'.

Following a series of focus groups with consumers and front line staff from a number of ABTA Members, feedback highlighted ABTA's unique position in providing confidence at the heart of travel. The aim was to better reflect this in its messaging, identity and communications. The outcomes resulted in a series of recommendations aimed at helping to improve consumers' understanding of ABTA and what it offers them, as well as highlighting the importance of looking for the logo when booking a holiday.

ABTA launched the new 'Travel with confidence' strapline and messaging via a programme of Member and staff engagement, and ran a print advertising campaign in January and June 2015 telling consumers 'We see travel from your point of view'.

DID YOU KNOW?
60 per cent of people think less positively of companies that are not ABTA Members.

ABTA has also runs a number of consumer awareness campaigns in partnership with organisations as diverse as the Foreign & Commonwealth Office, the City of London Police and Get Safe Online. Campaigns have included highlighting the importance of buying adequate travel insurance, preparing for ski holidays and swimming safety. Its fraud awareness campaign has achieved extensive coverage across major media outlets, broadcast, print and online.

73% 👍
OF PEOPLE FEEL MORE CONFIDENT BOOKING WITH AN ABTA MEMBER

Brand History

1950	The Association of British Travel Agents is founded by 22 leading travel companies.
1955	ABTA merges with the Institute of Travel Agents (ITA) to form the Association of British Travel Agents and Institute of Travel Agents Ltd.
1959	The first tour operators are admitted as affiliated Members.
1960	The first Code of Conduct is formally adopted at ABTA's AGM.
1965	ABTA sets up a fund to help repatriate stranded holidaymakers, refund deposits, or provide alternative holidays.
	Tour operators become full Members.
1987	A new logo is introduced.
1988	ABTA Benevolent Fund is established.
1993	ABTA Insurance Company is set up to provide shortfall insurance for tour operators.
1996	The travel Industry Partner scheme launches.
2007	The company change its name from Association of British Travel Agents Ltd to ABTA Ltd. A new logo introduced.
2008	ABTA and the Office of Fair Trading work together to eliminate misleading price advertising.
	ABTA and the Federation of Tour Operators amalgamate.
2014	ABTA launches its new consumer strapline and messaging, 'Travel with confidence'.

Brand Values
The ABTA brand stands for support, protection and expertise. This means consumers have confidence in ABTA and a strong trust in ABTA's Members. These qualities are core as they ensure that holidaymakers remain confident in the holiday products that they buy from ABTA Members.

amecfw.com

Amec Foster Wheeler is a global player in energy and related markets, with a proud 150-year heritage of delivery. The result is a 40,000-strong team offering engineering, project management, operations and construction services, project delivery and specialised power equipment services in more than 55 countries.

Oil & Gas

Clean Energy

Market

Amec Foster Wheeler designs, delivers and maintains strategic and complex assets across oil and gas, mining, clean energy, power generation, pharmaceutical, environment and infrastructure markets. Its work extends from environmental and engineering design at the start of a project, through to decommissioning at the end of an asset's life.

Product

In Oil & Gas, its largest market, Amec Foster Wheeler operates across the whole value chain – from production through to the refining, processing and distribution of derivative products. In the upstream market, it has capability in offshore and onshore oil and gas production and processing facilities.

Amec Foster Wheeler has extensive experience across all phases of liquefied

natural gas and gas monetization. In the downstream market it works on new-builds, major expansions and revamps, and owns leading refining and residue upgrading technologies. Amec Foster Wheeler has more than 60 years of experience in the chemicals industry.

The Environment & Infrastructure (E&I) teams provide services to all of the markets with skills that are transferable across customers in the water, transportation/ infrastructure, government and industrial/ commercial sectors. Amec Foster Wheeler provides compliance and due diligence services, ranging from geotechnical and environmental to materials and water resources consulting.

In its Mining markets, Amec Foster Wheeler works in a diverse range of commodities,

Environmental & Infrastructure

Mining

including potash, iron ore, copper and gold, offering mining consultancy including ore resource estimation, mine planning and feasibility studies, design, project and construction management services and has whole-life service capabilities, with a strong emphasis on managing emissions and discharges.

Amec Foster Wheeler's Clean Energy offering is wide-ranging. In renewables, it provides a full service engineering, procurement and construction solution for wind, solar, biomass and biofuels projects. Its nuclear capability has developed over 60 years, positioning it to support the full lifecycle of nuclear energy, from new build and reactor support to decommissioning and waste management. In transmission and distribution, its experience stretches from traditional power and gas networks to the latest carbon capture and storage technologies.

Its Global Power Group is rated the number one global market position, offering a full range of combustion and steam generation equipment, clean air technologies, aftermarket products and services to the power, industrial, and waste-to-energy sectors.

Achievements

In 2015, Amec Foster Wheeler won over 14,000 new contracts and more than 1,500 new customers including provision of engineering services for the expansion of the Çöpler Gold Mine in Turkey, which combines its gold-processing expertise with its Turkish operation's successful project delivery track record in the region.

The ability to offer integrated solutions across clients' asset lifecycle in the E&I market differentiates Amec Foster Wheeler. In Africa, E&I worked with one of its largest Oil & Gas clients to complete a large-scale remediation of an acid tar site, which entailed neutralisation, stabilisation and encapsulation of acid tar refinery waste in a lined and capped containment cell.

Another example is the Samcheok green power project, which marks a significant development in clean coal power combining advanced technology experience with Amec Foster Wheeler's capabilities in delivering large-scale quality projects.

Recent Developments

Amec Foster Wheeler has recently refreshed its internal global Academy, which helps it attract, train and retain talent to ensure it continues to serve customers to the highest standard.

The company launched its new sustainability strategy focusing on solving tomorrow's natural resource challenges. This is underpinned by three pillars that are key to making a positive social and environmental impact: people, innovation, delivery.

Amec Foster Wheeler has also rebuilt its early careers website, investing in the engineers of tomorrow to take forward business, sustainable solutions and ideas.

DID YOU KNOW?
Amec Foster Wheeler provided boilers for the Royal Yacht Britannia.

Promotion

Amec Foster Wheeler's new identity embodies a bright sense of purpose – Connected Excellence – bringing together skills, knowledge and expertise from across the global network to deliver excellence for stakeholders.

Amec Foster Wheeler combines traditional and innovative media in its award-winning external and internal communications, brand

Amec Foster Wheeler has reached
21,000
beneficiaries across
17 COUNTRIES
with SOS Children's Villages

and marketing initiatives. Using multiple languages and creative technology, it promotes the knowledge, expertise and skills of its people globally, regionally and locally.

Brand History

1848	Matthew Hall opens a lead work business in Lambeth (becoming an early UK specialist in plumbing and sanitation).
1883	Leonard Fairclough starts a stone business in the UK.
1884	The Water Works Supply Company is created by the Foster family.
1891	Wheeler Condenser & Engineering Company is established.
1913	William Press & Son is founded.
1927	Foster Wheeler Corporation (FWC) is formed from a merger of two US companies.
1929	FWC is first listed on the New York Stock Exchange.
1939	Matthew Hall & Co exceeds £1 million turnover and employs 2,700 people.
1960	William Press establishes Costain & Press to undertake mechanical works for oil companies overseas.
1982	William Press and Fairclough construction groups merge to form AMEC plc.
1988	Matthew Hall Group of Companies, operating from the UK, Australia, Holland and the US, employing 10,000 people, is brought into AMEC group.
1993	AMEC plc is listed on the London Stock Exchange.
2005	Foster Wheeler is relisted on the Nasdaq Stock Exchange.
2014	AMEC and Foster Wheeler combine on 13th November.

Brand Values

Amec Foster Wheeler's strong core values underpin the way it does business. It connects globally as one team and delivers on its promises. Sustainability and integrity are important, as is putting safety first. Amec Foster Wheeler believes in treating people with respect, including employees, customers and those in the communities in which it works.

arco®

arco.co.uk

Experts in Safety

Arco is the UK's leading safety company, distributing quality products and delivering training and expert advice to help keep people safe at work. Founded in 1884, with a heritage spanning four generations, Arco integrates traditional family values with pioneering innovation to offer a world-class range of more than 170,000 quality assured products.

Market

Since the company was first formed, Arco has continued to evolve, and today plays a leading role in shaping the UK safety agenda. Arco is the leading brand in the safety business, putting people and their well-being at the centre of everything it does. Arco offers training and consultancy services, managing customers' risks and provides personal protective equipment and workplace solutions to ensure safety in the workplace.

Arco understands that each industry has its own hazards and specific needs when it comes to safety clothing and equipment. It provides solutions across all sectors including manufacturing, food, utilities, transport, oil and gas, as well as construction. Arco also has many customers across the public sector and supplies numerous central and local government organisations.

Product

Arco offers the most extensive range of workwear and safety equipment in the UK and is able to supply more than 170,000 branded and own-brand products, for head-to-toe protection across all industries. The range of products includes personal protective equipment, clothing, footwear, gloves, workplace safety and hygiene products with specific solutions to meet most requirements and a price range to suit every budget.

Arco works with strategic suppliers to offer premium industry brands; it also invests its own expertise in the design and development of innovative new products, working with customers to understand their needs. This provides solutions that have been designed by experts, tested to the right standards and are fit for the job.

DID YOU KNOW?
Over 100,000 people climb over The O2 each year wearing Arco Safety kit.

Arco is the only safety distributor to have its own in-house, Product Assurance Laboratory. This is accredited by United Kingdom Accreditation Service and SATRA, recognised authorities in the industry. The laboratory gives the ability to test products to the limits and beyond, complementing routine certification and due diligence testing regimes, offering unrivalled quality assurance.

EVERY YEAR, ARCO DISTRIBUTES

1.75 MILLION PARCELS

EVERY DAY, ARCO EMBROIDERS

23 MILLION STITCHES

Achievements

Arco prides itself on achieving a positive, healthy and happy working environment for all employees throughout the company and was recently awarded 'One to Watch' status, in The Sunday Times Best Companies Survey, recognising very high colleague engagement levels.

Arco's continued growth and commercial success enables it to put more back into the communities in which it operates. Arco is dedicated to its Corporate Social Responsibility programme supporting local charities by donating in excess of 1 per cent of pre-tax profits annually.

As for sponsorships, the company's most recent partnership is with iconic London attraction, The O2. Its safety equipment ensures the 100,000 people who climb over the dome every year are kept safe and comfortable with bespoke designed climb suits and shoes, as well as safety harnesses to ensure the best possible experience.

Arco is a proud supporter of the Yorkshire Air Ambulances, which provide a rapid response

emergency service to five million people across Yorkshire. Arco provide hazardwear, including flight suits, for the paramedics.

Arco has also partnered with the Bloodhound SSC project as it planned, designed and built a supersonic car to raise the world land speed record to 1,000mph. Arco is providing expert advice and protective equipment to keep engineers and designers safe during the build and testing process.

Arco was the first distributor in the safety industry to become a member of the Ethical Trading Initiative, a groundbreaking alliance of companies, trades unions and voluntary organisations who work in partnership to improve the lives of workers across the globe.

Recent Developments

Following Arco's focus on safety from the 1960s, it has continued to build the strongest team of safety experts in the industry. To ensure customers' hazards and risks are managed in the best way possible, Arco has a dedicated Training and Consultancy

Division. This was recently expanded with the acquisition of two leading companies in its field. Total Access is the UK's leading supplier of Height Safety Training and Services. Confined Space Training Services Ltd are a specialist confined space, health and safety education provider. These acquisitions further expand Arco's services proposition into hire and rescue services, firmly establishing it as a market leader in the provision of working at height and confined space safety training and consultancy services.

Promotion

The Arco brand is displayed across retail outlets nationwide and has grown through the commitment of the 1,500 colleagues who each uphold its brand values and deliver expert advice to customers. Arco is proud to promote its mission to keep people safe at work through its award-winning communication platform 'It's not just safety gear', recently awarded Best Brand Campaign in the B2B Marketing Awards. Arco's partnership with The O2 allows it to communicate directly with millions of people who experience their entertainment at London's premier venue, knowing they are kept safe through Arco's products and services. Arco prides itself on the best quality, service and value, and ensures that customers can access these in the most convenient way possible.

Brand History

1884	The company is founded as Arthur Stanley Morrison & Co. in Duke Street London.
1898	It relocates to Hull and changes its name to Asbestos & Rubber Company Ltd.
1903	The Martin Family, now in its fourth generation, join the company.
1941	The King Edward Street shop in Hull is destroyed during the Blitz.
1967	The acquisition of Budgen & Hare heralds the development of the Arco branch network.
1980	The company officially changes its name to Arco Ltd.
2000	The National Distribution Centre opens, launching the first publication of a single integrated catalogue: The Big Red Book.
2003	Arco Clothing Centre opens in Preston. Arco Charity Committee was set up by Jo Martin (who died in 2008).
2008	Arco announces support for over 200 charities, winning the Corporate Social Responsibility Award at National Business Awards.
2009	The company receives the the 'Big Tick' Award for Excellence from Business in the Community for its ethical supply chain work.
2010	Becomes a member of Sedex, the Supplier Ethical Data Exchange. ACC accredited by BSI for ISO 9001 Quality Management.
2014	Arco opens independently accredited Product Assurance Laboratory ensuring unrivalled quality across product portfolio.

Brand Values

Arco believes that everyone who goes to work each day has a basic human right to return home safely to their loved ones. Arco aims to help customers do just that by offering expert advice and safety products to prevent accidents in the workplace and save lives. The company's core values are: Respect for people, Excellence in reputation, Hard work and enterprise.

autoglass.co.uk

Autoglass® is a leading consumer and business automotive brand, providing vehicle glass repairs and replacements to over one million motorists every year. With the widest reaching auto glazing network in the UK, Autoglass® has more than 1,200 mobile technicians. Autoglass® is part of Belron® Group, operating in 34 countries and serving over 11 million motorists worldwide. It operates 24 hours a day, 365 days a year.

AUTOGLASS® HAS SERVED MORE THAN

30 MILLION CUSTOMERS

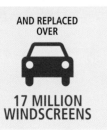

AND REPLACED OVER

17 MILLION WINDSCREENS

Market

Over the last 30 years, windscreens have evolved to play an integral role in modern automotive design and today's cars typically use 20 per cent more glass than in the 1980s. Windscreens can also incorporate complex technology such as rain and light sensors, wire heating, cameras and heads-up display components.

The modern windscreen is important for vehicle safety – its correct fitting and bonding can ultimately save lives if the vehicle is involved in an accident. As vehicle glass and the technology delivered through it become ever more complex, the importance of choosing a true expert vehicle glass repair and replacement partner

grows even further. Unrivalled commitment to innovation, technical excellence and superior customer service make Autoglass® a reliable partner for the road ahead.

Autoglass® handles the vehicle glass claims for nine of the top 10 UK insurance companies, providing a world-class service to their policyholders, as well as to a number of fleet and lease partners and their drivers. Autoglass® understands the complex needs of the business sector and continues to deliver peace of mind, high quality and added value to partnerships. The company also has a dedicated specialist glazing division, Autoglass® Specials, repairing and replacing glass on vehicles as diverse as coaches, buses, agricultural vehicles, motorhomes and trucks.

Product

Autoglass® fixes broken glass on any make, model or age of vehicle. The company operates a 'Repair First' philosophy ensuring that wherever possible, it will repair a chipped windscreen rather than replace it; a safe solution that saves time and money, and

DID YOU KNOW?

The 'Repair First' philosophy at Autoglass® saves, on average, 13,000 tonnes of CO_2 equivalent emissions plus over 5,000 tonnes of waste, every year.

is better for the environment. If the damage is beyond repair, Autoglass® will replace the glass. It only uses original equipment specification glass, ensuring that each replacement windscreen is as good as the original. As part of its commitment to the environment, Autoglass® reprocesses any laminate screens it removes.

Appointments can be made by phone or online and customers can also arrange for

Brand History

1972 Autoglass Supplies Ltd is launched, providing mobile vehicle glass replacement across northern England.

1982 Autoglass Ltd becomes part of Belron®, the world's largest vehicle glass repair and replacement company.

1983 The company merges with Bedfordshire based Windshields Ltd and becomes Autoglass Windshields, rebranding to simply Autoglass® in 1987.

1990 The windscreen repair service launches.

1994 Autoglass® becomes a registered trademark.

2005 The Heroes advertising campaign launches.

2007 The company becomes the first vehicle glass repair and replacement company to offer online booking at Autoglass.co.uk.

2009 The Autoglass® Specials brand is launched.

2010 The brand's mobile phone app, Facebook page and Twitter presence are launched.

2011 The brand becomes one of the first service brands in the UK to utilise F-Commerce, with appointment booking via Facebook.

2012 Autoglass® introduces its own unique Repair Resin and wins the prestigious Best of Belron® competition.

2013 The driver efficiency tool is rolled out across the entire fleet at Autoglass® and 400 Vanbrellas® are introduced.

2014 Autoglass® serves its one millionth online customer.

2015 The company is first in its sector to launch live online appointment booking.

Autoglass® leads the industry with investment in Advanced Driver Assistance Systems (ADAS) calibration.

one of the company's technicians to come out to a location of their choice.

Achievements

Autoglass® has received more than 44,000 customer reviews online, the highest number of reviews from any UK-based vehicle glass repair replacement specialist. Of these reviews, the average score was 4.4 out of five from happy customers who spoke positively about their experiences with the brand and the service it provides. In July 2014, The Institute of Customer Services ranked Autoglass® within the top 50 UK organisations in its United Kingdom Customer Satisfaction Index (UKCSI) for delivering excellent service. The volume of customer reviews held by Autoglass®, in addition to its latest ranking by the UKCSI, underline its commitment to delivering high quality service to every customer.

Recent Developments

Autoglass® takes an innovative approach to its business, investing in research and development to ensure it continues to deliver work of the highest standard.

Vehicles are constantly evolving and more and more safety features are now being integrated onto their windscreens. Advanced Driver Assistance Systems (ADAS) collectively

describe the advanced features in modern vehicles. They include systems which evaluate the vehicle's surroundings and warn the driver of hazards (for example Lane Departure Warning) and more advanced systems that actually take some level of control of the vehicle, such as Autonomous Emergency Braking. Typically these safety technologies are controlled by cameras which are located on the windscreen and therefore require a calibration if the windscreen is replaced to ensure the system operates correctly.

Autoglass® has invested heavily in understanding the implications of these technologies and is committed to removing the hassle out of calibration for its customers. The ADAS calibration solution by Autoglass® uses a custom-made diagnostic tool and was extensively piloted in 2015 ahead of a full national rollout.

Autoglass® is committed to achieving continual improvement in environmental as well as health and safety management. It is certified to ISO 140011 and OHSAS 180012 standards and constantly strives to reduce its relative use of non-renewable fuel and CO_2.

DID YOU KNOW? The 'Autoglass® Repair, Autoglass® Replace' jingle has been translated into 12 different languages and is now used by Belron® subsidiaries in over 20 countries.

Promotion

Autoglass® became a household name in the 1990s after becoming the main sponsor of Chelsea Football Club. Since then it has invested in a number of high profile brand campaigns to ensure it remains at the forefront of motorists' minds. In 2005, the testimonial-style Heroes campaign was first launched, featuring real technicians from Autoglass® explaining the benefits of repairing or replacing windscreens. This format has been extended throughout all of the company's brand communications, with staff appearing on vans, lorries and online.

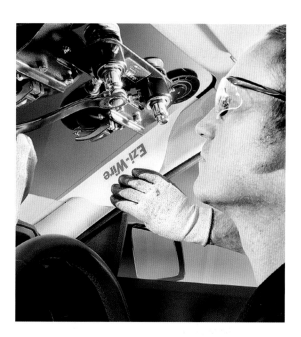

Brand Values

The Autoglass® vision is to be the natural choice by valuing its customers' needs and delivering world-class service.

home.barclays

Barclays is an international financial services provider engaged in personal, corporate and investment banking, credit cards and wealth management with an extensive presence in Europe, the Americas, Africa and Asia. Barclays' purpose is to help people achieve their ambitions – in the right way.

With 325 years of history and expertise in banking, Barclays operates in more than 50 countries and employs more than 130,000 people. Barclays moves, lends, invests and protects money for customers and clients worldwide.

Market
Barclays is a focused international bank with four core businesses: Personal and Corporate, Barclaycard, Investment Bank and Africa. The business divisions work together to provide customers and clients the best offerings across its markets.

Product
Barclays' longevity is the result of pioneering innovation that puts customers at the heart of all product and service solutions. This spirit continues today in the new digital arena.

Barclaycard's bPay wearable devices enable customers to make fast and secure contactless payments from a wristband, while the Sign Video allows customers with hearing impairments to use a smartphone to connect securely to a British Sign Language interpreter who will facilitate a conversation with a Barclays advisor. Premier Banking customers are able to contact Barclays via video call 24/7, helping them control when and how they do their banking, and business customers no longer need to remember a series of passwords to log in to their accounts – the finger vein scanner can identify customers using the unique vein patterns in their fingers.

Achievements
Barclays continues to be an award-winning business and was named 'Brand of the Year' in the UK Banking category at the 2015 World Branding Awards. It also collected two gold and two bronze awards at the Financial Communications Society's 21st Annual Portfolio Awards in New York, recognising Barclays' Investment Bank for brand and marketing excellence.

A committed proponent of Diversity and Inclusion, Barclays won Marketing Campaign

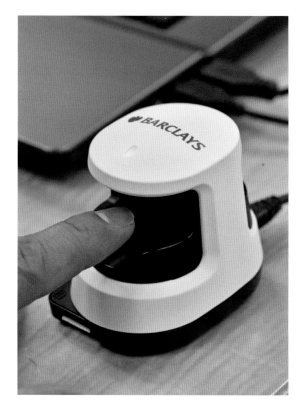

IN 2007 BARCLAYS LAUNCHED THE **UK'S FIRST CONTACTLESS PAYMENT CARD**

Brand History

1690 John Freame and Thomas Gould start trading as goldsmith bankers in London.

1728 Freame and Gould move to 54 Lombard Street, beneath the sign of the Black Spread Eagle.

1900s Barclays helps finance two of the fastest passenger ships in the world.

1920 Investment in William Morris helps him become the biggest car manufacturer in the UK.

1958 Barclays appoints the UK's first ever female branch manager, Hilda Harding.

1966 Barclaycard, the UK's first credit card, is launched.

1967 Barclays unveils the world's first ATM.

1975 Barclays sponsors the British-led expedition to conquer the South West face of Everest.

1987 Barclays launches the UK's first debit card.

2009 Banking on Change launches in 11 countries.

2012 Barclays Pingit launches, the first payment service allowing customers to transfer money via their mobile phones.

2013 The Purpose and Values launches.

2014 Barclaycard launches bPay wearable payment devices.

2015 Barclays launches Rise, a community for fintech startups to connect, co-create and scale innovative ideas.

DID YOU KNOW?
In 1975 Barclays sponsored a British expedition led by Sir Chris Bonington to the top of Mount Everest via the previously unconquered South West Face.

of the Year at the European Diversity Awards with its '#freedom to make a statement' campaign for Pride in London 2014. The bank was also named a Top 50 Employer for Women by The Times (UK) and was granted Star Performer status in Stonewall's 2015 Top Employers list. In partnership with Stonewall, Barclays has launched a global allies campaign to engage straight allies: a global programme of events and awareness raising activities that will enhance the visibility of each sexual orientation strand in different countries across the world.

Recent Developments

In 2015 Barclays marked its 325th anniversary, which makes Barclays older than the USA. While the core purpose has remained unchanged since 1690, a new strategy was announced in 2013 with the launch of the Barclays Purpose and Values proposition. These are fundamental to Barclays' long-term success and represent the set of standards under which everyone at Barclays works. They are integral to the Barclays Way and progress is measured as part of the Balanced Scorecard. The Balanced Scorecard sets out eight specific commitments across the 5Cs (Customers & Clients, Colleague, Citizenship, Conduct and Company) against which people can monitor how Barclays is doing. For employees, measurement and reward is based not just on commercial results, but on how they live the Values every day.

Barclays' recent focus has been continuing to build the business in a way that delivers shared growth – for Barclays and the communities it

serves – and focusing on being a balanced international bank across its four core businesses.

A prime example of shared growth in action is the Barclays Women in Leadership product suite, an industry first. Launched in 2014, it offers institutional investors a way to contribute meaningfully to promoting gender-based change in the boardrooms of major companies in the US market.

In addition, from 2012 to 2014 Barclays has supported 4.19 million young people and is on track to meet its '5 Million Young Futures' commitment by the end of 2015. Through the programme, Barclays employees invest time and expertise to deliver community initiatives that enhance the employability and financial skills of young people globally.

Equipping young people for the future is a constant theme running through Barclays' Citizenship strategy and every October, thousands of employees around the world

participate in the annual 'Make a Difference' campaign. Like one team from Mumbai who, for the past three years, have supported Snehasadan Homes for Hope, volunteering more than 1,200 hours to help the 260 young people that live there at any one time.

Promotion

As with all activity at Barclays, Purpose and Values sit at the heart of its marketing strategy. In 2015 an above-the-line campaign to promote Barclays Digital Eagles – employees who help people become more confident with technology – demonstrated digital innovation and a commitment to helping people in the community achieve their ambitions.

Across Africa, the Prosper brand campaign focuses on the concept of prosperity through storytelling, encouraging people of all ages, cultures and gender to share what the word 'prosper' means to them. The campaign shows Barclays' commitment to helping its customers and clients achieve prosperity through relevant products and services.

The Barclays LifeSkills programme focuses primarily on young people aged 11 to 19. In 2015 Barclays focused on inspiring young people to get job ready by 'presenting your best self online'. The integrated campaign teaches young people to think about the impact their online personas and activities could have on their ability to secure a job, and the skills they need for a better future.

Brand Values

Barclays' Purpose is to help people achieve their ambitions – in the right way.

Barclays' Values are: Respect, Integrity, Service, Excellence and Stewardship.

bbc.co.uk

Tony Hall, Director-General of the BBC, says, "Every week, the BBC informs, educates and entertains almost everyone in Britain. As the cornerstone of the UK's creative industries, the BBC is also an engine for growth, supporting jobs and businesses in the wider economy. The BBC. British, Bold, Creative".

Market

The BBC is the world's leading public service broadcaster. Operating under a Royal Charter it is funded by the licence fee paid by UK households, the BBC is constantly innovating to adapt to a rapidly changing media landscape. Income from the licence fee is used to provide the UK with a wide range of different services including national TV channels, regional programming, national and local radio stations, and an online presence. Commercially, BBC Worldwide delivers and promotes BBC content and formats to international audiences, with over two-thirds of BBC Worldwide revenue coming from outside the UK.

Approximately 46 million people across the country use the BBC every day, with an average of around eight-and-a-half hours of TV and more than ten hours of BBC Radio

per person. As technology has changed, the BBC has set the pace. Its top 10 apps have been downloaded 80 million times and BBC sites are the third most popular overall on mobile devices in the UK (Source: The Future of the BBC 2015).

Product

The BBC purpose is to make programmes and services that inform, educate and entertain. Its job is to discover and invest in the best British creative content and people and connect them with an audience both at home and abroad. It wants to perform a unique, distinct function in its media ecology – great British content, a trusted guide, for everyone. It is the largest single investor in British creative ideas and talent.

At the heart of the philosophy behind the BBC is a very simple, very democratic idea: everybody should have access to the best, whoever they are, wherever they live, rich or poor, old or young. The BBC is here to bring the best to everyone.

Achievements

In 2015 EastEnders celebrated its 30th anniversary with a live episode. It was watched by more than 21 million people – 37 per cent of the UK population and generated over one million tweets – the most ever for a UK drama. The BBC Two series Wolf Hall attracted six million viewers at its launch and became the channel's highest-rated drama series since 2002. The BBC Weather app reached five million downloads within eight months of relaunch, an average of 15 downloads per minute. Futhermore, 6 Music became the first digital-only radio station to reach two million weekly listeners. And Radio 4 Extra has now achieved a weekly audience of over two million listeners. Great British Bake Off continued to be as popular as ever with an audience of over 15 million tuning in.

DID YOU KNOW?
In 2015, a record 283 million people accessed the BBC's Global News services per week.

97% OF UK ADULTS USE BBC TV, RADIO OR ONLINE EVERY WEEK

Brand History

1922 British Broadcasting Company (BBC) is formed by a group of leading Wireless manufacturers.

1927 The BBC gains its first royal charter, ensuring its independence from Government, political and shareholder interference.

1953 On 2nd June around 22 million people watch the Queen's Coronation live on the BBC – a historic event that changes the course of television history.

1967 BBC Two begins transmission of the first regular colour television service in Europe.

1980 After 25 years, Children in Need becomes an event with a whole evening of dedicated programming – and raises £1 million for the first time.

1998 BBC Choice, the first BBC digital TV channel, launches. It becomes BBC Three in 2003.

2007 BBC iPlayer launches at Christmas and transforms media consumption in the UK, with 360 million views in its first three months.

2008 The first full digital switchover takes place in Whitehaven, Cumbria.

2010 BBC Television Centre, the world's first purpose-built television building, celebrates its 50th anniversary.

2011 The BBC marks the 75th anniversary of the first regular TV service broadcast from the BBC studios at Alexandra Palace, North London.

2012 The BBC broadcasts the 2012 Olympic Games, the UK's biggest national television event and the world's first truly digital Games.

2013 BBC Playlister, a new digital service for music fans, launches.

2014 BBC Music launches with a special reworking of God Only Knows by 27 artists forming 'The Impossible Orchestra'.

2015 The BBC unveiled the BBC micro:bit, a pocket-sized codeable computer with motion detection, a built-in compass and Bluetooth technology, which is to be given free to every child in Year 7, or equivalent, across the UK.

18.3 HOURS

LENGTH OF TIME AUDIENCES SPEND WITH THE BBC EACH WEEK

Recent Developments

The BBC has launched a number of new initiatives to make it a more open BBC for the internet age. With the 'Make it Digital' initiative, it is working with a host of partners who will put almost a million programmable devices into schools across the country – one for every child aged 11 and 12. It is also working with a number of organisations to reach up to 5,000 unemployed young people around the country and to help boost their digital skills. It has launched both BBC Arts and BBC Music as online destinations; created a successful new arts slot on Saturday nights on BBC Two; inspired school children to play classical music through the Ten Pieces project; brought TV and radio services together for the Hay and Edinburgh festivals, and created the BBC Music Awards.

Along with new initiatives, the iPlayer also had a revamp with the programme viewing

window being extended from seven to 30 days. Alongside the creation of BBC Store, audiences have more opportunities to watch and listen to the BBC content they love.

Promotion

In 2015, the BBC launched a new brand strategy to reposition the BBC as a life-enhancing brand and help audiences to access the full range and breadth of content it produces. As part of that strategy the BBC has launched a new brand campaign, The Golden Thread, to highlight the role it plays in people's lives and showcase its content and services. This year also saw the launch of a unique audience feedback mechanic, the 'Heart Button' that encouraged online audiences to enter a personal relationship

with the BBC in order to get more content tailored to their interests. This product launch was supported by an on-air marketing campaign, If You Love Something Let It Show featuring the legendary Beatles track All You Need is Love re-recorded by a BBC Introducing artist. This has also been a very active 12 months in social for the BBC with multiple campaigns successfully encouraging audiences into a more personal and participatory relationship.

Brand Values

Public-service, trust and responsibility, creativity, innovation, unity, respect for and love of BBC audiences.

ba.com

Throughout its 95-year history, British Airways has been at the forefront of innovation in aviation. Its pioneering spirit has led to numerous industry and world firsts; the first commercial scheduled service, the first commercial jet and supersonic services as well as the first fully flat beds on its aircraft. British Airways has committed to putting the customer at the heart of everything it does and 2015 saw a renewed focus on improvements to customer experience.

Market
British Airways, part of International Airlines Group, is one of the world's leading global premium airlines and the largest international carrier in the UK. The carrier has its home base at London Heathrow and flies to over 170 destinations in more than 70 different countries. British Airways carries almost 40 million customers a year and has a fleet of 288 aircraft.

Product
British Airways offers a range of flights to UK domestic, short haul and long haul destinations. From the flagship premium cabins of First, Club World and Club Europe to the World Traveller Plus and economy cabins of World Traveller and Euro Traveller,

all customers enjoy a full service experience that conveys British style and sophistication.

Last year saw the addition of the Boeing 787-9 to the fleet, featuring a new First cabin that will fly to Delhi, Abu Dhabi, Muscat, Austin and Kuala Lumpur.

Achievements
Along with its 2015 Consumer and Business Superbrands award, British Airways has continued to win awards including Best Long and Short-Haul airlines at The Times Travel Awards and Conde Nast Awards, Best European Airline at the Independent Travel Awards and Best Airline at the Travel Weekly Globe Awards. Its Executive Club frequent

DID YOU KNOW?
Last year British Airways welcomed more than 175 apprentices onto 12 different schemes.

flyer programme recently won Best Airline Loyalty Programme at the Business Traveller Awards.

Recent Developments
In 2015, British Airways' focus on customer service has seen the airline launch a new first class cabin on the airline's 787-9 aircraft, complete the new cabins on all short-haul aircraft and a refresh of many of the airline's 747 jumbo jet fleet with new in-flight entertainment systems. Celebrations were held to mark the 500th issue of Highlife in-flight magazine, published since 1973, along with the launch of a new Chinese language edition and a refreshed First-Life magazine for First class customers.

Customers in World Traveller and World Traveller Plus cabins can now upgrade their catering from a choice of luxury meals including Gourmet Dining and Great British Breakfast.

At Heathrow, British Airways completed its move from Terminal 1 to Terminal 3 with new check-in facilities and refreshed lounges. New lounges have opened in Singapore and Dubai, with Concorde Bars for the exclusive use of First Class customers.

EVERY YEAR, BRITISH AIRWAYS SERVES ITS CUSTOMERS

| 36 MILLION+ MEALS | 35 MILLION CUPS OF TEA | 3.7 MILLION BOTTLES OF WINE |

During 2015 British Airways launched a range of new routes, including Reykjavík and a return to Kuala Lumpur. A further 12 new routes have been announced including Lima in Peru, Costa Rica, San Jose in California, Palermo and Inverness. Codeshares with both Vueling and TAM Brazil mean customers have more choice of destinations than ever before.

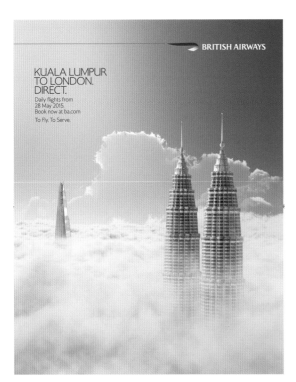

In April, a new version of the British Airways mobile app was launched with specific features for Apple watch, showing time to departure along with gate numbers and flight status. For customers using the airline's lounges, iBeacons are being used to activate push notifications, with the app including Wi-Fi login details and boarding information. The British Airways app has been downloaded more than five million times and is the highest rated airline app on Apple Store.

At the start of the year the airline relaunched its SME loyalty programme OnBusiness in collaboration with partners American Airlines and Iberia, offering a more rewarding relationship with small and medium sized companies globally. It also launched a Customer Service Apprentice scheme, with 72 apprentices joining the company in October along with 51 Graduate Trainees.

Promotion

At the start of 2015, British Airways launched an innovative partnership with eBay, a bespoke campaign that showed the public a comparison of the price of relevant items for sale on eBay to the cost of British Airways flights to major European cities.

The airline has continued to launch engaging campaigns on social media, including two campaigns that focused on the photographic talents of its customers. #inspireus challenged customers to send in their best holiday snaps for a chance to win a European break. Over 10,000 entries were submitted and the best were showcased in a physical marketing campaign around London. To celebrate the 500th issue of Highlife, 500 travel photographs from BA's customers were chosen from Instagram to make up the cover of the edition.

In June, Kidzania London, a children's entertainment and education experience launched in Westfield White City. As its airline partner, children entering Kidzania check in at British Airways terminal and can even enroll at the British Airways Flight Academy to finesse their piloting skills on a number of flight simulators.

In September 2015, British Airways launched its No Place Like Home campaign in the US and Canada, encouraging British Expats to return home for Christmas with a tongue-in-cheek viral video on the weird and wonderful festive traditions in the UK.

The airline's Flying Start charity partnership with Comic Relief has continued its successes in 2015, reaching its £12 million fundraising target. In addition, on-board collections for the Nepal Earthquake Appeal raised over £300,000. Furthermore, colleagues at seven US airports ran events to celebrate the first US Red Nose Day, including a vintage uniform fashion show in New York.

Brand Values

Four simple words capture the essence of British Airways: 'To Fly. To Serve.' These words describe the passion and expertise that British Airways sets out to demonstrate to customers every day; delivering a unique combination of iconic British style, thoughtful service that is personal and knowledgeable, and unrivalled flying know-how.

The airline's reputation is built on its heritage of excellence in all areas of flying, its uncompromising standards of safety and security, and its commitment to set new standards for the future.

Brand History

1919 AT&T operates the first commercial scheduled flight.

1924 Imperial Airways is formed as the UK's first nationalised airline to operate UK air services.

1936 British Airways Ltd is formed from United Airways, Hillman Airways and Spartan Airlines.

1974 BOAC and BEA merge to form British Airways.

1987 British Airways is privatised.

1988 Club World and Club Europe cabins are launched. British Caledonian joins British Airways.

1999 The oneworld® alliance launches with British Airways, American Airlines, Canadian Airlines, Iberia and Qantas as the founding members.

2008 British Airways' new home at London Heathrow's Terminal 5 is opened.

2009 Club World London City launches.

2010 A redesigned first class cabin is unveiled and a joint business with American Airlines and Iberia launches.

2011 British Airways merges with Iberia to form the parent company IAG.

British Airways moves into a new state-of-the-art home at London Gatwick.

2012 IAG acquires bmi and integrates into British Airways. The brand sponsors the London 2012 Olympic and Paralympic Games.

2013 British Airways welcomes the first new aircraft types in 17 years – the Airbus A380 and Boeing 787 Dreamliner.

2014 British Airways is voted as Britain's number one Consumer Superbrand.

2015 British Airways is voted as Britain's number one Consumer and Business Superbrand.

British Airways launches the new 787-9 aircraft, complete with a newly remodelled luxury First class cabin.

British Heart Foundation

bhf.org.uk

The British Heart Foundation (BHF) is the UK's number one heart charity. For more than 50 years it's funded pioneering research that has saved thousands of lives and transformed the landscape of heart disease. Its vision is a world where people do not die prematurely or suffer from heart and circulatory disease. Since 1961, the number of heart and circulatory disease related deaths in the UK has fallen by more than half.

Heart Disease is Heartless 2015

Market

In the UK more than one in four people still die from heart and circulatory disease. The BHF aims to reduce premature deaths from heart and circulatory disease by 25 per cent by 2025, but the challenges are huge, because although heart and circulatory disease is a serious issue causing one death around every three minutes in the UK, it is not seen as a major concern for the public.

The BHF's ambitious targets reflect the need to raise even more money and become even more efficient in order to power its life saving research. All of the BHF's work is funded by the public. From growing its eBay operation, to putting on engaging events, it is always looking for new ways to grow its income.

Product

The British Heart Foundation is a research pioneer, funding thousands of research projects around the UK. Since 1961 the charity has funded studies that have revolutionised how heart disease is treated, resulting in more people surviving a heart attack or cardiac arrest than ever before.

The Nation of Lifesavers is a UK-wide BHF campaign to give people the skills they need to carry out CPR. There are more than 30,000 out-of-hospital cardiac arrests in the UK each year. By teaching people how to perform CPR, the BHF could save up to 5,000 lives a year.

The British Heart Foundation also supports health professionals on the front line, who are helping to support

those diagnosed with heart or circulatory conditions. It also pilots new models of service delivery to demonstrate improved clinical outcomes and patient care.

DID YOU KNOW?
The BHF aims to spend around £100 million on new research each year.

The British Heart Foundation is the nation's heart charity and one of the most recognisable brands on the high street.

The heartbeat symbol was created in 1969 by a member of staff and, after a few tweaks over the years, is one of the

most recognisable logos in the UK. In recent testing, 93 per cent of people recognised the heartbeat as the BHF – even with the name removed.

Achievements

The British Heart Foundation has a heritage of creative innovation which has been recognised in the industry. Across the course of 2015, BHF won the September/October 2015 Thinkboxes award for TV ad creativity with its 'Heart disease is heartless' campaign and Gold in the Best Use of Digital to Aid a

Brand History

1961 The British Heart Foundation is born. Concerned doctors launch the BHF to address the epidemic of cardiovascular disease.

1963 BHF starts funding research – an early grant goes to Dr Aubrey Leatham who later implants the first UK pacemaker.

1968 Surgeon Donald Ross performs first the UK heart transplant following five years of BHF-funded research.

1970 BHF Professor Magdi Yacoub pioneers 'the switch' operation for babies born with an otherwise deadly congenital defect.

1976 BHF Professor Michael Davies proves a blood clot causes a heart attack.

1980 BHF funds clinical trials that lead to beta-blockers, clot-busting drugs, aspirin and ACE inhibitors transforming heart attack treatment and reversing death rates worldwide.

1994 BHF-funded studies show the life saving benefit of statins in preventing heart attacks and strokes, cutting the nation's heart disease risk.

1996 BHF funds its first public access defibrillator.

2000 BHF launches its Heart Helpline.

2013 BHF funds three Regenerative Medicine Centres to help find a cure for heart failure.

2014 BHF announces its ambition to save more lives of people who suffer a cardiac arrest by starting a revolution in CPR training to create a 'nation of lifesavers'.

The Clot Thickens: Fraser Macrae, University of Leeds.

CPR Campaign for its 'Nation of Lifesavers' campaign at the Digital Impact Awards. Prior to this, BHF won Gold in the Not-for-Profit Campaign category at the 2014 Chartered Institute of Public Relations Awards with its 'Nation of Lifesavers' Scotland launch. In 2012 it collected several accolades, including two Gold awards at the British Arrows Awards for its 'Hands-only CPR' in the Charity Advert and Public Service Advertising categories; Gold for Best Use of Integrated Media for the 'Hands-Only CPR' campaign at the Cannes Lions; and Media Grand Prix at the Media Week Awards for its 'Angina Monologues' campaign.

Recent Developments

In 2015, BHF began a marketing strategy to shift the public's perception of heart disease and show the sudden devastation it can cause. This builds on its strong campaign history, including the 2012 to 2015 three hero campaigns – 'Bag it. Beat it', 'Wear it. Beat it' and 'Fight for every heartbeat' – which were promoted at key points across all areas of the charity. Prior to 2012, the focus was educating the public on different areas of heart health. Campaigns included Vinnie Jones 'Hands-only CPR', 'Watch your own Heart Attack' and 'Fatty Cigarette'.

DID YOU KNOW? The majority of BHF's charitable expenditure goes to research.

In 2015 the public donated more than ever before to the fight against heart disease, with the BHF's charitable income increasing by 9 per cent and more than 50,000 people signing up to give a regular donation.

The latest brand campaign, 'Heart disease is heartless', was the first step of a long-term marketing strategy to show the sudden devastation heart disease can cause. In the TV advert and supporting digital content, a young boy loses his father suddenly to heart disease.

Carolan Davidge, Director of Marketing and Engagement, said: "This campaign aims to shift the way people think about heart disease. We want to give people an emotional wake-up call, showing them that heart disease can rip people away from friends and family without warning."

OVER 90,000 PEOPLE RAN, SWAM OR CYCLED IN BHF FUNDRAISING EVENTS IN 2015

Brand Values

BHF's brand strategy 'Fight for every heartbeat' tells the story of its winning history of scientific achievements and their relentless determination to beat heart disease. The brand values – brave, informed, compassionate and driven – influence external marketing and staff behaviours, inspiring everyone to come together and raise money to fund vital research.

bt.com

BT is one of the world's leading providers of communications services, serving customers in more than 170 countries. It supplies networked IT services to government departments and multinational companies, and is the UK's largest communications provider to consumers and businesses.

BT has five lines of business: BT Consumer, BT Business, BT Global Services, Openreach and BT Wholesale.

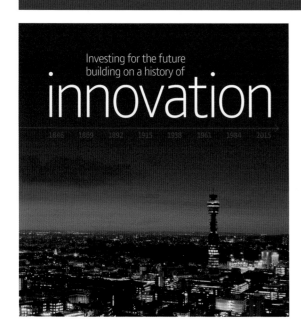

Market

BT operates in a thriving, multi-trillion pound global industry. In recent years the boundaries between telcos, IT companies, software businesses, hardware manufacturers and broadcasters have blurred. BT is innovating fast in this rapidly converging market.

Product

BT is the leading provider of consumer phone and broadband services in the UK.

Since 2008, BT has invested more than £3 billion in fibre broadband. The rollout has been one of the fastest in the world and more than three-quarters of the UK is now covered by BT's fibre network. More than

99 per cent of UK premises have access to basic broadband – this is the best in the G8. In fact, a higher proportion of UK premises can access fibre broadband than in any of the other four major European economies (Germany, France, Spain, and Italy).

BT's TV offer has continued to go from strength to strength. In 2015/16 BT has exclusive live football from UEFA Champions League and UEFA Europa league. This is in addition to its continued rights for FA Premier League football.

In March 2015, BT moved back into the consumer mobile market, offering plans that combine 4G, unlimited texts, unlimited access to BT Wi-Fi hotspots in the UK and to the BT Sport app, at no extra cost.

For around one million business customers, BT builds communications solutions of all sizes, serving small start-ups to global enterprises. BT also caters to small and medium-sized enterprises, offering fixed-voice, data, mobility and IT services.

BT also provides services to around 6,500 large corporate and public sector customers in more than 170 countries worldwide. They operate in a wide range of sectors including banking and financial services,

Brand History

1984 British Telecom is privatised, making it the only state-owned telecommunications company to be privatised in Europe.

1991 British Telecom is restructured and relaunches as BT. This structure focuses on specific market sectors, reflecting the needs of different customers. These changes gave BT the means to expand into overseas markets.

2003 BT unveils its current corporate identity, reflecting the aspirations of a technologically innovative future.

2005 Following the Telecommunications Strategic Review, BT signs legally binding undertakings with Ofcom to help create a better regulatory framework.

2006 Openreach launches and is responsible for managing the UK access network on behalf of the telecommunications industry.

2008 BT becomes the official communications services partner, and a sustainability partner, for the London 2012 Olympic and Paralympic Games.

2009 BT installs a giant LED screen at the top of BT Tower in London, which counted down the days to the start of the Olympic Games.

2012 BT is at the heart of London 2012, the most connected Olympic and Paralympic Games ever.

2013 BT Sport channel launches, with studios at the Queen Elizabeth Olympic Park, and is in over five million households to date.

2014 BT and Alcatel Lucent demonstrate the world's fastest transmission of data over fibre.

In December, BT celebrates 30 years since the company was privatised.

2015 BT Tower celebrates its golden anniversary by opening its world-famous revolving restaurant to the public for two weeks during the summer.

IN OCTOBER 2015, BT CELEBRATED

50 YEARS
SINCE THE OPENING OF THE BT TOWER

 189 METRES

DID YOU KNOW? The Brand Z ranking – a major ranking of brand value by Millward Brown – shows the BT brand is now worth US$18 billion.

manufacturing, logistics, pharmaceuticals, and consumer goods. Public sector customers in the UK include health, central and local government, and government organisations worldwide.

Achievements
BT's contribution to the UK economy is considerable. The company employs around 72,000 people in the UK.

It has been estimated that BT is responsible for generating £1 in every £80 produced in the UK. According to an independent report by Regeneris Consulting, BT spent £6.5 billion with UK suppliers during the 2014/15 financial year and gave an £18 billion boost to the country's economy.

The report estimates that the equivalent of 217,000 full-time UK jobs are supported through BT's direct employment, its spending with contractors and suppliers and the spending of employees.

BT takes corporate responsibility seriously and every year at least one per cent of BT's pre-tax profits go into programmes that benefit the communities in which BT operates. Since 2012, BT has raised £231.4 million for good causes and 26 per cent of BT people took part in volunteering activities in 2014/15.

Recent Developments
BT has announced plans to transform the UK fibre broadband landscape from superfast to ultrafast. Using G.fast technology, it will be possible to offers speeds of up to 500Mbps, available to most of the UK within a decade.

Promotion
In April 2015, BT launched its new TV advertising campaign. Called 'Behind the Scenes', the campaign gives viewers a humorous look at the making of an advert.

The first ad featured actor Ewan McGregor as well as BT Sport Ambassadors and footballers Robin Van Persie and Alex Oxlade-Chamberlain. Subsequent executions have featured actors including Willem Dafoe and Rebel Wilson.

As a long-term supporter of Paralympic sport, BT continues to support a number of Paralympic athletes including 100m gold medal winning sprinter Jonnie Peacock and 100m and 200m gold medal winner, wheelchair racer Hannah Cockroft. BT was the founding partner of the British Paralympic Association (BPA) when it was formed in 1989, and was the first BPA partner to extend its partnership through to Rio 2016.

coca-cola.co.uk

The Coca-Cola Company is the world's largest beverage company and leading drinks brand. Since 1886, Coca-Cola has connected with more people and grown to become the world's most universally recognised brand. In 2015 highlights for Coca-Cola Great Britain included celebrating 100 years of the iconic contour bottle, the launch of a new marketing strategy for Coca-Cola and sponsorship of the Rugby World Cup 2015.

DID YOU KNOW?
Coca-Cola is the second most widely understood term in the world after "OK".

Market

Coca-Cola is one of the most successful and innovative brands in the world today. Within Great Britain, the MyCoke portfolio is worth more than £1 billion and reinforces its position as market leader in the soft drinks category through ongoing brand and product innovation. Coca-Cola remains the most popular soft drink within the market, closely followed by Diet Coke.

Product

The Coca-Cola portfolio comprises of Coca-Cola, Coca-Cola Life, Coca-Cola Zero and Diet Coke. Alongside the Coca-Cola range there are a number of other brands within the 19-strong brand portfolio in Great Britain including Sprite, Fanta, Dr. Pepper, glacéau smartwater and vitaminwater as well as the Schweppes range.

Achievements

Coca-Cola is constantly striving to create innovative and exciting marketing campaigns globally. In 2015 Coca-Cola Great Britain won awards, including a Cannes Lion and an Ad Week award, for the world's first fully personalized broadcast video on-demand campaign as part of the Share A Coke campaign. Coca-Cola delivered four million personalised ads across 4oD that saw viewers served a personalised advert featuring their name on a Coca-Cola bottle.

Recent Developments

In 2015 Coca-Cola introduced a new approach to marketing Coca-Cola, Coca-Cola Life, Coca-Cola Zero and Diet Coke, bringing the four together under the Coca-Cola brand. For the first time all four Coca-Cola variants were featured together across marketing campaigns to promote the choice offered throughout the range and awareness of the no calorie options, Coca-Cola Zero and Diet Coke. The move also included a change in packaging with each can and bottle now featuring the same iconic style with a different colour to signify the variant.

Also in 2015, Coca-Cola launched a new website, Coca-Cola Journey. With a greater focus on storytelling, the platform brought together all aspects of Coca-Cola for the first time, including what the brand and company is doing, both locally and globally. Coca-Cola Journey provides original content, designed to tell the story of Coca-Cola in a new way.

Promotion

Coca-Cola celebrated 100 years of the iconic contour bottle in 2015. The 100th anniversary was celebrated through the unveiling of "I've Kissed…", a global marketing campaign that featured icons including Elvis Presley, Marilyn Monroe and Ray Charles being 'kissed by' the Coca-Cola contour bottle. The campaign included a television commercial demonstrating how the bottle has been a part of moments of happiness and celebration over the past 100 years. A pop-up Contour Centenary Bar in Soho was also created to celebrate the anniversary in London.

Brand History

1886 Coca-Cola is created by John Pemberton and served at Jacobs' Pharmacy in Atlanta, USA.

1893 The Coca-Cola Spencerian script trademark is registered.

1915 The contour bottle prototype is designed by Alexander Samuelson and patented. Today, the original glass bottle is the most recognised bottle in the world.

1983 Diet Coke is launched – the first brand extension of Coca-Cola in Great Britain.

2005 Coca-Cola Zero becomes the third brand in the Coca-Cola family in Great Britain.

2009 The MyCoke portfolio becomes the first brand to top the £1 billion retail sales mark.

2011 The Coca-Cola Company celebrates the 125th anniversary of Coca-Cola.

2014 Coca-Cola Life becomes the fourth brand in the Coca-Cola family in Great Britain.

2015 Coca-Cola launches 'one brand' strategy, uniting the four distinct brands; Coca-Cola, Diet Coke, Coca-Cola Zero and Coca-Cola Life, under the umbrella of Coca-Cola for the first time.

In March 2015, Coca-Cola announced a change to its marketing strategy to unify the Coca-Cola range, bringing Coca-Cola, Diet Coke, Coca-Cola Zero and Coca-Cola Life, under a new 'one brand' strategy to promote the full choice of Coca-Cola variants. The lower and no sugar and calorie Coca-Cola variants were presented in the final frames of all Coca-Cola television advertising, and 2015 media investment in the lower and no sugar and calorie variants of Coca-Cola doubled. The Choose Happiness campaign ran throughout the summer and included the first TV adverts under the new strategy, bringing the variants together for the first time.

In 2015, the UK saw the arrival of the EKOCYCLE™ brand, launched in Harrods. A joint collaboration between The Coca-Cola Company and will.i.am, the project pushed the boundaries of sustainable fashion and design. The brand's ambition is to educate and empower consumers to proactively seek out more sustainable lifestyle choices by identifying everyday household products and recycling them into wearable and useable items. The result was an inspiring, aspirational collection that challenged preconceived notions of products made from recycled materials.

During the summer, Diet Coke revealed its latest fashion collaboration with a new limited edition Diet Coke bottle designed by leading British fashion designer J.W.Anderson.

As a sponsor of the Rugby World Cup 2015, Coca-Cola launched its biggest ever rugby on-pack giveaway to support the sponsorship, giving away up to one million Coca-Cola Gilbert rugby balls throughout the summer. The tournament was the first sports sponsorship under the new marketing strategy for Coca-Cola and saw all four variants featured, with Coca-Cola Zero playing a leading role.

Brand Values

Since 1886, Coca-Cola has embodied values of happiness, opportunity, authenticity and togetherness, shaping the brand through its 129-year plus history and spreading optimism to people across the globe.

IF ALL OF THE COCA-COLA BOTTLES IN THE WORLD WERE LAID END TO END

THEY WOULD REACH THE MOON AND BACK MORE THAN 1,677 TIMES

continental-tyres.co.uk

As an international tyre manufacturer and leading automotive supplier, Continental develops intelligent technologies for transporting people and their goods. The corporation sets the future in motion with its five strong divisions – Chassis & Safety, Interior, Powertrain, Tyre and ContiTech.

Market

Generating sales of €34.5 billion in 2014 and currently employing 208,000 people in 53 countries, Continental's market position as a leading premium tyre manufacturer is underlined by winning four out of five independent tyre tests in Europe. Offering best in braking across all weather conditions, Continental tyres are fitted to one in three new cars across Europe. The German manufacturer is much more than just a tyre brand; it is also one of the world's leading automotive suppliers, shaping the automotive landscape for a safer future with the advent of autonomous technologies.

Product

With a rich heritage of developing groundbreaking technologies and mobility solutions over the last 140 years, Continental offers a broad range of tyre fitments for cars, vans, trucks and also bikes. Continental works with manufacturers to develop groundbreaking solutions such as ContiSilent – the tyre with a foam inner liner that reduces interior noise by up to nine decibels. It invests heavily across its ranges, with its latest SportContact 6, for high performance vehicles, offering perfect grip in all situations.

At the forefront of tyre development, Continental offers unique products such as the Conti.eContact for the hybrid car market, right through to industry leading developments such as Taragum dandelion rubber for a truly sustainable future. As well as delivering the highest quality products to its customers,

DID YOU KNOW?
A tyre is made up of more than 30 different ingredients including steel and nylon, as well as both synthetic and natural rubber.

Continental also prides itself on its supply chain performance and working closely with retailers.

Achievements

The market-leading approach of Continental has been frequently recognised with a range of UK tyre test wins and international awards. In 2015, it took first place in both the Auto Express and evo summer tyre tests.

The company also won Tyre Manufacturer of the Year 2014 and was honoured for its ContiLifeCycle plant in Hanover by the trade journal Tire Technology International. The brand's approach to developing sustainable tyres from dandelions was also honoured at the GreenTec Awards 2014.

Continental's commitment to technical excellence and innovation ensures its tyres deliver superb braking, handling and

performance. It is the only tyre manufacturer to have an automated braking test centre, enabling year-round testing. Continental completes more than 700 million test miles annually and more than 200 rubber compounds daily.

Continental is the leading tyre choice for the world's top car manufacturers, with over 500 current model approvals. To be a 'factory fit', the tyre must have achieved the required levels of excellence set by the car manufacturer, passing up to 120 stringent tests to become an integral part of the vehicle's equipment. So if the manufacturer trusts its tyres, drivers can too. Independent magazines regularly test Contintental's tyres and it consistently takes top places in reviews that assess performance over and above the EU tyre label. It is regularly Best Buy and Testers Choice in the key press.

Continental works hard to develop relationships with international press; all supported through a range of bespoke media events. The Black Chili Driving Experience offers such an experience, putting its tyres to the test in Southern Spain, demonstrating the ultimate braking abilities whilst fitted to high performance vehicles from leading manufacturers.

Recent Developments

Over recent years Continental has developed a range of partnerships to maximise its brand awareness across audiences. As lovers of football on the world stage, Continental is a longstanding supporter of UEFA's European Championship and is looking forward to France 2016. It has an extensive grassroots programme, and was a founding sponsor of the Women's Super League and a proud supporter of the Lionesses who finished third in the World Cup. It supports the Football Association (FA) to develop coaching via its innovative Contiwarmup programme, as well as becoming a partner of the FA Centre of Excellence at St George's Park. Continental's commitment to the game also recently won it the Sponsor Impact Award for support of the FA Girls' Football Festivals. Working closely with adidas, Continental brings advanced tyre technology to the soles of trainers, creating rubber compounds with exceptional grip in both wet and dry conditions. Better grip means faster times and adidas is deploying this technology across much of its range, with three marathon world records in the last three years. Continental proudly maintains its

partnership with adidas to the running community through Conti Lightning Run and Conti Thunder Run, endurance races to test the ultimate traction off road.

Continental is also a 'Partner in Excellence' at Mercedes-Benz World, the pioneering brand experience centre located at Brooklands motor racing circuit. Adrenaline-filled driving experiences demonstrate that together the brands deliver the ultimate combination of high performance with a shared passion for safety.

Promotion

Continental's communication concept focuses on peace of mind. Whatever the road condition or weather, its tyres will perform at the best level of safety in terms of shorter braking distances. Continental adopts a safety-first approach to everything it does and is a proud member of TyreSafe, working together with the industry to raise awareness of the importance of tyres.

Over recent years, its five-strong divisions have helped establish Continental as one of the top automotive suppliers globally, with such technologies contributing to zero accidents and fatalities in the future, known as Vision Zero. A partnership with the New Car Assessment Programme through its 'Stop the Crash' campaign has further enhanced Continental as a leader in automotive technology and safety.

Brand History

1871	Continental-Caoutchouc- und Gutta-Percha Compagnie is founded in Hanover.
1882	The rampant horse is adopted as a trademark.
1904	Continental presents the world's first automobile tyre with a patterned tread.
1914	There is a triple victory for Daimlers fitted with Continental tyres at the French Grand Prix.
1979	The takeover of the European tyre operations of Uniroyal, Inc., USA, gives Continental a wider base in Europe.
1993	Continental has approximately 2,000 tyre retailers and franchises in 15 European countries.
1998	Continental now adds sites in Argentina, Mexico, South Africa and Slovakia.
2001	Majority holdings are purchased in two Japanese companies.
2003	The world's first road tire approved for speeds up to 360Km/h – the ContiSportContact 2 Vmax – is unveiled.
2006	Continental acquires the automotive electronics business of the company Motorola, Inc..

1 IN 3

NEW VEHICLES PRODUCED IN EUROPE COME FITTED WITH CONTINENTAL TYRES

Brand Values

With its technologies, systems and service solutions, the future starts earlier with Continental. Its contributions make driving an exciting experience, with a long-term vision of its tyres and associated technologies contributing to making mobility and transport safer, more comfortable, more individual and affordable.

dulux.co.uk

Manufactured for more than 80 years, Dulux™ paint has an enviable and established reputation for quality, whilst offering the tools and services that make it easy for consumers to decorate. The brand is instantly recognisable thanks to its iconic Dulux mascot, the Old English Sheepdog, that made his debut in a TV advert in 1961. In recent years the brand's remit has expanded to offering not just high quality paint but also inspiration, support and reassurance throughout the decorating process.

Market

With 174 million litres of paint sold in the UK last year, the DIY market is highly competitive. However, Dulux remains a strong market leader in the category, and continues to drive innovation throughout its products, services and guidance to inspire beautiful living spaces.

Product

Dulux provides a comprehensive portfolio of home decorating products, with its primary focus being on its paints and primers, to deliver leading colour. With a wide range of paint products, Dulux has always led the market in terms of innovation such as its unique product, Light & Space, with its patented LumiTec™ formulation for brighter and more spacious rooms. The last year has

been no different in the long line of innovation launches, with the introduction of Dulux Travels in Colour and Dulux Amazing Space.

Dulux Travels in Colour is a range of colours inspired by beautiful places. The Dulux team of colour and design experts have curated a series of three co-ordinated colour palettes that reflect the mood of the destination; Day at the Beach, Country Retreat and City Getaway. Each of the themes consists of tonal colours, soft neutrals and off-whites designed to go together perfectly, making it easy to create beautiful, contemporary colour schemes.

In 2015, Dulux launched Amazing Space, an innovative, online interior design service that enables people to create affordable, personalised living spaces. For £75, this service brings professional designers directly into people's homes.

The 2014 innovations continue to perform strongly in the market; MixLab, with its easy to follow four-step process, which allows consumers to add functionality and bespoke finishes to their perfect colour; and exclusive Chromalock technology with polymer technology that creates paint with excellent durability, shielding walls from the wear and tear of everyday life.

Brand History

1919	Naylor Brothers, long-established varnish makers, set up a factory in Slough.
1926	Nobel Chemical Finishes acquires Naylor Brothers.
1932	Dulux paint is sold to the building trade for the first time.
1940	Nobel Chemical Finishes becomes known as ICI (Paints) Ltd.
1953	The Dulux brand is introduced to the consumer market for the first time.
1961	Dash – the first Dulux dog – makes his debut in a black and white TV advert.
2004	Dulux Easy Living Editions™ range launches, comprising a palette of 'new neutrals'.
2006	The Light & Space™ range launches, introducing a paint that reflects up to twice as much light as existing paints.
2007	Dulux unveils its new campaign – 'We Know the Colours that Go' – sparking a new wave of personalisation and colour.
2008	Dulux launches PaintPod™ – the biggest innovation in painting since the roller and tray – and AkzoNobel acquires ICI.
2011	The Dulux dog celebrates his 50th anniversary as company mascot and the Ecosense™ paint range launches.
2013	Dulux launches the 'Dulux Let's Colour Awards'.
2014	It is the 10 year anniversary of ColourFutures™.
2015	Dulux Amazing Space design service launches.

200,000 LITRES OF PAINT ARE REDISTRIBUTED BY DULUX TO COMMUNITY GROUPS, CHARITIES AND VOLUNTARY ORGANISATIONS EVERY YEAR

Achievements

For Dulux and the brand owner, AkzoNobel, environmental sustainability is fundamental to its strategy of connecting value creation to resource efficiency. In the UK specifically this year, AkzoNobel's environmental progress was recredited with Carbon Trust Triple Standard for carbon, waste and water reduction for the second time. It is the only DIY company to have achieved all three awards.

Over a decade of Colour Futures™ was marked in 2015 with a global launch in the UK. This annual publication showcases the Dulux forecasted trends for the home, which have been globally inspired and consolidated by a team of experts across design, colour and fashion. It is this level of commitment to colour and design research, for over a decade, which has given integrity to the Dulux brand message 'Let's Colour'.

Dulux also had a successful year at the PRCA Awards, which celebrates the best activity within the PR industry. Dulux won the consumer award for its Colour Britain campaign, which demonstrated the emotional power of colour, positioning Dulux as a transformational brand.

Recent Developments

In 2014, Dulux launched its revolutionary new augmented reality app, the Visualizer, which allows consumers to try colours on their walls in real time. Winner of the most innovative app at the UK IT industry awards in 2014, the Dulux Visualizer app is able to detect the difference between wall space, furniture and fixtures and paint around contours. The decorating tool can be used to pan around a room and, once the walls are identified, will track the colour live – giving decorators the chance to visualise the space as it could be.

Dulux hosted its third successful Dulux Let's Colour Awards in 2015. With the heritage of Dulux rooted in colour, these awards allow Dulux to celebrate and recognise the power and impact of colour across every aspect of its customers' lives. The awards include best use of colour across a variety of categories, including Colour Moment of the Year.

Launched in 2013, the Let's Colour Guarantee is designed to give consumers confidence when choosing colour. Dulux understands that choosing the right paint colour isn't always easy, but if consumers don't get their colour right first time, they can get another free of charge.

Dulux also produces the Let's Colour magazine, which is a high-quality inspirational guide for people actively decorating or thinking about decorating. The magazine helps them to visualise their project and gives them the knowledge and confidence they need to progress.

Promotion

Through all communication in 2015 Dulux focused on making it easy for consumers to decorate. The TV campaign featured Travels in Colour to help consumers create colour schemes with confidence, whilst the Let's

Colour Guarantee provided support and reassurance to consumers that Dulux is there to help with a replacement colour if their first choice isn't quite right.

DID YOU KNOW? The volume of Dulux paint sold in the UK in the last year would fill over 23 Olympic sized swimming pools.

Brand Values
Through Adding Colour To People's Lives™, Dulux aims to transform people's surroundings, their moods, their views and attitude to life. Dulux hopes to inspire consumers to decorate by celebrating the power of colour and the ongoing positive change that comes from creating a beautiful living space.

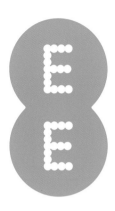

ee.co.uk

EE is the largest, most advanced digital communications company in Britain – providing customers with everything from phones and tablets to fibre broadband and digital TV. It pioneered the UK's first superfast 4G mobile service and offers the UK's biggest and fastest mobile network.

EE SERVES MORE THAN
31 MILLION
CUSTOMERS 𝕚𝕚𝕚𝕚𝕚𝕚𝕚𝕚𝕚𝕚
𝕚𝕚𝕚𝕚𝕚𝕚𝕚𝕚𝕚𝕚𝕚𝕚𝕚𝕚𝕚𝕚𝕚𝕚𝕚𝕚

Market
EE is the UK's largest mobile network operator, with a third of all UK mobile users on its network. With approximately 15,000 employees and 550 retail stores, EE looks after more than 27 million customers on EE, Orange and T-Mobile plans – providing them with mobiles, tablets, broadband, landlines, TV and more.

Product
EE is best known for being the first digital communications company in Britain to offer 4G and fibre broadband together. EE's 4G network now covers 95 per cent of the UK population, and its fixed broadband services reach 15 million households in the UK.

One of EE's goals is to make sure as many people in the UK as possible can benefit from access to 4G, so EE products include the UK's first £1 pay as you go 4G plan. EE also introduced the UK's first shared 4G plans, allowing customers to connect up to five devices to a single mobile plan.

EE TV debuted in November 2014, marking the launch of EE's quad-play offering (mobile, landline, broadband and TV). EE used its understanding of how people watch video on phones and tablets to create a TV experience with mobile at the centre, which is easy to use and accessible in every room of the home.

EE also has a range of own-brand products including smartphones, tablets, 4G Wi-Fi devices and the UK's first 4G Car Wi-Fi. In 2015 EE added the 4GEE Action Cam – the world's first action camera that can live stream over 4G – to its device portfolio.

Achievements
Launching the UK's first 4G network has been EE's most famous achievement to date. But creating the network is something EE has always seen as a starting point.

In 2015, EE also became the first operator in Europe to launch Wi-Fi Calling, allowing customers to make calls in areas with no reception, including basement flats, rural homes and the London Underground.

EE now provides 4G+ (what Apple calls LTE-A) in major cities, following its London launch in 2014. This technology gives customers access to some of the fastest mobile internet speeds in the world, delivering real world mobile data speeds of 150Mbps to a smartphone.

In September 2015, EE hosted the second National Techy Tea Party Day: a nationwide

scheme that sees more than 500 retail stores close their tills so staff can help people improve their basic digital skills over a cup of tea. EE also uses its powerful position as one of the country's biggest companies to boost youth employment.

EE's achievements haven't gone unrecognised either. Over the last few years it has been named Fastest Network at the Uswitch.com Mobile Awards in 2014; as well as best

Brand History

2012 EE launches in October following the merger of Orange and T-Mobile, and switches on the UK's first 4G network.

2013 EE hits one million 4GEE customers just 10 months after launch, four months ahead of target.

EE hits two million 4GEE customers in January.

2014 EE becomes the first mobile network operator to offer contactless mobile payments through Cash on Tap available on London's Underground, DLR and Overground networks.

EE switches on its 4G+ network in central London in October, delivering speeds over 150Mbps in the capital.

EE TV – a new multi-screen TV service offered free with EE broadband to mobile customers – launches in November. There are now six million customers on EE's 4G network.

2015 EE trials the fastest mobile speeds anywhere in Europe, offering visitors to Wembley Stadium speeds of up to 400Mbps.

EE launches WiFi Calling for EE customers, allowing people to make and receive calls and text in areas with no coverage.

EE switches on its 10,000th 4G mast as coverage hits more than 90 per cent.

EE reaches more than 14 million 4G customers by the end of the year, remaining the largest 4G operator in Europe.

DID YOU KNOW?
EE's 4G network covers more than 95 per cent of the UK population, including over 600 towns and cities with a population of more than 10,000, and over 6,000 smaller towns and villages.

network at The Mobile Choice Awards 2015, What Mobile Awards 2015 and the Mobile Industry Awards 2015. For the past two years, EE has also been awarded Best Overall Network by RootMetrics®, the most thorough mobile network performance analysts in the industry.

In the last 12 months EE has made a major difference to public sector groups, including police constabularies and the NHS. Building on this, in late 2015, EE signed a contract with the Home Office to provide the world's most advanced 4G voice and data network, powering Britain's 300,000 Emergency Services workers, helping them save time and save lives.

Recent Developments

Building on the strength of its network and technology, in 2015 EE increased its focus on becoming the market leader for

customer service. The company developed a major retail investment programme including store refits, mobile tablet tills and new service-in-store capabilities. These have had a really positive effect – increasing in-store issues resolutions by 80 per cent and Net Promoter Scores by 55 points, while complaints to Ofcom have halved.

Further service improvements have included digital platforms and a new operations hub for EE's broadband customer service team. These have led to a 31 per cent year-on-year reduction in customer service calls, and the creation of 500 new roles.

Promotion

EE has the UK's biggest, fastest and most reliable network, and this has been the main focus of a number of multi-million pound campaigns featuring A-lister Kevin Bacon. Through TV, cinema, out-of-home and digital, Kevin brings the benefits of EE's network to life, demonstrating the brand's key products and services in the process. EE also bolsters its marketing with a special Apple partnership, allowing EE to feature live demos of the iPhone – the first time Apple has authorised third-party use of the iPhone in this way.

Elsewhere, EE and Glastonbury continued their partnership in 2015. As well as providing phone charging for festival-goers, EE installed a bespoke 4G network on site alongside a number of 4GEE hotspots and created the official festival app.

EE also continued its partnership with the British Academy Film and Television Awards, supporting the EE Rising Star Award, the only BAFTA award voted for by the British public.

Finally, EE is the first lead partner for Wembley Stadium. The six-year partnership was launched in 2014 and aims to see Wembley become the most connected stadium in the world. EE has already doubled 3G and 4G capacity and trialled 400Mbps 4G and 4G broadcast, which allows a full multimedia experience.

Brand Values

EE's brand vision is to show everyone in the UK how the magic of technology can make the everyday better. Its role is to enable people. So if they ever thought they couldn't do this, or they couldn't do that... now they can.

fedex.com/gb

FedEx Express invented express distribution and is the industry's global leader, providing rapid, reliable, time-definite delivery to more than 220 countries and territories, connecting markets that comprise more than 90 per cent of the world's GDP within one to three business days. Unmatched air route authorities and transportation infrastructure, combined with leading-edge information technologies, make FedEx Express the world's largest express transportation company, providing services for more than 3.6 million shipments each business day. FedEx UK provides road distribution and logistics services for the UK, delivering in excess of 200,000 shipments every day from 62 depots.

Market
FedEx Corp. (NYSE: FDX) provides customers and businesses worldwide with a broad portfolio of transportation, e-commerce and business services. With annual revenues of US$48 billion, the company offers integrated business applications through operating companies competing collectively and managed collaboratively, under the FedEx brand. Consistently ranked among the world's most trusted employers, FedEx aims to inspire more than 325,000 team members to remain 'absolutely, positively' focused on safety, the highest ethical and professional standards, and the needs of its customers and communities.

Product
FedEx Express offers time-definite, door-to-door, customs-cleared international delivery solutions, using a global air-and-ground network to speed delivery. It can deliver a wide range of time-sensitive shipments, from urgent medical supplies, last-minute gifts and fragile scientific equipment, to bulky freight and dangerous goods. Each shipment sent with FedEx Express is scanned 17 times on average, to ensure that customers can track its location online 24 hours a day.

In addition to the international product range offered by FedEx Express, FedEx UK provides customers with a wide range of

options for domestic shipping. Within the UK this includes time-definite, next-day and Saturday delivery services. All services are supported by free and easy-to-use automation tools, allowing customers to schedule pick-ups and track their packages online.

FEDEX HAS THREE CORE FOCUS AREAS THAT ITS INVESTMENTS CAN IMPACT ON IN IMPORTANT AND MEANINGFUL WAYS:

 EMERGENCY AND DISASTER RELIEF

 CHILD PEDESTRIAN SAFETY

 ENVIRONMENTAL SUSTAINABILITY

LOCAL PASSION — EUROPEAN AMBITION

Achievements

FedEx Express, which started life in 1973 as the brainchild of its founder Frederick W. Smith, CEO of FedEx Corp., has amassed a long list of 'firsts' over the years. FedEx Express originated the overnight letter, was the first express transportation company dedicated to overnight package delivery, and the first to offer next day delivery by 10.30am. It was also the first express company to offer a time-definite service for freight and the first in the industry to offer money-back guarantees and free proof of delivery. In 1983 Federal Express (as it was then known) made business history as the first US company to reach the US$1 billion revenue landmark inside 10 years of start-up, unaided by mergers or acquisitions.

This history has resulted in multiple awards and honours. In 1994 FedEx Express received ISO 9001 certification for all its worldwide operations, making it the first global express transportation company to receive simultaneous system-wide certification. In 2008 FedEx Express and FedEx UK were granted the highly regarded, internationally accepted ISO 14001:2004 certification for environmental management systems. In March 2015 FedEx Express was named as one of Britain's Top Employers.

DID YOU KNOW?
FedEx works with a number of relief organisations including, The Salvation Army, American Red Cross, Direct Relief and InterAction.

Recent Developments

Connecting to the communities where FedEx lives and works is a really important part of who FedEx is and what it believes in. That is why FedEx team members run a global campaign called FedEx Cares, and volunteer their personal time to support their local communities. In 2015, in Europe alone, FedEx Cares Week volunteer programme drew 1,574 participants. In total, FedEx team members volunteered 3,338 hours across 58 events that saw 2.2 tonnes of food raised for various causes, over 692 blood donations, and thousands of euros raised for various organisations. FedEx is proud to play an active role in improving life in the communities it serves.

Promotion

FedEx has signed an agreement with UEFA in which FedEx will take the Main Sponsor position in the UEFA Europa League. The sponsorship commenced with the start of the 2015/16 season and will extend for three seasons through to 2017/18. A major European football cup competition, the UEFA Europa League, spans 192 teams across 54 European nations, which aligns with FedEx's presence and network in the region. The sponsorship also extends into UEFA's digital channels across desktop and mobile platforms. In addition, FedEx will deliver the trophy to the stadium for the final, where it will be hand-delivered to a UEFA delegate before making the journey to pitch side. The sponsorship builds on FedEx's history of sports partnerships, including sponsorship of the ATP World Tour and 2014 Ryder Cup.

Brand Values

The FedEx corporate strategy, known to FedEx employees as the 'Purple Promise', is to 'make every FedEx experience outstanding'. The Purple Promise is the long-term strategy for FedEx to further develop loyal relationships with its customers. The FedEx corporate values are: to value its people and promote diversity; to provide a service that puts customers at the heart of everything it does; to invent the services and technologies that improve the way people work and live; to manage operations, finances and services with honesty, efficiency and reliability; to champion safe and healthy environments; and to earn the respect and confidence of FedEx people, customers and investors every day.

Brand History

1973 Federal Express establishes operations.

1983 Federal Express reaches US$1 billion in revenue – the first US business to achieve this status without merger or acquisition.

1985 Regular scheduled flights to Europe begin.

1991 ExpressFreighter® is introduced to provide overnight delivery between the US, Europe and Asia.

1994 FedEx launches fedex.com, the first transportation website to offer online package status tracking, enabling customers to conduct business via the internet.

1997 FedEx launches an around-the-world flight, which significantly reduces transit times from Europe to the Middle East, the Indian subcontinent and Asia.

1999 Launch of an improved FedEx International Priority® service through the new FedEx EuroOne® network, featuring later pick up times and earlier deliveries for European customers.

2003 FedEx is successfully recertified for the revised ISO 9001:2000 international quality management standard for its entire worldwide operations.

2009 FedEx Express introduces FedEx International Economy® service for less time sensitive shipments from more than 90 countries and territories around the globe.

2013 FedEx Express surpasses its self-imposed vehicle fuel efficiency improvement target ahead of schedule with more than 22 per cent cumulative improvement in fuel economy for its vehicles.

2014 FedEx marks a European growth milestone by opening its 100th new station in Seville, southern Spain.

2015 FedEx Express celebrates 30 years of operations at the Stansted Gateway (UK).

garmin.com/en-GB

Garmin products are world renowned for their accuracy, durability, build quality and attractive design. For more than 25 years Garmin has pioneered new GPS navigation and wireless devices designed for people who live an active lifestyle. Garmin products are as diverse as activity trackers, sports watches, outdoor handhelds, marine equipment, aviation, cycling computers, satellite navigation (sat nav), dash cams and action cameras, all made to enhance customers' lives. Garmin has more than 11,400 associates worldwide in over 50 locations.

Market

As a leading worldwide provider of GPS navigation, with a history of excellence in research and engineering, Garmin has harnessed technological expertise from multiple sectors and remained at the forefront of innovation. Its 'vertical integration' business model keeps all design, manufacturing, marketing and warehouse processes in-house, giving more control over timelines, quality and service.

Garmin's user-friendly products are not only sought after for their compelling design, superior quality and best value, but they also have innovative features that enhance the lives of its customers.

Product

Garmin designs and delivers solutions for a wide range of customers across automotive, outdoor and recreational, fitness, marine and aviation.

Garmin's automotive products feature valuable tools including situational awareness of traffic, exits, lane-departures, spoken directions, school zones, back-up cameras and much more. These help customers have a safer and more confident driving experience. The devices include personal navigation devices for cars, motorcycles, trucks and caravans.

Garmin's outdoor products are known for ruggedness, reliability, and intuitively simple operation. Customers can rely on the security of always knowing where they are, where they've been and where they're going. The outdoor range includes wrist-worn and mounted devices for hiking, camping, geocaching, golf and hunting.

Garmin also creates high-quality, state-of-the-art products to help customers achieve their fitness goals. Whether returning to a healthy lifestyle or championing the highest levels of competition, Garmin fitness devices provide innovation and inspiration for athletes of all levels. The range has wrist-worn and mounted devices for running, swimming, cycling, golf and other sports, with the ability to monitor heart rate and speed, as well as the ability to track, store and share activities on Garmin Connect.

In 2015, Garmin was named Manufacturer of the Year and received the honour of being the most recognised company in the marine electronics field by the National Marine Electronics Association (NMEA®). Garmin's portfolio includes some of the industry's most sophisticated chartplotters and touchscreen multifunction displays, sonar technology,

high-definition radar, autopilots, high-resolution mapping, sailing instrumentation and other products and services that are known for innovation, reliability and ease-of-use.

Garmin's industry-leading aviation technology has made the skies easier to navigate. From portables to panel-mounts to integrated glass flightdecks, Garmin innovation is modernising the way people fly. Human factor testing ensures advanced Garmin avionics are a seamless extension of the pilot. This range offers OEM, aftermarket and portable avionics for aeroplanes, helicopters

DID YOU KNOW?
Over 10 million people use Garmin Connect, Garmin's online fitness community.

as well as sport aircraft, particularly focusing on satellite weather, traffic, terrain and situational awareness, navigation and communication, transponders, indicators, instruments, and autopilot.

Achievements

Garmin won the Which? Best Buy Awards Sat Navs category in April 2015 for the Garmin nüvi 55LM, 65LM and Garmin nüvi 2599LMT-D sat navs. It was also the Eurobike Award Winner 2015 for the Garmin Varia Bike Radar.

Garmin vivoactive GPS Smart Watch with Sports Apps also won several awards last year, including Men's Running Gold, Women's Running Bronze and the T3 Platinum award. In addition, Garmin vivosmart won the Which? Best Buy Award for Activity Trackers August 2015.

Recent Developments

Garmin has now expanded into different active markets with the Varia range, Index Smart Scales and performance enhanced products, such as Forerunner 235 and Fenix 3.

Garmin has also recently launched Index Smart Scales, providing a full Circle of Wellness and Weight Management, and the vivosmart HR and Forerunner 235, both with wrist-based heart rate and smart notifications. In addition to this, Garmin has launched the Varia range, the first bike radar in the world.

Promotion

Garmin had a number of advertising campaigns over the course of 2015. The 'Forerunner. For Runners' campaign focused on the idea that no runner is the same, and neither are Garmin's products. The campaign advertised the wide range of devices available so customers could find a training partner that is right for them.

The 'Beat Yesterday' campaign featured across video, print, digital and social media, with the aim of turning consumers' global data from Garmin Connect to LetsBeatYesterday.com – a motivational site that creates goals based on previous achievements, inspiring consumers to do a little better than the day before. The campaign championed the feeling of success whilst turning consumers' attention to the Garmin devices that make data tracking possible.

Garmin also sponsors a range of sporting teams across its product sectors. It is the official navigation and fitness partner for Southampton Football Club and Saracens Rugby Club, has previously championed support for Cannondale Garmin cycling team and the Clipper Round the World Race, in addition to having a Garmin pilot and aeroplane in the Red Bull Air race.

GARMIN HAS SOLD MORE THAN
144.9 MILLION DEVICES

Brand History

1989 Garmin is founded by Gary Burrell and Dr. Min Kao.

1993 The company introduces the first GPS with a moving map (GPS 95) and goes on to pioneer the GPS market for automobiles with the first portable mapping GPS for automobiles (StreetPilot®).

1997 Garmin innovates the digital cockpit with the GNS® 430 and 530.

1998 The first car sat nav is announced, the StreetPilot®. Detailed routes can be manually created in software and there are no spoken directions.

1999 Garmin creates the first dedicated walking handheld GPS device, the eTrex®.

2000 Garmin goes public on the NASDAQ stock market.

2003 The first wrist-based GPS is announced. The Forerunner 101 uses the GPS signal to calculate time, pace and distance.

2005 The nüvi 300 series launches and is the first modern-shaped (rectangular and portable) sat nav made by Garmin.

2007 Garmin launches the Garmin Connect website to enable customers to upload and share their fitness data.

2009 Garmin launches its first triathlon watch – Forerunner® 310XT.

2014 Garmin enters the Action Camera and Wellness markets with the VIRB and VIRB Elite action cameras and the vívofit wellness band.

Brand Values

The foundation of the Garmin culture is honesty, integrity, and respect for associates, customers, and business partners. Each associate is fully committed to serving customers and fellow associates through outstanding performance and delivering what it promises to do.

haagen-dazs.co.uk

One of the world's first super-premium ice creams, Häagen-Dazs was introduced in 1961 by Reuben Mattus, whose vision was to make the best ice cream in the world using only the finest ingredients. In doing so, he pioneered a new luxury category in the ice cream sector. The brand has remained true to its founder's principles and is so proud of its original vanilla ice cream that the recipe has not changed in over 50 years.

Market

Häagen-Dazs is one of the most successful and indulgent brands in the world, sold in 80 global markets. It is a leading player in the UK's luxury ice cream sector, currently number two in the luxury pints and mini cups market (Source: Nielsen ScanTrack, Total Coverage, Value Sales, w/e 6th November 2015).

creamy texture and innovative products all reflect a deep commitment to quality. It took six years, for example, to find strawberries perfect enough for its Strawberries & Cream flavour.

Starting in 1961 with only three flavours – Vanilla, Chocolate and Coffee – the brand currently has 19 flavours in retail.

DID YOU KNOW?
The name Häagen-Dazs doesn't actually mean anything. The founder, Reuben Mattus, invented the name to sound Danish, as a tribute to Denmark's extraordinary treatment of the Jews during World War II.

Product

The ultimate indulgent treat, Häagen-Dazs is created from a base of 100 per cent real milk and cream, as well as yolks from free-range eggs. Its mouth-watering flavours, dense,

Achievements

Häagen-Dazs is currently valued at £43 million in a category worth £153 million (Source: Nielsen ScanTrack, Total Coverage, Value Sales, w/e 6th November 2015).

Recent Developments

Haagen-Dazs recently relaunched a heritage flavour in the UK, Coffee. With it's smooth texture and balanced flavours, Häagen-Dazs Coffee ice cream uses only five ingredients, combining Brazilian coffee with real cream, milk, egg yolks and sugar. The coffee

HÄAGEN-DAZS USES
REAL CREAM AND MILK
FROM SOME OF THE
BEST DAIRY COWS IN EUROPE

beans are sourced from specially selected regions of Brazil. Once harvested, each coffee bean is then lightly roasted and blended to create a fuller, richer flavour. Then it is combined with Häagen-Dazs ice cream to create a unique flavour.

Following this the brand also introduced a limited edition range called Little Gardens. Inspired by nature, this unique range includes two botanical flavours – Apricot & Lavender and Lychee, Raspberry & Rose.

For the Apricot & Lavender flavour, Häagen-Dazs uses apricots from Morocco and France and lavender from the Mediterranean coast to create an ice cream that is both fruity and floral. The Lychee, Raspberry & Rose flavour is crafted with rose extract originating from Turkey.

The Little Gardens packaging has been designed by the Jardins de Babylone, specialists in plant inspired creations.

Häagen-Dazs also invests in bringing excitement and new news to the category with its programme of seasonal flavour variants. The brand has been celebrating its tradition of craftsmanship and ice cream expertise by delighting the world with exquisite, limited edition Christmas Ice-Cream Cakes. Now in its eighth year, Häagen-Dazs has collaborated with one of the most iconic interior designers, Paola Navone, to ensure that their 2015 Christmas cake goes down in memory as one of the most stunning examples of gastronomic design ever seen.

DID YOU KNOW?

Häagen-Dazs has a very low overrun (the amount of air incorporated into the product during freezing) which is why it takes longer to be able to scoop once it comes out the freezer, providing the creamy, thick, indulgent texture.

Proposing an edible advent calendar design, Navone worked with Häagen-Dazs pâtissiers to create 31 pillars of ice cream to represent the 31 days from 1st December to New Year's Eve. In order to make it truly special, they agreed on a sumptuous white chocolate coating, velvety base and ice cream hidden within each pillar, covered in either edible gold or edible silver leaf.

Häagen-Dazs has left its luxury mark on the arts world through its partnership with the Royal Albert Hall as well as with iconic theatres and venues across the UK. Over 4.5 million mini cups are sold in such venues every year (Source: Nielsen ScanTrack, Total Coverage, Value Sales, w/e 6th November 2015).

Promotion

In 2014, Häagen-Dazs began an exciting new direction with a renewed commitment to the brand's founding principles of craftsmanship and quality ingredients through the 'Nothing is Better than Real' campaign.

Häagen-Dazs has had continued success with this theme. The hashtag #realornothing brings the brand to life, whilst also making people aware of the quality ingredients that go into Häagen-Dazs ice cream.

Brand History

1921 Reuben Mattus, founder of Häagen-Dazs, helps in his mother's ice cream business selling fruit ice and fruit ice pops from a horse-drawn wagon in the bustling streets of the Bronx, New York.

1940 Ice cream becomes a year-round treat due to improved refrigeration. Mattus expands the product line to include pints, quarts, half-gallons, bulk ice cream and novelty items.

1950 Mattus introduces innovations including colour-coded packaging, year-round retail distribution and round pint containers.

1960 The original Häagen-Dazs range launches with three flavours: Chocolate, Vanilla and Coffee.

1961 The Häagen-Dazs name is registered by Mattus to market the single best ice cream available.

Häagen-Dazs super-premium ice cream starts to be sold in gourmet shops in New York City.

1990 Häagen-Dazs opens a flagship store in Leicester Square, London, and begins retail distribution.

1992 The new manufacturing facility in Arras, France is established.

2013 The new Salted Caramel ice cream launches, which quickly rises to become a top five flavour for the brand.

2014 The 'Nothing is Better than Real' advertising campaign launches.

2015 Häagen-Dazs relaunches its heritage Coffee flavour.

2016 The limited edition range, Little Gardens, launches.

Brand Values

Today Häagen-Dazs is more committed to its founding values of quality and craftsmanship than ever, using the finest quality ingredients possible to create a super-premium ice cream.

hallmark.co.uk

On 10th January 1910, an 18 year-old boy called JC Hall stepped off a train in Kansas with nothing to his name but two shoeboxes full of picture postcards, big dreams and entrepreneurial spirit. He quickly sold the cards, taking orders for many more, and Hallmark Cards was born. More than 100 years and billions of good wishes later, Hallmark continues to thrive and remains the world's largest supplier of greeting cards.

Market

Since 1910, Hall's vision has been to create a world-class product that encompasses creativity and a way to bring people together. His passion for design, innovation and quality has been the foundation of everything Hallmark puts its name to and continues to be the driving spirit that has made this family business the iconic international brand it is today.

Even in the digital age, sending a 'physical' card remains a cornerstone of British life. Be it birthdays, special occasions, Christmas, Valentine's Day or just to say hello, the British public sends more than £1 billion worth of cards every year, with the greeting cards industry remaining one of the largest retail categories, larger than tea, coffee or biscuits.

In the 100 years since JC Hall established Hallmark Cards many things have changed, but Hallmark's passion for quality and creativity has not. Working with key high street retailers and grocers, more than 1,500 independent card shops across the country and 150 Gold Crown stores, Hallmark leads the way in category expertise as well as nurturing the best creative talent in the industry. Hallmark's New Designers programme helps more than 50 graduate designers a year come into the industry. Hallmark was the first greeting card company to sponsor New Designers – the UK design degree showcasing over 3,000 of the best in graduate design talent.

Product

Hallmark operates in more than 100 countries worldwide, employing some of the world's best designers, creating over 10,000 new cards per year. The company believes in partnering with the very best brands and licenses to give its customers more choice. The offerings include ranges from Star Wars, Disney and Warner Brothers to Hello Kitty, RSPCA and The Simpsons, to name but a few. The Forever Friends brand continues to be one of the most loved and commercially successful brands within the portfolio, together with the global collectable

DID YOU KNOW?
Around 10,000 new greeting cards are launched annually by Hallmark's Kansas City headquarters. (Source: Hallmark Corporate Facts).

sensation, Itty Bittys, appealing to a wide range of ages and tastes. In January 2014, Hallmark launched its exclusive 'Handpicked' brand for independent retailers and May 2015 saw the Hallmark family tree extending to launch the Hallmark Studio, targeting a new generation of card lovers with quirkier, 'of the moment' humour, to premium ranges such as Hall & Co.

Whatever the genre or design, Hallmark believes in creating the very best products, using authentic editorial with a high refresh rate, which ensures the best mix of products at the right prices.

AT HALLMARK WE HAVE A LITTLE MANTRA:

leave your mark

IT'S WHAT WE DO.
THIS IS HOW WE MAKE OUR MARK

Achievements

Hallmark stays close to what's going on in people's lives, with some of the best insight in the industry, working exclusively with the Kantar world panel, alongside substantial investment in market research. As category leaders, Hallmark is continually striving to be first to market, with a track record of innovation that has been recognised by the industry with 21 Henries awards (Greeting Card Association awards for new product innovation – voted by industry buyers). In a challenging market with cheaper product alternatives, Hallmark has stayed true to its principal of careful stewardship of the environment. In the UK Hallmark ensures that 100 per cent of products use certified, well managed, or recycled, materials.

Recent Developments

In a world where consumer needs are changing, Hallmark leads the way in trend analysis and innovation. From its innovation team of more than 2,000 people in the US to local designers in Yorkshire, Hallmark has pioneered new production techniques, in addition to introducing innovative technology which offers customers customisation options, delivered via hubs in the US. New proprieties, such as the collectable Itty Bittys, have grown in appeal beyond cards and created fun for customers old and young. This also goes for Hallmark's retailer programme, Gold Crown, partnering with independent retailers in the UK and Ireland to roll out its 'LIFE' retail space with fresh and exciting displays.

Promotion

Globally, Hallmark remains the leading consumer card brand with iconic advertising campaigns, keeping it in the front of customer minds and impressing its inextricable link to quality. Campaigns such as 'Care enough to send the very

HALLMARK HOLDS LICENSING AGREEMENTS
WITH 4 OF THE TOP 5
BIGGEST LICENSED PROPERTIES

best', encouraging consumers to flip over the envelope to see the famous Hallmark embossing, have kept preference high. Embracing social media has renewed relevance to younger generations and seasonal campaigns, such as Mother's Day, #mumsmoment, have helped people stay connected and express their feelings easily.

AND BECAUSE OF ALL OF THAT, WE CAN DO LOVELY THINGS LIKE THIS.

Brand Values

In 2015 Hallmark launched its new brand essence 'Leave your mark'. This is underpinned by a simple promise that for the moments that matter, Hallmark cards will help leave a more enduring mark. By producing the very best to help people communicate and connect, Hallmark has established a brand that is synonymous with caring and quality, creativity and innovation. Today's brand statement brings together all these values, at the same time as connecting it to the original dictionary definition of the word 'hall-mark', a sign of distinctiveness and quality.

Brand History

1910 Joyce Clyde Hall jumps on a train from Nebraska to Kansas City with big dreams and two boxes of postcards under his arm.

His brothers Rollie and William join him. Hall Brothers is formed.

1928 Hall Brothers becomes Hallmark Cards.

1958 Hallmark UK opens for business in its London offices.

1959 Hallmark UK's first Spring Seasons range launches.

1966 Hallmark International is set up in the UK to co-ordinate all activities outside of the US.

1968 The company starts supplying Don Lewin, founder of Clinton Cards, with greeting cards. Clinton Cards begins business.

1972 Fine Arts is established in Ireland to print all of Hallmark's requirements in Europe.

1984 WN Sharpe's in Bradford is acquired.

1994 The company acquires The Andrew Brownsword Collection and bring Forever Friends and Country Companions into the Hallmark portfolio.

1998 Hallmark Cards UK forms – merging all the previous acquisitions into one business.

Creative Publishing is acquired, including Tigerprint – a sole supplier to Marks and Spencer today.

2001 Hallmark Cards plc forms.

2005 The first national television advert launches for Hallmark UK.

2008 The company website, Hallmark.co.uk, launches.

2011 The flagship store in Leeds opens, along with the Hallmark brand's relaunch to give a new vision, look and feel.

2015 The company launches its Hallmark Studio brand and the 'Leave your mark' brand positioning.

ESTD
HARDYS
1853

hardyswines.com/uk

The world's leading Australian wine brand and the number one selling wine in the UK, Hardys was established in Australia in 1853 by Thomas Hardy. From humble beginnings, it has grown to a position where it is enjoyed in more than 100 countries and is into the fifth generation of the Hardy family. Represented by William (Bill) Hardy who, in 2015, was named 2015 South Australian Legend of the Vine by Wine Communicators in Australia. This longevity of a proud tradition in winemaking is at the heart of Hardys' success, with the brand having won more than 7,000 wine awards to date.

Market
Hardys has long been one of the most successful wine brands in the competitive UK market with the top three players holding less than a 13.3% market share. Over the past year, Hardys has reinforced its position as the UK's market-leading wine brand with retail sales worth in excess of £309 million per annum. It continues to gain share in this category with annual growth of six per cent in value (Source: ACNielsen 52 Weeks to 12/09/2015).

DID YOU KNOW? Two million glasses of Hardys are enjoyed daily in more than 100 countries.

Product
Hardys has an extensive portfolio, spanning a variety of price points and wine varietals. These include the well-known Hardys VR, Hardys Stamp of Australia, Hardys Crest and Hardys Nottage Hill sub-brands – all of which have been available in the UK market for over two decades. A more recent addition to the range in 2012 was the William Hardy range of wines, created as a tribute to the Hardy family's proud heritage and dedication to winemaking, and to recognise the 40-year contribution of fifth generation family member, Bill Hardy. In 2014, this range saw a brand refresh with an upgrade to premium quality cues in the packaging.

Recent Developments
Hardys has recently aligned itself with the UK's number one summer sport, cricket, by partnering with England Cricket as its Official Wine Partner.

Promotion
In 2014, Hardys became the Official Wine of England Cricket, signing a three-year sponsorship deal. The England Cricket partnership affords Hardys global reach via extensive in-ground and perimeter advertising at all England

IN 2014 HARDYS SOLD MORE THAN 70 MILLION BOTTLES OF WINES IN THE UK

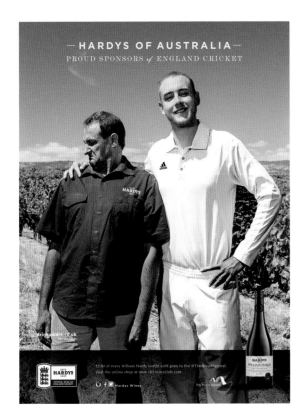

home games. Hardys complemented the deal by sponsoring Sky Sports' broadcast coverage of England Test and IT20 home matches.

The second year of the partnership, 2015, saw the Australians return to England for Test cricket's premier series, the Ashes. Having the Australians in town provided Hardys with the opportunity to juxtapose the irony of an Australian wine brand sponsoring the England cricket team in the brand's above-the-line and below-the-line campaigns. The campaign, which featured England cricketer Stuart Broad, captured the reactions of Hardys' Australians employees discovering that their company sponsor the old enemy in a fun, light-hearted manner, and the adverts generated extensive positive sentiment.

The 360 cricket campaign also included an on-pack consumer competition where cricket tickets were given away every 24 hours, as well as a focused PR and digital campaign, utilising cricketing ambassadors including Stuart Broad, Sir Ian Botham, Glenn McGrath and Michael Vaughan. Hardys also ran a wine sales unit at all England international matches throughout the summer, allowing fans to enjoy an extensive range of Hardys wines in-ground.

Outside of the cricket, Hardys continued its journey to re-educate consumers on the heritage and quality of the Hardys brand with the 'Five Generations of Devotion' campaign, which focused on the pioneering and progressive nature of the Hardys family. The campaign was symbolised by objects from the family's history, handed down from generation to generation and was brought to life via outdoor media, press and digital.

In addition, May 2014 saw the culmination of Hardys 'All About Chardonnay' campaign, with a three-day pop up bar in central London.

Achievements
At the pinnacle of Hardys' offering are the internationally acclaimed Eileen Hardy wines. This iconic range was born in 1973 when

the matriarch of the Hardy family turned 80. Since then, the winemakers select the very best handpicked parcels of fruit to carry the label each vintage.

In 1882, Thomas Hardy made history by producing the first Australian wine to be awarded the prestigious Gold medal at the International Wine Show in Bordeaux. Recently, Hardys won gold medals across the range for Eileen Hardy Chardonnay at the 2015 International Wine Challenge awards and gold for Thomas Hardy Cabernet Sauvignon at the 2015 Decanter World Wine awards.

It was also acknowledged as the world's leading Australian wine or spirit in the Power 100 Intangible Business Report 2014.

DID YOU KNOW?
More than 70 million bottles of Hardys are sold per year in the UK.

Brand Values
Hardys has built a tradition of great endeavour in winemaking; Thomas Hardy's vision was to produce wines that would be prized in the markets of the world by showing outstanding innovation and resourcefulness, directed at making wines of quality and character. The expertise and devotion driven by the Hardy family since 1853 is in every sip of its wine.

Brand History

1850 Thomas Hardy leaves Devon for Australia, where he finds work with John Reynell, South Australia's first winemaker.

1853 Thomas purchases his first property at Bankside and establishes Hardys.

1857 Thomas produces his first Bankside vintage and becomes one of the first exporters of Australian wine.

1870 Thomas launches his Oomoo range and purchases the Tintara vineyards and winery in McLaren Vale.

1882 Thomas' wines become the first Australian wines to be awarded two prestigious Gold medals at the International Wine Shows in Bordeaux 1882 and Paris 1889.

1884 Thomas Hardy's nephew, Thomas Hardy Nottage, joins the family business.

1912 Thomas Hardy dies. His son, Robert Burrough Hardy, takes over the business.

1953 A centenary celebration is held at the house of Eileen Hardy.

1976 In recognition of her contribution to the Australian wine industry, Eileen Hardy is awarded an OBE.

1988 Hardys Stamp of Australia range launches at the World Exposition in Brisbane.

2012 To celebrate the 40 years of dedicated service from fifth generation family member, William (Bill) Hardy, the William Hardy range launches.

2013 Continuing the vision of its pioneering founder, the entire Hardys range is revitalised with a new packaging design.

2014 Hardys announces a major three-year sponsorship deal as the brand becomes Official Wine of England Cricket.

2015 Hardys launches a cricket campaign which plays on the juxtaposition of an Australian wine brand sponsoring the English cricket team.

Heathrow

Making every journey better

heathrow.com

Heathrow is the UK's gateway to the world. Each year, over 74 million passengers choose Heathrow as a springboard for travel and adventure, spending time with friends and family – or forging international business links. Heathrow helps more passengers with their journeys than any other airport in Europe. Along the way, they enjoy some of the best airport facilities, services and shopping in the world.

Market

As Britain's only hub airport, Heathrow is home to 82 airlines, serving more than 180 destinations with over 8,000 international flights weekly – including six of the world's 10 busiest intercontinental routes. In passenger volume, Heathrow is the largest in Europe (and third largest globally) handling an average of more than 200,000 passengers each day, with 37 per cent of these connecting between flights. Its busiest ever day on record was 22nd May 2015 with a passenger total of 246,000.

Product

At Heathrow, passenger experience is everything. This is defined by its purpose: 'Making every journey better'. Its priority is to offer a stress free and memorable journey between home or onward connection and air travel. This means Heathrow is constantly working to improve every aspect of the through-airport journey. This includes the ease with which passengers travel to and from the airport, find their way around, and the punctuality of flights.

It encompasses the quality and value of shopping and food – including retail services such as Passenger Ambassadors who collectively speak over 38 languages, as well as Personal Shoppers, Shop & Collect and Reserve & Collect.

Heathrow partnered with luxury lifestyle group and concierge service company, Quintessentially, to conduct an in-depth review of its retail service offerings to ensure Heathrow brings to life its corporate vision – to deliver the best airport service experience in the world.

The introduction of new independent lounges throughout the airport means that passengers can find a lounge in every terminal to relax, refresh and prepare for their flight. It also extends to opportunities for passengers to enjoy spa facilities, exhibitions and other special events. Passenger confidence in safety and security, and staff courtesy as well as attentiveness are equally important priorities.

Achievements

In 2015, Heathrow was awarded the Best Airport in Western Europe accolade for the first time and Best Airport Shopping for the sixth year in a row. Terminal 5 was voted, for the fourth consecutive year, the World's Best Airport Terminal with Heathrow's overall competitive position in the World's Best Airport category continually improving. The airport is now ranked eighth in the world in 2015, jumping forward two places since 2014 (Source: Skytrax Awards).

DID YOU KNOW?
The total size of Heathrow airport is 1,227 hectares.
It has 470,695 flights annually, or 1,290 per day on average.
Its cargo volume is 150 million metric tonnes per year.

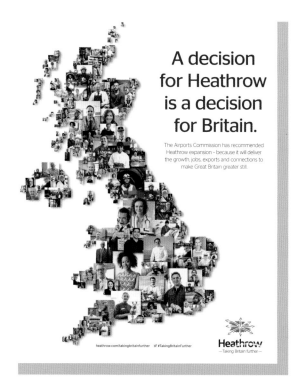

A decision for Heathrow is a decision for Britain.

The Airports Commission has recommended Heathrow expansion - because it will deliver the growth, jobs, exports and connections to make Great Britain greater still.

heathrow.com/takingbritainfurther ⅋#TakingBritainFurther

Heathrow
—Taking Britain further—

HEATHROW'S MOST POPULAR DESTINATIONS ARE:

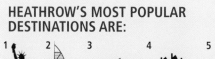

1 NEW YORK 2 DUBAI 3 DUBLIN 4 HONG KONG 5 FRANKFURT

Because your holiday means everything to us, too.

Kids Eat Free — While you've been thinking of the beach, at Heathrow we've been thinking of how to help get you there in holiday mood.

We want the excitement to start at the airport, so there are free play areas for your little ones – and VAT-Free shopping and exclusive offers for you.

Free play areas

There's Kids Eat Free in restaurants. Free beauty treatments. And helpful Heathrow people everywhere, from check-in to boarding gate.

We know your holiday is something you really look forward to. So at Heathrow this summer, we've everything to help it take off. Look forward to seeing you.

VAT-Free shopping

Heathrow
Making every journey better

heathrow.com/summer

Brand History

1946 London Airport opens on the current site.

1966 The British Airports Authority is created and London Airport is renamed Heathrow Airport.

1977 The London Underground reaches Heathrow.

1997 The Terminal 5 public planning inquiry – the longest in UK history – comes to an end.

1998 The Heathrow Express rail service begins.

2008 Terminal 5 opens and the first commercial A380 flight arrives at Heathrow.

2010 Terminal 2 is demolished and work starts on its £1 billion replacement.

2012 Heathrow welcomes the world as Host Airport for the 2012 Olympic Games and Paralympic Games.

2014 Terminal 2: The Queen's Terminal opens in June.

2015 Expansion of Heathrow is recommended by the Airports Commission.

In 2015, Heathrow received the ECO-Innovation Award from the Airports Council International, the Private Sector Fleet of the Year (Medium-Large) Award 2015 by Green Fleet Magazine and the 8th Biodiversity Benchmark Award (The Wildlife Trust). Heathrow also received a four out of five rating by the Business in the Community Index, the UK's leading benchmark of responsible business practice. Responsible Heathrow 2020 continues its commitment to supporting the UK and local economies and reducing Heathrow's environmental impacts, while looking after passengers and people.

Recent Developments

In January 2015, Terminal 5 revealed a fashionable new look, unveiled by style icon Laura Bailey. As part of the reopening, Louis Vuitton opened its first ever European airport store joining Fortnum & Mason, Cartier, Rolex and Bottega Veneta in the luxury brands line up at Terminal 5. Heathrow also welcomed a new airline partner to the airport, Vietnam Airlines. The airline launched its new 787-9 Dreamliners from the UK's hub operating at Terminal 4 with direct services four times a week to and from Vietnam.

Heathrow Rewards loyalty programme continued to strengthen member benefits with the introduction of Emirates as a partner of the programme. Members also receive free Wi-Fi and benefit from Instant Rewards at a range of stores including World Duty Free, Jo Malone and Dixons Travel where points can be redeemed instantly for a discount. Points can now be converted to air miles with Emirates Skywards in addition to existing partners Avios, British Airways Avios, Eithad Guest, Virgin Atlantic's Flying Club and Miles & More.

Heathrow Rewards has over one million members and throughout the year, has given its loyalty members £1.2 million of vouchers to spend on their future visits to the airport.

Another important activity, Heathrow Academy, has continued to work with the five neighbouring boroughs to provide pre-employment training, recruitment and apprenticeships for roles within retail, construction, aviation and logistics, as well as customer service.

Promotion

Advertising communications in 2015 continued to build on delivering the brand promise of 'Making every journey better' by promoting its focus on passenger experience and the sheer pleasure of travel. The summer campaign brought to life the service-focused initiatives for holiday travellers, such as family-friendly security, free play areas and 'kids eat free' offer. Each advertising campaign is tailored to showcase the very best of Heathrow for all the different reasons passengers travel through and their different needs; starting from before they reach the airport through to their choice of shopping, eating and relaxing while at the airport.

Heathrow was also the focus of a three-part documentary series called 'Britain's Busiest Airport – Heathrow' that was filmed between June 2014 and January 2015, transmitted on ITV1 in June 2015. It achieved around 3.5 million viewers.

Brand Values

A fleeting impression when connecting. A last look before departure. An emotional welcome home. Heathrow wants every experience of its airport to be the best it can possibly be for each of its 74 million-plus passengers. Heathrow knows that, for them, it's their journey that matters most. That's why Heathrow does everything it can to make it an experience that shows modern Britain at its very best.

Hotpoint

hotpoint.co.uk

For more than 100 years, Hotpoint's mission has been simple; make life at home easier. Whatever the need, Hotpoint has developed a product tailored to it. From small to large appliances, freestanding or built-in, Hotpoint's range of products deliver outstanding performance through a combination of innovative technology and stylish design.

Market

Operating in the highly competitive home appliances market – in which approximately 12 million appliances are sold each year – Hotpoint is one of the UK's leading manufacturers, selling an appliance every 19 seconds (Source: AMDEA, 2015). Hotpoint appliances are sold both online and in-store, through a distribution network that includes many of the UK's leading electrical retailers.

Product

Hotpoint's range comprises a complete choice of freestanding, built-in and small appliances that together provide the complete kitchen solution. Its products are manufactured in centres across the world, including 12 factories in the UK and Europe. The built-in collection includes stylish ovens, hobs and hoods, which provide outstanding cooking performance, as well as integrated appliances across laundry, dishwashing and refrigeration. The freestanding range covers laundry, dishwashing, refrigeration and cooking, with each product featuring unique technologies designed to deliver superior performance.

In 2013 Hotpoint launched HD Line; a new collection of small appliances that incorporate everything from food and drink preparation to microwaves and coffee machines, plus floor and garment care. Today, that range has grown to incorporate MY Line and the new Ultimate Collection of premium small appliances.

In 2015, Hotpoint continued to build on its reputation for creating innovative appliances with the launch of two new ranges. The new Ultima S-Line washing machine removes more than 100 stains at just 20°C, keeping colours and fabrics safe with Direct Injection technology, whilst the new Ultima fridge freezers include the latest in cooling technology to help maintain the first day freshness of food for up to 14 days.

DID YOU KNOW?

Hotpoint got its name by creating the first electric iron; an iron that was literally 'hot to the point'.

As well as delivering outstanding performance, Hotpoint understands the importance of good design in delivering both functionality and style, which is why all its products are designed by internationally renowned product designer, Makio Hasuike.

A commitment to quality is at the heart of Hotpoint's design and manufacturing process. Every product goes through a rigorous testing process designed to simulate 10 years of use – the equivalent of thousands of hours. For this reason, Hotpoint can be confident in the quality and reliability of its appliances, which is why all large appliances now come with a 10-year parts guarantee for extra peace of mind.

Achievements

Hotpoint has been part of the fabric of Britain for over 100 years and today two in every three households have at least one Hotpoint appliance. Each year, over

Brand History

 1911 Hotpoint is founded and launches its first major product, the Hotpoint iron.

1920 -30s The first washing machine is launched, and vacuum cleaners, travelling irons, kettles and portable clothes dryers are added to the range.

1961 The Hotpoint Home Centre opens in London's Oxford Street, providing demonstrations, lectures and films showing all aspects of homemaking.

 1970 -80s Hotpoint establishes itself as market leader in the home appliance sector.

 1990s Hotpoint introduces its first 'Frost Free' fridge freezer.

 2006 The first Aqualtis washing machine launches.

2011 Hotpoint celebrates its 100th birthday.

2013 Hotpoint returns to its roots with the launch of the HD Line of small appliances.

HD technologies – including Zone Wash, Active Oxygen and Direct Injection – are introduced to the market.

Hotpoint launches Next Generation – a range of its most energy-efficient appliances ever.

2014 Lisa Faulkner is revealed as Hotpoint's official brand ambassador.

2015 Hotpoint launches the #LoveYourKitchen campaign and embarks on new digital content partnership with BBC Good Food.

800,000 products are manufactured from the Hotpoint factory in Yate, near Bristol. The company employs more than 2,200 people across the UK and boasts a market-leading service and logistics operation, which includes the largest white goods service team in the UK and Ireland. Each member of the service team is a fully trained Hotpoint specialist, which is why 90 per cent

of customers recommend the Hotpoint after-sales service. With a reputation built on quality, reliability and innovation, Hotpoint has more than 60,000 independent consumer reviews via Reevoo – more than any other appliance brand – with an average score of 9/10.

Recent Developments

As with other sectors, there has been a significant increase in the number of consumers researching and then buying home appliances online; 80 per cent of consumers will research an appliance online before purchasing and over 50 per cent are now making that purchase online (Source: Google Consumer Barometer, 2015).

This shift means consumers now have more information and choice than ever before. For this reason, Hotpoint has transformed the way it communicates with consumers, with a greater emphasis on digital communication to support this change in the customer purchasing journey. Enhanced product content, detailed videos, 'Buy now' functionality and consumer reviews are all now prominently featured on the hotpoint.co.uk website, to ensure a consumer has all the information they need. This also means that content needs to be device responsive to ensure a better consumer experience, as 80 per cent of consumers will use their smart phone to view product content, even when they are in a store.

Technology and energy efficiency has also moved on significantly, however, there is still a tendency to hold on to old, inefficient appliances. Today, more than 30 per cent of appliances in the UK are more than 10 years

DID YOU KNOW?
Hotpoint's Ultima S-Line washing machine removes more than 100 stains at just 20°C.

old. Hotpoint continues to address this issue through its 'Change for the Better' initiative, which aims to educate consumers on the improvements and cost savings the latest home appliance technologies can offer.

Promotion

Hotpoint's aspiration is to become the most-loved appliance brand for the kitchen. To support this ambition, Hotpoint teamed up with leading author, TV cook, actress and former Celebrity MasterChef winner, Lisa Faulkner. Lisa now acts as the brand's ambassador and fronts all major brand campaigns for cooking, including a national TV advertising campaign showcasing the innovative Dual Flow cooking system. Hotpoint also continued a sponsorship agreement with the Good Food TV Channel, which incorporates programme advertising as well as activation online, in print, via social media and through consumer events including the BBC Good Food Show. This

THERE ARE APPROXIMATELY
16 MILLION
HOTPOINT APPLIANCES IN
HOMES THROUGHOUT THE UK

has been further enhanced by the new #LoveYourKitchen campaign, which features media partnerships with BBC Good Food Magazine as well as Jamie Oliver's Food Tube channel, ensuring cooking content featuring Hotpoint appliances is seen by millions of UK consumers. The #LoveYourKitchen campaign also includes a series of national promotions, designed to offer added-value to consumers whilst demonstrating how Hotpoint appliances care for the things that consumers and their families love most, be it their clothes, fresh food or cooking.

Brand Values

By creating appliances that combine stylish design with innovative technology that improve lives through performance, Hotpoint's mission is to become the most-loved appliance brand for the kitchen.

HOWDENS
JOINERY CO.

MAKING SPACE MORE VALUABLE

howdens.com

Howdens Joinery was founded in 1995 in order to serve the needs of small builders undertaking routine joinery and kitchen installation work. Howdens is now the UK's leading supplier of integrated kitchen and joinery products, all of which are available to the trade all the time from local stock. Howdens' local depot managers are entrepreneurs with a high degree of autonomy and responsibility for the performance of their own depot.

Market

Howdens Joinery operates within the trade or 'done for you' kitchen market, its core customer base comprising local builders and skilled professionals.

The company believes that project management by local builders is the best way to install a kitchen. The constantly increasing sophistication of products, services and end-users' expectations, combined with the need to keep abreast of legislation governing every aspect of materials and installation, has driven strong growth in this market.

Howdens helps builders to manage their businesses by guaranteeing product availability from local stock with rigid

cabinets that are ready to install, saving builders time and money as well as allowing them to plan effectively. Its versatile supply chain ensures its depots, and in turn its customers, receive a high level of service. Specifically within the trade sector, key competitors are Magnet Trade, Benchmarx and Travis Perkins.

Product

Howdens sells integrated kitchens – encompassing appliances, accessories, handles, worktops, sinks and taps – and joinery, such as doors, flooring, stairs and hardware.

The company has the UK's largest kitchen range available from stock and ensures a constant flow of new product by gathering

feedback from its depots. As all depots hold stock locally, they are also able to offer local delivery to site for a small charge. A free survey and state-of-the-art computer-aided design (CAD) service, which includes a site visit, is also available. Howdens has developed an exclusive appliance, sink and tap brand, Lamona, and all appliances come with a two-year guarantee.

Achievements

Since it was established 20 years ago, with just 14 depots and sales of £1 million, Howdens has demonstrated strong growth. Sales in 2014 were in excess of a milestone £1 billion and by November 2015, the business was operating from 614 depots nationwide.

In 2014, Howdens supplied over 365,000 complete kitchens, 650,000 appliances and 2.3 million doors to over 330,000 building trade professionals who serve homeowners, private and public landlords, and housing associations.

In 2015, Howdens Joinery was awarded the Royal Warrant of Appointment to Her Majesty The Queen, as a Supplier of Fitted Kitchens.

DID YOU KNOW?
Howdens recycles more than 98 per cent of all manufacturing waste produced.

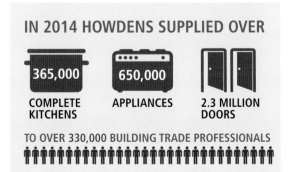

IN 2014 HOWDENS SUPPLIED OVER

365,000	650,000	2.3 MILLION
COMPLETE KITCHENS	APPLIANCES	DOORS

TO OVER 330,000 BUILDING TRADE PROFESSIONALS

Howdens has been in partnership with Leonard Cheshire Disability for 11 years. As well as employee volunteering and fundraising activities, Howdens supports and funds Leonard Cheshire's 'Can Do' project, which gives young adults with disabilities the chance to volunteer in their own communities. Howdens also works with Leonard Cheshire Disability services across the UK to develop affordable, attractive and practical kitchen facilities for people with disabilities. Its 'Inclusive Kitchen' collection is sold through its depots and many kitchens are donated to Leonard Cheshire care homes.

Recent Developments
Product development remains key to the company's focus on continued growth. In 2015, Howdens introduced 17 new kitchens across all price points and styles, bringing its total range to more than 50. Other key developments include the introduction of affordable granite worktops, AEG and Neff appliances, and premium additions to the Lamona appliance range.

The company has been awarded FSC® and PEFC™ chain of custody certificates for a number of its joinery products, worktops and kitchen ranges, and it continues to work to gain further certification. All of its manufacturing and warehouse sites maintained ISO 14001 for environmental standards, and it also remains certified under the Carbon Trust's prestigious Energy Efficiency Accreditation Scheme, an accolade that it has held for more than 10 years.

Promotion
Howdens puts the relationship between local depots and builders at the heart of its promotional strategy. As such its literature is specifically designed to help builders in discussion with their own customers. Local marketing is critical and each depot tailors its promotional activity to meet customer needs. Howdens continues to develop its range of Lamona cookbooks and cast iron trivets, which are given to customers when they have a kitchen planned.

To further raise awareness of the brand, Howdens attended 13 county shows and agricultural fairs across the country in 2015. The stands were manned by local depot staff who spoke to visitors about the company and handed out literature and promotional items.

Howdens continues to invest in digital communications and now has over 180 product movies available on its website and YouTube channel. In every depot there is a 'virtual showroom' to enhance the customer experience. A large TV or projector and media player allows presentations of customer CAD plans and product movies.

Since 2009 Howdens has published 16 'Truly Local' books to tell the stories behind individual customer relationships and to illustrate some of the ways in which a Howdens depot is an integral part of its local community. Many depots choose to make donations to local charities and community projects, including sponsorship of grassroots football and rugby teams.

DID YOU KNOW?
Howdens employs over 7,000 people across the UK.

Brand History

1995	Howdens Joinery starts trading in October with 14 depots.
1999	Howdens opens its 100th depot.
2004	Howdens sets the standard in the trade kitchen market with its new format, high quality Kitchen Brochure.
2006	Howdens launches a market-leading Joinery Brochure featuring doors, joinery and flooring.
2007	The Howdens website launches in April and the 400th depot opens.
2008	The launch of the first Howdens-branded delivery trailers and home interest magazine advertising.
2009	The Lamona appliance, sink and tap brand, exclusive to Howdens, is launched.
2010	The concept of kitchen 'families' is introduced.
2011	Howdens opens its 500th depot.
2013	Howdens introduces the 25-year cabinet guarantee.
2015	Howdens celebrates its 20th anniversary, and is awarded the Royal Warrant of Appointment to Her Majesty The Queen.

Brand Values
Howdens supply integrated kitchen and joinery requirements from local stock nationwide to the small builder's ever-changing routine, assuring best local price, no-call-back quality and confidential trade terms.

investec.com

Investec

Investec is a distinctive Specialist Bank and Asset Manager, providing a diverse range of financial products and services to a niche client base. The business has three divisions: Specialist Banking (including services for private clients as well as corporates), Asset Management and Wealth & Investment, and employs 8,500 people. Investec strives to be 'out of the ordinary' in everything it does. It is involved in a range of sponsorships in its key markets of South Africa and the UK, sponsoring various events and initiatives in fields including hockey, cricket, equestrian, music and horticulture.

Market

Founded in South Africa in 1974, Investec currently has a market capitalisation of £4.9 billion globally and maintains principal offices in London and Johannesburg, with origination, sales and distribution channels in Australia, Asia, Europe and North America.

Investec manages to differentiate itself in the notoriously competitive financial markets in which it operates by bringing unusual thinking to the table. Investec's original approach and challenging nature are often called upon when 'out of the ordinary' solutions are

required. Investec's people are driven by a common spirit; they challenge, question and explore all possibilities in order to deliver for clients. In short, Investec is a company of ideas.

Investec was founded by a group of like-minded individuals with a passion and desire to build a new company with a unique attitude in the finance world. The business has survived world recessions and has seen growth that has made it a FTSE 250 company, and the 16th largest bank in the UK, where it is also a top three private client wealth manager.

Paradoxically, Investec is seen as both a thought leader and a challenger-brand. It has an international presence and is a South African success story. Investec is an organisation where the people it employs embody the brand values and continues to build its reputation in markets worldwide.

DID YOU KNOW?
Stephen Koseff, Investec's CEO is the longest-serving CEO of a UK listed bank.

Product

Based on a deep understanding of the financial challenges its clients face, Investec has developed a wide range of products and services to respond to individual client needs. From private banking, finance and lending, to investing, treasury

IN 2015 #INVESTECASHES APPEARED ON TWITTER OVER **600 MILLION TIMES**

Brand History

1974 Investec is founded in South Africa.

1989 Investec Limited is listed on Johannesburg Stock Exchange.

1992 Investec is established in the UK, with its first international acquisition.

2000 Investec searches for an 'Out of the Ordinary' advertising campaign to stand apart from the cluttered market; the zebra joins the brand.

2002 Investec is listed on both the London Stock Exchange and Johannesburg Stock.

2015 Investec plc is a FTSE 250 company, 16th largest bank in the UK and a top three private client wealth manager in the UK.

and trading, Investec prides itself on being ideas led and solution driven. By connecting capabilities and sharing insights, Investec can advise clients on the best strategy to achieve their objectives.

While focused on providing creative and successful solutions, Investec delivers its services in a unique way. Investec knows it can't be all things to all people, so it focuses on on what it does best – being distinctive in the market.

Achievements

Since its founding, Investec has grown significantly, establishing itself as a household name in South Africa as well as having offices in Australia, Botswana, Channel Islands, China, Hong Kong, India, Ireland, Mauritius, Namibia, Switzerland, Taiwan, the UK and USA. The brand has received many industry awards including Best Private Banking Current Account; Best Structured Product Provider; SME Champion of the Year; and Best service from an Asset Based Finance Provider.

Recent Developments

The Investec brand goes from strength to strength as it continually adapts to changing economic and customer behaviours. Underpinning this at all touch points of the brand are Investec's core strategic values. As customers desire to be more aligned to the brands they choose to deal with, Investec responds by offering a more joined-up and inclusive experience. Investec has always used brand differentiation to separate its offer from that of its competitors. It is this cultural difference that is the focus of Investec bringing its clients closer to the Investec brand.

DID YOU KNOW? Investec is the fifth largest bank in South Africa.

Promotion

The name 'Investec' was first introduced in the 1970s to reflect a combination of investment and technology, its core strengths at the time.

The focus symbol, seen today, was first designed in the 1980s; to show an organisation that was focused and had its clients' goals in sight at all times. Since then the shape and style of the focus symbol has evolved, moving to its current position in 2000 and changing colour to sky blue in 2009.

The Investec zebra has become the most instantly recognisable brand element and the visual trigger for most global communications. The Investec zebra has proved to be a flexible marketing tool, providing brand consistency at all levels and represents the values and aspirations of Investec. The now familiar icon supports the distinctive undertone of the company and remains true to the 'out of the ordinary' positioning. There are now over 100 zebras in the Investec brand library, each of them named after a member of the company's marketing teams.

Brand Values

The Investec brand is built around attitude and personality: energy, creativity, performance and focus. Its mission statement declares 'We strive to be a distinctive specialist bank and asset manager, driven by our commitment to our core philosophies and values'.

Investec is a meritocracy, a tightly focused business and determined to cultivate an environment that stimulates extraordinary performance. Investec's positioning is an assertion of confidence, creativity and implies that extraordinary standards are the norm. The company demands the exceptional from its staff and promises to deliver it to clients.

Out of the Ordinary*

⊕ Investec
Specialist Bank

Great business minds don't think alike

Ideas, Advice, Financing, Risk Management.
Strategies for your business success

Investec's attitude is reflected in its sponsorships and advertising. As Investec's products are not mass market, being distinctive and exceptional is central to all of its promotions. Across the brand, Investec's sponsorships provide a key avenue for engaging with its target market, whether through TV coverage, activation at events, creative and unusual hospitality, stand out advertising or innovative PR. Thinking beyond the conventional is key to its relationship with any sponsorship whether it is the Investec Test Series and the Investec Ashes; the Investec Derby Festival; Investec Super Rugby in New Zealand; or across a multitude of other sponsorship assets including opera and horticulture.

investorsinpeople.com

Investors in People is the Standard for people management. The Standard exists to enable every individual and team to succeed by realising the potential of their people. The prestigious accreditation is a mark of excellence held by 14,000 organisations worldwide. At its heart, Investors in People is a high performance framework, developed to enable every person to achieve their full potential. Why? Because good people make a great business. It's a simple idea that drives everything Investors in People does.

Market
The Standard was launched in 1991 to raise the performance of UK businesses relative to international competitors. Today, the world of work and business is transformed. In September 2015, Investors in People launched the sixth generation of its management Standard to reflect the very best of modern workplaces.

Product
The new Standard, which is comprised of nine indicators for high performance, is an internationally recognised mark of excellence. From Australia, the Philippines, Europe and the United Arab Emirates,

Investors in People has created a global community of like-minded organisations.

Alongside the launch of the new Standard, Investors in People is pulling ahead as a leader in the B2B marketing field and has transformed its approach to communicating the product. The launch of the new Standard in 2015 won the prestigious B2B Marketing 'Best Brand Initiative', strengthening the brand's position as one of 2016's Superbrands.

Promotion
The 2015 'Outperformance' campaign defined Investors in People's core messaging in line with the revised product offer. New core benefits such as industry benchmarking, a performance focus, a unique progression model and the launch of a Platinum award were revealed through the campaign. The campaign ran in partnership with Sir Dave Brailsford, former Team GB Olympic cycling coach, as a brand spokesperson. Sir Brailsford's commitment to measurable increases in performance and continuous improvement made him a natural spokesperson for Investors in People and the Outperformance creative.

SINCE 1991 MORE THAN
10 MILLION PEOPLE
HAVE WORKED IN AN ORGANISATION
RECOGNISED BY INVESTORS IN PEOPLE

ORGANISATION AMBITION

09 CREATING SUSTAINABLE SUCCESS
01 LEADING AND INSPIRING PEOPLE
02 LIVING THE ORGANISATION'S VALUES AND BEHAVIOURS
03 EMPOWERING AND INVOLVING PEOPLE
04 MANAGING PERFORMANCE
05 RECOGNISING AND REWARDING HIGH
06 ...UCTURING ...WORK
LEADING

Recent Developments

Last year also saw the second Investors in People member awards held at the iconic Tower of London. Businesses from across the globe came together to recognise and celebrate the people that make their organisations great. In 2016, Investors in People will host its third awards ceremony, celebrating the very best of its organisations and drawing applications from across the Investors in People global community. With 2016 being the 25th Year of Investors in People, the Awards programme promises to be the largest and most talked about event in the industry.

Brand Values

The Investors in People visual brand identity reflects the simple belief that it's the people that

DID YOU KNOW? Investors in People is celebrating 25 years of excellence in people management.

make the difference. Its values are engrained in the Investors in People culture, underpin its strategy, and are embedded in its product:

People first – Everything Investors in People does is guided by the belief that organisations succeed by realising the potential of people. Achieving this ambition starts with building trusted relationships with its people, partners and clients.

Excellence – Upholding standards is Investors in People's business and is at the heart of its brand. Its people, products and approach to clients is driven by the belief that if it's worth doing, it's worth doing well.

Continuous improvement – Better tomorrow than today. Learning from the best and seeking to outperform is Investors in People's habit. This starts with learning and always listening to bring this insight to customers through its market leading product.

Sustainability – Investors in People believe in making decisions for the long term. This means paying close attention to big trends and drivers in the economy, workforce demographics and technology, as well as bringing a focus on sustainability through its product.

Leadership – Inspiring and motivating customers starts with inspiring and motivating Investors in People's own people. This begins with vision, focus and motivation at every level of the business. This enables it to lead the discussion and ensure that everyone sees the benefit of investing in people.

By capturing and sharing these factors, the Investors in People Standard reflects the features of organisations that consistently outperform industry peers, helping to deliver tangible results for members.

Achievements

In 1991, Investors in People was a government-led initiative offered with grant subsidy to employers. Today its product competes in the market as a value proposition, generating £20 million in commercial revenue and supporting 14,000 client organisations, as well as a network of more than 400 highly trained practitioners. This strategic re-positioning has enabled the sustainability of the business, greater focus on client value, and a stronger member community.

As a brand, Investors in People has maintained significant awareness amongst UK businesses, and retained its position as the dominant B2B people management accreditation. The UK Commission's Employer Perspectives Survey of 18,000 employers reported that 74 per cent of the UK business audience are aware of the Standard, and 47 per cent of businesses report to know about the product (Source: UKCES, 2014).

In November 2015, Investors in People won Best Brand Initiative at the B2B Marketing Awards, for the 'Outperformance' campaign with OgilvyOne Business, fronted by former performance director of Great Britain's cycling team, Sir Dave Brailsford.

Brand History

1990 The Employment Department is tasked with developing a national standard of good practice for training and development; Investors in People is born.

1991 The first 28 Investors in People organisations are celebrated at the company's formal launch.

1993 Investors in People UK forms as a business led, non-departmental public body.

1995 The first review of the Standard occurs and an operation is established in Australia.

2004 Investors in People launches the latest version of the Standard and the Champions programme is introduced.

2007 Investors in People 'Interactive', a free online support tool, launches.

2008 7,771,357 employees are in organisations working with Investors in People.

2009 An extended framework introducing Bronze, Silver and Gold recognition launches.

2010 The Health and Wellbeing Good practice Award is launched and ownership of the Investors in People trademark transfers to the UK Commission for Employment and Skills.

2012 Investors in People operates in 80 countries worldwide.

2013 Investors in people undergoes a brand refresh.

2014 The annual Investors in People awards launch at London's Landmark Hotel. More than 1,000 employers are involved in the re-design of the new Investors in People Standard and Framework.

2015 Investors in People launches the sixth generation Standard at The Bridgewater Hall in Manchester.

2016 Investors in People hosts its third award ceremony, alongside celebrating 25 years of excellence in people management.

ironmountain.co.uk

Iron Mountain is a leading global provider of storage and information management services. The company's solutions help organisations to lower storage costs, comply with regulations, recover from disaster and use their information to promote business advantage. Founded in 1951, Iron Mountain stores and protects billions of information assets, including business documents, backup tapes and electronic files as well as medical data, music recordings and more for organisations around the world.

Market

The information management market continues to grow as businesses recognise the need to protect and manage the information they receive and create. The market in Europe is dominated by a small group of international companies as well as a large number of local players. Iron Mountain is the worldwide market leader with 67 million sq ft of real estate across more than 1,000 facilities in 36 countries, and a global turnover of US$3 billion.

Product

Information management is Iron Mountain's core business. It has more than 60 years' experience in managing information for organisations large and small. It continually invests in its people and services to ensure that information is protected at every touchpoint.

Its records management service looks after the classification, storage, access and security of active or archived paper records. Its off-site data protection service provides secure and reliable storage and retrieval of customers' electronic backup media.

The Iron Mountain box, a key feature of its records management business, has long served as a testament of its unwavering commitment to safeguarding customers'

information. Over the course of six decades, it has gone beyond the box to develop innovative new services. From intelligent scanning and digitising, to records retention solutions, technology escrow, tape storage and archive tape management for e-discovery, Iron Mountain offers services and solutions at every stage of the information lifecycle.

Achievements

Iron Mountain's experience, dedication and stability make it one of the most trusted names in the business. It works with more than 85 per cent of the FTSE 100 companies and 156,000 organisations worldwide. Investing in a network of facilities and experts across the globe ensures that its quality standards are applied on every continent. Iron Mountain operates in North America, Latin America, Europe and Asia Pacific. Recently, Iron Mountain has achieved significant growth in international markets.

Iron Mountain strives to meet internationally recognised standards in information security, protection, management and resilience. Companies entrust Iron Mountain with approximately 500 million boxes of paper records and more than four petabytes of

data. It maintains the highest level of ethical and security standards, derived from industry best practices. All of its 17,500 employees are security vetted and it has invested in achieving the ISO 27001 security standard and PCI DSS in the UK.

Recent Developments

Iron Mountain creates new solutions to help businesses identify ways to save time, money and space, stay secure and compliant and access information more quickly. Advances in records management include a new service that compiles and delivers records retention guidance to Iron Mountain customers. In

the data field, Archive Tape Management Services offer an efficient approach to managing growing tape catalogues and e-discovery requests.

Iron Mountain stores a vast and growing archive of wills and letters of probate on behalf of Her Majesty's Courts and Tribunals Service (HMCTS). The precious documents span six generations from 1858 to the present day. In 2013, Iron Mountain and HMCTS initiated a project to digitise 230,000 World War I soldiers' wills. The award-winning PR campaign helped bring more than one million visitors to the online portal, where the entire archive of 41 million digital copies of the wills was available to be ordered by the end of 2014.

Growing the business in international markets is key to Iron Mountain's growth strategy. Its 2014 acquisitions included 10 organisations in North America and one in Belgium. Iron Mountain also bought out its joint venture partners' interests in Serbia, Denmark, Russia and the Ukraine, and acquired ALCZ, a provider of records management services in the Czech Republic. To expand its footprint in emerging markets, the company purchased Keepers Brazil, which operates five storage facilities across Sao Paulo. In 2015, Iron Mountain

completed the purchase of Crozier Fine Arts and US-based Box Butler. Both decisions reflect strengths in secure storage.

Building a sustainable business is a priority. In 2014, Iron Mountain published its first Corporate Social Responsibility report, Taking Care, which outlines a commitment to working with its customers, team and suppliers to look after the environment, its communities, its people and its business. Iron Mountain has pledged to cut its absolute greenhouse gas emissions across North America and the UK to five per cent below 2012 level, and has been recognised with awards for its Green Fleet and environmental operations. It has an ongoing partnership with CyArk, a non-profit organisation dedicated to the scanning and digital preservation of 500 world heritage

DID YOU KNOW?
Iron Mountain's secure vaults store the wills of Princess Diana, Dickens and Darwin; the 1959 patent of the Red Delicious apple; and the original recordings of Frank Sinatra and Jimi Hendrix.

sites. Last year saw the digitisation of the Brandenburg Gate to celebrate 25 years of German unification.

Promotion

Recent marketing strategies have supported growth in new markets and in particular with mid-market companies across Europe. In 2015, Iron Mountain, in conjunction with Pricewaterhouse Coopers (PwC) created the first-ever value index enabling organisations across the world to measure how well they manage information for advantage. Iron Mountain continues to innovate through integrated marketing campaigns using social, PR, online, direct mail and event channels.

Investments in thought leadership have focused on helping businesses understand the future of information management and the goal of balancing risk and value.

Brand Values

Complete Confidence is Iron Mountain's brand promise at the heart of what it does and what it delivers. It reminds the organisation of what is most important: its customers' trust, and its trust in its people. Iron Mountain's core values are security, total customer satisfaction, candour, integrity, accountability, action orientation and teamwork.

GLOBALLY, IRON MOUNTAIN STORES
500,000,000
BOXES OF RECORDS AND
4,000,000,000,000,000
BOXES OF DATA TAPES

Brand History

1951 Iron Mountain Atomic Storage is founded in Boston, MA, USA. Herman Knaust converts a former iron ore mine into a bunker for vital records.

1962 Businesses seek a blast-proof vault for protecting vital records amid fears of nuclear war.

1996 In February, Iron Mountain becomes a public company with annual revenues exceeding US$100 million.

1999 Iron Mountain opens its first UK office in Southwark, London.

2005 Iron Mountain offers Intellectual Property Management services and Technology Escrow in Europe.

2010 Iron Mountain commits to a social responsibility programme, Iron Mountain Taking Care.

2011 Top analyst firm, Gartner, recognises Iron Mountain as a Leader in Enterprise Information Archiving.

2012 Iron Mountain and PwC create Europe's first Information Risk Maturity Index.

2013 Iron Mountain and HMCTS digitise 230,000 soldiers' wills from World War I.

2014 Iron Mountain invests US$150 million to acquire international records and information management businesses.

2015 Iron Mountain and PwC create the first global information value maturity index.

Iron Mountain purchases Crozier Fine Arts and Box Butler and moves into the art storage and consumer storate fields.

JEWSON

BLOG

jewson.co.uk

With more than 600 branches across the country, Jewson is the UK's leading supplier of sustainable timber and building materials. It offers the widest range of quality materials and products from everyday core essentials to the latest sustainable innovations.

Jewson also has specialist landscaping, joinery, insulation, tool hire, brick, kitchen and bathroom centres up and down the country.

Market

Jewson has over 300,000 customers ranging from trade professionals, small to medium builders, national contractors, house builders, homeowners, architects and construction companies.

Such variety allows Jewson to specialise in key areas, offering technical product information and support across all branches. It is committed to delivering a great customer experience through sustainable, mutually beneficial, long-term partnerships.

It is part of the Saint-Gobain group, one of the largest construction businesses in the UK and is a world leader in design, production and distribution of materials,

delivering innovative products and services with tomorrow in mind.

Product

Jewson offers an extensive range of more than 600,000 products, including a significant number of renewable technologies and sustainable solutions. Every branch stocks a comprehensive range of quality products including heavy and light building materials, sustainable timber, sheet materials, doors, joinery and plumbing materials.

Many branches also offer kitchen and bathroom showrooms, landscaping centres, roofing centres and dedicated tool hire services. Jewson prides itself on its friendly, knowledgeable employees providing high

levels of customer service and the first class partnerships it holds with all key product suppliers across the UK.

Achievements

In October 2015, Jewson was named 'the best builders merchant for self builders' in the Build It Awards. Over the past year Jewson has invested in its self build offering, ensuring support is on hand via the new dedicated Jewson Self Build Team – a group of assigned customer service experts helping customers through every stage of their build.

October also saw the Jewson Tools website receiving an eCommerce Award for Excellence in the Best Business2Business

eCommerce category. The Jewson Tools website replicates the reliable service that customers have come to expect when they visit a Jewson branch.

The website was recognised by an independent panel of judges – digital experts from companies including Google and Tesco – for delivering a high-class customer experience with advice on offer via live chat and a quick checkout process.

Furthermore, Saint-Gobain UK was named as a Top Employer in 2015 for the third year running, awarded by the Top Employer Institute. In particular, the group was singled out for its managerial culture, training and professional development.

Recent Developments

To celebrate and support communities across the UK, Jewson launched a competition to give away a total of £100,000 to fund the renovation of community buildings. Over 2,000 entries were received with a wide range of nominations – from community gardens and village hall refurbishments to wheelchair boxing facilities and services for the elderly.

The 14 winners were invited to a Building Better Communities celebration event at the Greenworks Training Academy in Birmingham. Penlee RNLI Lifeboat Station in Penzance received the top £50,000 prize for its appeal to re-erect the 31-year-old lifeboat base.

Developed by Jewson and its sister brands, the Academy has become an authority in sustainable building products and solutions. The Academy helps customers to advance knowledge and skills in sustainable building by providing unbiased training, consultancy and in-depth advice on solutions in new markets.

JEWSON HAS OVER 600 LOCATIONS NATIONWIDE

CUSTOMERS ARE NEVER MORE THAN A 16-MINUTE DRIVE FROM A BRANCH

DID YOU KNOW?

The first Jewson branch opened in 1836 – for 180 years it has been supplying building materials and supporting the trade.

The Jewson Pro Build Training Tour was launched last year to provide vital support for trade professionals through local Jewson branches. Free to attend, the events offer customers the chance to gain updates on the latest product innovations, talk to experts about best practice installation methods and ensure compliance with changing Building Regulations.

Last year Jewson opened a new, innovative Customer Experience Centre in Binley, Coventry. The centre is home to the Customer Experience Team, who support the Jewson Operations Team to improve experience and customer service levels of Jewson. The team answers email and phone requests, providing customers with advice, information and guidance on Jewson products and services. The team also conducts Jewson Customer Score surveys (based on the Net Promoter Score), to continuously monitor feedback.

The working environment at the centre has been designed to have a positive impact on employees' health and well-being. It comprises a quiet room where mobile and laptop use is prohibited, a Fit for Work Zone with exercise machines and a social area. Working with the charity Business in the Community, it has been able to provide work experience placements for local unemployed people.

Promotion

Jewson is a multi-channel builders' merchant with customer experience at the core of all its promotions. It offers targeted marketing campaigns, with regular trade promotions on specific everyday products or services through direct mail and online channels.

E-business is an instrumental part of Jewson's marketing strategy. The Jewson website includes detailed information for more than 16,000 core products, a suite of tools to support the trade customer and up-to-date industry news items. The website also offers an online account management service available to all account holders, providing access to order history and current balance, to credit limit reviews 24/7.

Jewson has focused on friendly employees in-branch for 180 years, meaning a wealth of knowledge is directly shared with customers every day. Trade professionals, whatever stage in their career, still want to be able to take advantage of face-to-face advice from an expert.

Brand History

1836	George Jewson buys a company in Earith, dealing in coal, timber, lath, bricks, cement and salt. The Jewson brand is born.
1882	Jewson wins its first major contract, supplying wooden paving to the city of Norwich.
1966	Jewson merges with Horsely Smith to create one of the largest timber and builders' merchants in the country.
1995	Jewson expands after the recession and acquires 21 Builders Mate branches.
1996	The acquisition of Harcros adds 201 branches to the Jewson network.
1998	Jewson relocates to Coventry, still the home of its Head Office today.
2000	Jewson becomes part of the Saint-Gobain group.
2010	The launch of the Sustainable Building Guide and the Greenworks Training Academy marks a new age for modern construction.
2011	Jewson celebrates its 175th anniversary.
2012	Jewson acquires Build Center and integrates 99 new branches into the network.
2015	Saint-Gobain celebrates 350 years of innovation.

Brand Values

Jewson's number one commitment is to maintain a safe and accident-free environment. The Jewson model has three pillars: colleagues, customers and suppliers. High-performing people are at the heart of the Jewson business – colleagues are its greatest asset: friendly, reliable and knowledgeable.

Jewson also values diversity and development to make sure its colleagues are representative of the local customers they serve. Delivering an excellent customer experience is at the centre of all Jewson's activities, resulting in long-term relationships. Its suppliers are crucial in helping Jewson remain a sustainable and ethical builders' merchant, which contributes to local communities in a positive way.

kingspan.com

The driving force behind the Kingspan ethos is to provide effective, lifetime value, low energy and low carbon solutions for the built environment. From thermally efficient, practical and beautiful building envelopes, to energy generation and water management systems, Kingspan delivers a whole host of innovative products, backed by the highest levels of technical support and customer service.

Market

Kingspan products can be found in buildings all over the world, in all sectors: community and amenity, education, healthcare, hotel and leisure, industrial, offices, housing and retail, including both new build and refurbishment projects.

With a growing global demand for energy efficient buildings and clean energy generation, Kingspan products can help reduce energy consumption both for space heating and cooling by providing sources of renewable energy, as well as other environmental solutions such as rainwater harvesting.

Product

The Kingspan Group has four operational divisions: Insulated Panels, Insulation,

Environmental, and Access Floors, each offering a wide selection of products for the construction industry. Each division offers high levels of customer support, including design, technical services, Building Energy Modelling, U-value calculations, field services, waste take-back schemes, after sales and comprehensive product guarantees.

Achievements

Following on from the launch of the ground-breaking ZerO Energy Lighting solution in 2014, Kingspan Insulated Panels continued to fulfil its role as a systems and solutions provider, investing in innovation across all product lines to create ever-more sustainable

buildings that deliver total lifetime cost reductions to building owners and occupiers. The introduction of new colours, finishes and materials brought more creative choices to architects throughout 2015.

In July 2015, Kingspan Insulated Panels announced the global launch of IPN-QuadCore – the company's biggest scientific breakthrough in insulated panel core technology for over a decade. Delivering industry-leading thermal performance, unique guarantees, superior fire protection and enhanced environmental credentials, IPN-QuadCore raises building performance to new levels. The vision for IPN-QuadCore is to become a hallmark of quality and a recognised brand within the global insulation industry. It will continue to roll out across all of Kingspan's markets worldwide throughout 2016.

Kingspan Insulation reached another milestone in its journey of continuous improvement after its manufacturing facility in Pembridge, Herefordshire was awarded World Class Operation Management (WCOM) Gold. The WCOM programme covers nine

DID YOU KNOW?

IPN QuadCore from Kingspan Insulated Panels offers a unique 40-year thermal and structural guarantee.

different areas including engagement, quality, maintenance, and production. Other sites within Kingspan Group are also working towards achieving WCOM Gold by 2018.

Find additional space where you never knew it existed.

The Pembridge site was also certified to energy management standard ISO 50001, complementing the ISO 9001 (Quality Management), ISO 14001 (Environmental) and OHSAS 18001 (Health and Safety) standards to which the site's fully integrated management system has already been certified.

In terms of firsts for the industry, Kingspan Insulation launched a new online U-value calculator – the first to feature calculations approved under the BBA / TIMSA competency scheme. Also, the Kingspan OPTIM-R panel became the first vacuum insulation panel to be granted a BDA Agrément®. While Kingspan Access Floors launched a new access floor pedestal adhesive that is believed to be the first in the industry to be phthalate free.

Following its most recent audit under issue 3.0 of BES 6001: Responsible Sourcing of Construction Products standard, Kingspan Insulation is the first insulation manufacturer

Recent Developments

Kingspan Insulated Panels has continued to grow through acquisition, geographical expansion and the launch of new core technologies and systems. The acquisition of the building products division of Canadian firm VicWest in late 2014 boosted Kingspan's ability to drive conversion of the North American market to more energy-efficient panels, coming at a time when the energy agenda is becomingly increasingly persuasive. The additional acquisition of Joris Ide in January 2015 – a pan European manufacturer and supplier of insulated panels with leading market positions in France and Benelux together with manufacturing facilities in Belgium, Germany, Romania and Russia – provided a complementary geographic

DID YOU KNOW?
In 2014 28 per cent of the Group's energy usage was from renewable sources. It is currently on track to exceed an interim target of 50 per cent in 2016.

to have products manufactured at its Pembridge and Selby facilities certified to the Excellent level.

footprint to Kingspan's existing European insulated panel business.

Finnish PIR insulation manufacturer, SPU, was acquired in July 2015 as part of the continuing programme of expansion of the Insulation Division. The acquisition will allow an unparalleled range of products and expertise to be offered to the northern European market.

Kingspan is also now the sole owner of premium performance pipework insulation manufacturer Kingspan Tarec, now renamed Kingspan Industrial Insulation Limited following the purchase of Recticel's 50 per cent stake in the business.

Promotion

Kingspan's communications strategy spans both traditional print and digital media, with technical articles, case studies, video content, Twitter, LinkedIn and active blogs, highlighting industry news and engaging with stakeholders.

The different divisions within the Group exhibit at major trade shows, such as EcoBuild and Batimat. Kingspan sponsor key industry events and provide CPD training in a number of different areas. There is also a strong track record on the Award scene, with regular wins across the board.

Brand History

1960s Founded by Eugene Murtagh, the Kingspan Group, a small engineering business, starts up with the manufacture of steel frame buildings.

1970s The business moves into the small-scale manufacture of environmental products.

1980s The Group starts to grow steadily, establishing a number of plants in Ireland and the UK, manufacturing Insulated Panels and Insulation products.

1990s The start of a significant Group growth period, with expansion and diversification into Europe, establishing facilities and sales teams in Benelux, Germany, Poland, Hungary and the Czech Republic.

2000s The focus turns to broadening the network and strengthening the Group's global presence across Europe, North America, Australia, and South East Asia. Further acquisitions lead to the creation of two new Divisions – Access Floors and Environmental.

2010s Investment in acquisitions, plant and product development provides the platform for continued growth.

36% OF KINGSPAN GROUP SALES CAME FROM ITS UK MARKET IN 2014

Brand Values

The Kingspan brand seeks to go beyond the simple manufacture and supply of products, to provide customers with significant added value in terms of service, support and product benefit.

The business actively develops solutions for current and future industry issues, making life easier for specifiers and contractors and making the built environment better. Its business aim is to become the world's leading provider of low energy building solutions.

lastminute.com

lastminute.com

In the late 1990s, Brent Hoberman was turning up at flash hotels trying to blag a top suite at a knockdown price. He was surprisingly successful. Once he joined forces with Martha Lane Fox, they decided that everyone should get a five-star lifestyle for three-star prices – and made this their mission. In 1998 lastminute.com was born, bursting with top-notch ideas to help people make the most of their free time, minus the extravagant price tag.

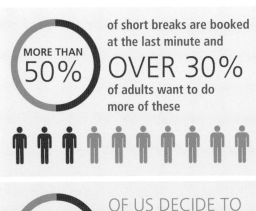

MORE THAN
50%

of short breaks are booked at the last minute and

OVER 30%
of adults want to do more of these

27%

OF US DECIDE TO BOOK A MAIN HOLIDAY IN LESS THAN TWO WEEKS

Market

lastminute.com serves up more things to do than anyone else in Europe and was the first to offer 'last minute' European travel and experiences online. Today, with smartphones and tablets enabling spontaneity like never before, this proposition is more relevant than ever, as customers hanker to milk the most out of every minute whether going out or going away. lastminute.com customers book, on average, a hotel six days before checking in. Furthermore 58 per cent of rooms are booked five hours before check-in.

lastminute.com's customers have seen every theatre show, tried every menu and are always looking for the next great experience. lastminute.com provide their spontaneity-seeking customers with an array of possibilities for adventure, be it local or global, theatre or spas.

Today's culture is one of 'now', and lastminute.com is perfectly placed to live at the heart of this. In fact, when lastminute.com asked independent researchers to discover which European brand people associated with 'last minute' travel and leisure, 94 per cent of them mentioned lastminute.com.

Product

lastminute.com's customers are always looking to do more good stuff. They wake up on Thursday and decide that they want to go to Barcelona on Saturday.

lastminute.com serves up not only hotels, but flights, city breaks, experiences, spa deals, theatre tickets, restaurant deals and a whole host of spontaneous and surprising gift ideas.

Achievements

In summer 2015, lastminute.com's brand team broadcast its brand new 'Love

DID YOU KNOW?

lastminute.com is the UK's largest provider of things to do worldwide with more than 1.65 million site visitors per week. Headquartered in Farringdon, London, lastminute.com also operates in Ireland, France, Germany, Italy and Spain.

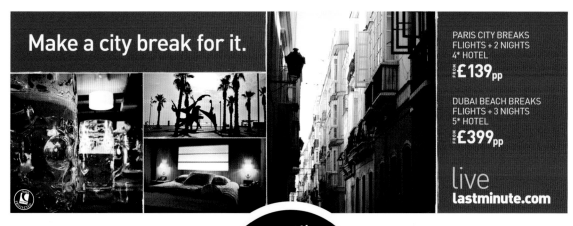

Make a city break for it.

PARIS CITY BREAKS
FLIGHTS + 2 NIGHTS
4* HOTEL
FROM **£139**pp

DUBAI BEACH BREAKS
FLIGHTS + 3 NIGHTS
5* HOTEL
FROM **£399**pp

live
lastminute.com

Every Minute.' European TV commercial. Last minute by name last minute by nature, it was produced and broadcast in a record-breaking two weeks. A marketing and advertising industry first. lastminute.com served a spontaneous brand masterstroke, by patching Wimbledon players' whites with its logo. The logo was seen on TV by 430 million people across the two week championship.

Recent Developments

Last year was the year that lastminute.com set out to strengthen its positioning as the first stop for those seeking last minute travels and leisure deals, by increasing its offerings and advertising. It reasserted its brand advantage: price, plus quality, plus expertise, for every last minute.

Through a new pan-European brand campaign, people were reminded of just how easy it is to be spontaneous, and all the reasons that lastminute.com can give them to love every last minute. Whether booking a city break at the best price available (or lastminute.com refunds the difference), or the freedom to decide on a last minute trip

DID YOU KNOW?
Short notice, spontaneous getaways boosts the UK's economy by £26.1 billion each year.

away with friends, lastminute.com means you can book then and there via mobile phone in less than three minutes. These products sit at the heart of the brand and allow it to give people the opportunity and the permission to embrace spontaneity.

Promotion

The campaign built around 'love every minute' has brought real meaning to that statement. In all its comms, at every touch-point, it is seeking to inspire people to say yes more often, to jump in and take advantage of everything life has to offer.

With this as its mantra, the brand has developed a campaign look and feel that is vibrant, colourful, energetic and inspirational. It uses multiple images, which together evoke the feeling of actually being in the destination or enjoying the experience being communicated.

lastminute.com wants these images to feel familiar to its audience – almost as if they are looking at the holiday photos of a friend – and are therefore able to project themselves into the moments captured. By doing this, it not only reminds people of how much spontaneous fun and adventure lastminute.com enables but also to inspire them.

Brand Values

Just like its customers, lastminute.com has the 'last minute' mindset. The brand caters to it by serving up experiences that inspire spontaneity (successful), grafting hard to build a brand customers can count on (trusted), knowing the 'last minute' like no one else (insightful), great ideas that keep the brand fresh, relevant and exciting (innovative) and by rewarding the impulsive (providing value).

Love Every Minute.

AMSTERDAM CITY BREAKS
FLIGHTS + 2 NIGHTS
4* HOTEL
FROM **£109**pp

TENERIFE HOLIDAYS
FLIGHTS + 7 NIGHTS
4* HOTEL
FROM **£249**pp

live
lastminute.com

Brand History

1998 lastminute.com launches in the UK.

1999 The brand branches into France and Germany, soon followed by more markets.

2000 lastminute.com reaches more than 500,000 regular users and expanded its offering into entertainment, gifts and more.

lastminute.com is floated on the London Stock Exchange.

2003 The brand acquires 15 businesses.

Top Secret® Hotels (posh rooms for not-so-posh-prices) launches.

2005 lastminute.com is acquired by Sabre Travelocity.

A Robbie Williams concert is the fastest selling show on lastminute.com, selling 12,000 tickets in nine minutes.

2006 On Valentine's Day, lastminute.com installs an inflatable church in London for last minute weddings.

2009 lastminute.com is the first to introduce flash sales ('WIGIG' – 'when it's gone it's gone').

2012 lastminute.com is voted the UK's coolest brand within its travel category in the CoolBrands® 2011/12 annual survey.

2013 Independent researchers find that when people want to take a trip within the month, they go to lastminute.com more than any other site in Europe.

2014 lastminute.com is voted the UK's best travel app (Source: EPiServer Research 2014).

2015 lastminute.com serves up a spontaneous brand masterstroke by patching lastminute.com logos on select Wimbledon players with the pink logo seen by 430 million people globally. lastminute.com is acquired by BravoflyRumbo Group.

LLOYD'S

lloyds.com

The world's specialist insurance and reinsurance market, Lloyd's, is at the heart of the City of London, the number one financial centre in the world. With revenues of £25.3 billion and operating in more than 200 countries and territories worldwide, Lloyd's has been able to retain its pre-eminent position in global insurance due to a combination of reputation, scale, governance, a unique working culture and continuing commitment to innovation and boldness.

Market

Lloyd's is a market comprising 94 syndicates, more than 200 licensed brokers, and almost 4,000 coverholders who bring business into Lloyd's. Much of Lloyd's business works by subscription, where more than one syndicate takes a share of the same risk. As the insurance and re-insurance market changes, so too must Lloyd's, and Vision 2025 aims to ensure that Lloyd's remains the global centre for specialist insurance and re-insurance.

Product

Lloyd's provides a platform for individual commercial businesses to thrive. It is a varied market, containing large international organisations and smaller niche businesses. Lloyd's syndicates cover risks that are often too complex for other insurers, including categories such as shipping, aviation, nuclear, climate, pandemics, political risk and cyber. Lloyd's pioneered the first cyber liability policy in 1999 and today there are 60 syndicates in the Lloyd's market providing coverage for cyber risks.

Lloyd's not only provides the market with infrastructure and transactional support, but oversees the operations of its participants, holds licenses with governments to write insurance in more than 80 countries worldwide and manages a central fund designed to guarantee policies underwritten in the Lloyd's market, should any syndicate be unable to meet its commitments.

Lloyd's is proud of its reputation for paying valid claims, most notably following the San Francisco earthquake in 1906 – a decision that encouraged the insurance market as a whole to re-evaluate its approach to risk management. Since then, it has constantly sought to respond quickly to events, lead change in the industry and in the last five years alone Lloyd's has paid £62.3 billion in claims.

Achievements

While insurance is seldom seen as exciting, the specialist cover Lloyd's provides plays an important role in economic progress. Originally created to insure shipping ventures 328 years ago, Lloyd's has covered arctic explorers, aid organisations and space missions, as well as key current global risks such as climate change and terrorism.

Lloyd's does not reduce risk, but the cover offered by its participants can give organisations confidence to go forward in the face of risk. Lloyd's is uniquely constituted to consider extremely risky proposals that other parts of the insurance market are unable to. Face-to-face negotiations between brokers

DID YOU KNOW?
Lloyd's has insured commercial space launchers including service launch providers Virgin Galactic and Space X and also insured space tourists en route to the International Space Station.

and underwriters have stood the test of time for over 300 years with the judgment of its expert underwriters helping brokers to come up with innovative solutions to risks.

As the world becomes more interdependent, the fall-out from risk is far-reaching. Lloyd's is well placed to meet the needs of the global economy with significant operations in Singapore, Shanghai, Beijing, Tokyo, Dubai and its business is continuing to expand in Latin America, as it opens offices in Mexico and Colombia alongside the established operation in Brazil.

Recent Developments

The challenges facing Lloyd's today are a far cry from the days when almost everything insured was marine. Now, Lloyd's is responding to the risks of cyber-attack, climate change or the Ebola infection.

Lloyd's worked with the University of Cambridge to outline the potential cost of a major cyber-attack in the USA – a scenario that could result in 93 million people without electricity, facing the US economy with potential losses of over US$1 trillion.

The debate on climate change is one that Lloyd's has been at the forefront of for a number of years, and in 2015 Lloyd's hosted the Governor of the Bank of England, Mark Carney, who spoke about the impact climate change could have on poverty, political stability and food and water stability. Lloyd's intends to continue to use its position to ensure the insurance industry plays a full part in this debate.

Lloyd's Corporate Social Responsibility initiative has expanded to include global projects and is championing diversity in the insurance industry by encouraging open and inclusive cultures. Inclusion@Lloyds hosted a three-day festival, Dive-In, in September 2015 where people came together to discuss these issues in the wider insurance market.

Promotion

Lloyd's is a name that resonates beyond its market. In addition to communicating to the specialist insurance and reinsurance market, it looks outward towards the markets in Latin-America, South-East Asia and India, as well as its more traditional markets in the UK, Europe and North America.

Lloyd's also uses its position in the marketplace to drive discussion on some of the key issues facing the global economy – from hosting seminars on how developments in financial technology, Fintech, are expected to change and benefit the insurance market, to Lloyd's work on the potential implications of a cyber-attack on the global economy.

In 2015 Lloyd's published its global City Risk Index which provided a detailed analysis of what the potential impact of 18 manmade and natural threats could have on 301 of the world's major cities. Lloyd's also continues to publish its series of Emerging Risk reports, looking at the issues likely to affect the insurance market in the coming years.

Brand Values

Lloyd's key brand values are Trust, Modernity, Innovation, Expertise and Global. Every two years Lloyd's conducts a survey to check brand health, which is published in the Annual Report.

Lloyd's is clear about its aim to be the global centre of specialist insurance and reinsurance, meeting the challenges of a changing world and accessing major overseas territories and emerging markets. It is a market where innovation is encouraged and entrepreneurs can thrive.

LLOYD'S PAID
£62.3 BILLION
IN CLAIMS OVER THE LAST FIVE YEARS

Brand History

1688 Lloyd's coffee house is recognised as the place for obtaining marine insurance.

1803 Lloyd's responds to the growing number of wounded soldiers from the Napoleonic wars by setting up its first charity, the Lloyd's Patriotic Fund.

1904 Lloyd's writes its first motor policy, cementing its reputation for innovation.

1906 Faced with the devastation of the San Francisco earthquake, Lloyd's underwriter Cuthbert Heath instructs prompt payment: "in full, irrespective of the terms of their policies." Lloyd's reputation is established and the USA goes on to account for nearly 40 per cent of Lloyd's business today.

1911 Lloyd's writes its first policy for aviation.

1965 Lloyd's underwrites the first ever space exploration risk.

2005 In the aftermath of Hurricane Katrina, Lloyd's emerges with only a small market loss and reinforces its commitment to help a devastated region rebuild.

2010 Lloyd's is granted a license to write direct business in China.

2011 Lloyd's celebrates 25 years in its iconic building although it proves a tough year with claims from the Japanese tsunami and other natural disasters.

2013 Lloyd's celebrates 325 years.

2015 Lloyd's reports 2014 profits of £3.2 billion and the 2015 interim results show Lloyd's outperforming insurance competitors for the fourth successive year. New offices are opened worldwide.

London
Stock Exchange Group

lseg.com

London Stock Exchange Group (LSEG) is a leading diversified market infrastructure group sitting at the heart of the world's financial community. It operates a wide range of markets and related businesses including London Stock Exchange, FTSE Russell, clearing house LCH.Clearnet and technology specialist MillenniumIT. Headquartered in London with significant operations in North America, Italy, France and Sri Lanka, the Group employs around 4,700 people.

Market
LSEG delivers the infrastructure, products and services that enable capital markets to thrive, including primary and secondary markets, market data, post-trade services and markets technology. The Group is an acknowledged global leader in its field, with a highly diversified portfolio across multiple asset classes and geographies.

With structural economic shifts and widespread regulatory change impacting the markets and communities served by the Group, the significance of neutral, trusted, well regulated and systemically important market infrastructure has never been more apparent. Against this background, LSEG is acutely aware of its responsibilities

in the wider world. Specifically, through capital raising and distribution, it plays a leading part in promoting market efficiency, enhancing market stability and enabling economic growth.

Product
The Group operates a broad range of international equity, bond and derivatives markets including London Stock Exchange; Borsa Italiana; MTS, Europe's leading fixed income market; and Turquoise, a pan-European trading platform. Through these markets the Group offers businesses efficient access to capital, while giving investors the opportunity to trade one of the world's most diverse ranges of securities.

The Group understands that ambitious smaller companies are key to driving growth and creating jobs in the real economy. The Alternative Investment Market (AIM) launched in 1995 has raised more than £90 billion in financing for these companies. LSEG has also created ELITE, an innovative and rapidly growing programme that provides private companies with education, support and access to a professional community of investors and advisers. Meanwhile, '1000 Companies to Inspire Britain', published by the Group, is an annual celebration of some of the UK's most dynamic small and medium-sized enterprises.

LSEG also offers its customers extensive real-time and reference data, market leading post-trade and risk management services, as well as high performance capital markets software. FTSE Russell, the largest global index company by assets under benchmark, is part of the Group.

DID YOU KNOW?
Originating in Italy, ELITE – LSEG's programme nurturing ambitious private companies – has now extended its support to over 320 businesses in 21 countries.

SINCE 1995, COMPANIES HAVE RAISED MORE THAN

£90 BILLION
ON LSEG'S AIM

Brand History

1698 At 'Jonathan's Coffee-house', John Castaing issues a list of stock and commodity prices called 'The Course of the Exchange and Other Things'.

1761 A group of 150 stockbrokers and jobbers form a club at Jonathan's to buy and sell shares.

1773 The brokers erect a building in Sweeting's Alley. Briefly known as 'New Jonathan's', the name soon changes to 'The Stock Exchange'.

1801 The first regulated exchange comes into existence in London and the modern Stock Exchange is born.

1812 The first codified rulebook is created.

1923 The Exchange receives its own Coat of Arms, with the motto 'Dictum meum pactum' (My word is my bond).

1973 The first female members are admitted to the market. The 11 British and Irish regional exchanges amalgamate with the London exchange.

1986 Deregulation of the market, known as 'Big Bang', allows ownership of member firms by outside corporations. Trading moves from face-to-face to computer and telephone.

1995 AIM, the international market for growing companies, launches.

1997 SETS (Stock Exchange Electronic Trading Service) launches.

2004 London Stock Exchange moves to new headquarters close to St Paul's Cathedral.

2007 London Stock Exchange merges with Borsa Italiana, creating London Stock Exchange Group.

2010 LSEG completes acquisition of MillenniumIT.

2011 The Group completes the acquisition of the remaining 50 per cent of FTSE.

2013 A majority stake in LCH.Clearnet is acquired.

2014 LSEG acquires Frank Russell Company.

2015 FTSE and Russell Indexes come together as FTSE Russell.

Achievements
In recent years LSEG has grown substantially to become a multi-asset, multi-platform business with an increasingly worldwide presence. Home to more than 2,300 listed companies from over 100 countries, it offers some of the most liquid markets, game-changing products and innovative services in the global capital markets universe.

Passionately committed to building enduring partnerships with customers and market participants, the Group also seeks to play a positive role in the multiple communities within which it operates.

Recent Developments
In 2013 the Group purchased a majority stake in LCH.Clearnet, the leading multi-asset global clearing service. This greatly enhanced its post-trade capabilities at a time when regulatory change has focused on the critical importance of post-trade to the safe, efficient functioning of markets.

The transaction was followed in 2014 by the Group's acquisition of Frank Russell Company, a world-class US-based financial services business. Russell's index and

DID YOU KNOW?
As well as providing the technology underlying LSEG's own markets, Group company MillenniumIT also serves over 40 other capital markets customers worldwide.

benchmarking arm, Russell Indexes, subsequently came together with the FTSE Group (already part of LSEG) to create FTSE Russell.

LSEG continues to partner with its customers to develop key innovations across the value chain – with further developments ranging from the pan-European rollout of the ELITE programme, to LCH.Clearnet's introduction of leading-edge compression and portfolio margining services.

Promotion
Targeting a diverse range of audiences, the Group concentrates its promotional activity on its four complementary business divisions:

Capital Markets, Post-Trade Services, Information Services and Technology Services.

Recently, the focus of corporate marketing activity has been on the Group's open access philosophy, which sets it apart from all its main competitors. Open access champions the ability of investors to choose where to trade and clear their products, free from the vertical silo model that has predominated in the past. Supported by European regulation, it is set to increase innovation as well as bringing customers economic benefits.

A growing number of partnership agreements, such as FTSE Russell's recent licensing deals with CME Group and the Chicago Board Options Exchange (CBOE), are already demonstrating the huge potential of open access.

Brand Values
Convinced that collaboration is the key to long-term growth, LSEG prides itself on working with its customers as a partner, not merely a supplier. The Group also cherishes a pioneering spirit that values fresh thinking, and a passion for delivering quality in everything it does. Finally, its motto – 'Dictum meum pactum' (My word is my bond) – expresses unwavering commitment to building markets based on transparency and trust.

These essential foundations for the Group's way of working are embodied in four core values: integrity; partnership; innovation; and excellence.

Marshalls

Creating Better Spaces

marshalls.co.uk

Marshalls is the UK's leading manufacturer of hard landscaping products and has been supplying superior natural stone and innovative concrete products to the construction, home improvement and landscape markets since the 1890s. Marshalls believes that the better its environment, the better it can be and strives to create products that improve the landscapes and create happier and healthier communities.

Market

In the public sector and commercial end market, Marshalls focuses on developing products that help architects, local authorities and contractors to create better spaces, whether it is street furniture, natural stone paving, block paving, water management or anti-terrorist products.

Marshalls' domestic customers range from DIY enthusiasts to professional landscapers, driveway installers and garden designers. Sales continue to be driven through the Marshalls Register of Accredited Landscapers and Driveway Installers.

Marshalls has an established and growing presence in Northern Europe, North America and China, and will soon be opening an office in the Middle East.

Product

Marshalls places a focus on innovation and quality. It is committed to producing new products that better any existing market offering, to make them from the best materials it can source and to care about the impact on society and the environment.

Marshalls has become synonymous with quality; supplying prestigious landmarks, such as Trafalgar Square, whilst also caring for the environment and communities in which it operates.

In 2015, Marshalls extended its commercial water management range with innovative drainage products, as well as adding a number of products aimed specifically at the rail industry.

For homeowners, Marshalls offers the inspiration and product ranges to create gardens and driveways that integrate effortlessly with people's lifestyles. In 2015, Marshalls launched a range of Vitrified paving, a relatively new material to the UK market, as well as a product called Pavesys which speeds up the installation of a patio by up to 50 per cent.

DID YOU KNOW?
Trafalgar Square is paved with Marshalls Yorkstone.

Achievements

Marshalls remains at the forefront of sustainable business. Marshalls was the first company in the hard landscaping industry to belong to the Ethical Trading Initiative (ETI), Marshalls is committed to the implementation of the ETI Base Code, pioneering the ethical sourcing of natural stone paving from India and China.

Building on its work with the ETI, in 2013 Marshalls announced a three-year partnership with UNICEF, aimed at tackling child labour in India's quarrying sector and furthering children's rights in China and Vietnam.

Following its acceptance in 2009, Marshalls remains a signatory of the United Nations Global Compact (UNGC) and its Group Marketing Director is Chair of the UNGC UK network.

In addition, The Carbon Trust has reaccredited Marshalls four times. Since 2009, the company has reduced its relative carbon footprint by more than 28 per cent and has made a commitment to reduce its carbon emissions by more than 3 per cent per year until 2020.

Marshalls remains the only organisation in the world to have carbon labelled its entire domestic range. It continues to be a constituent member of the FTSE4Good UK Index and an active member of Business in the Community.

Recent Developments

In October 2015, UNICEF launched the Marshalls-funded research into child labour in the quarrying sector in the northern Indian state of Rajasthan. It is hoped that the findings of this research will lead to long-term interventions that will help to tackle child labour in the stone quarrying industry in India.

Promotion

Brand communications for both the domestic and commercial markets focus on the company's mission to create better spaces for all.

In 2015, the domestic business ran an advertising campaign called 'Paving To Be Proud Of' to promote its products and the Register of Accredited Landscape Contractors and Driveway Installers to consumers.

DID YOU KNOW?
Marshalls stone clads the new Bloomberg building in the City of London.

The commercial business focused on the promotion of key growth areas of business, such as water management, internal stone paving, rail products and street furniture.

Marshalls has also continued to invest in its online presence with a focus on social media activity through Twitter, Facebook, YouTube and Pinterest.

Brand Values

Marshalls believes that everyone needs places that make them feel safer, happier and more sociable; places to be themselves where they can live, play, create and grow. Its core brand values are based on leadership, excellence, trust and sustainability.

Marshalls aims to be the supplier of choice for every landscape architect, contractor, installer and consumer, and for the brand to remain synonymous with quality, innovation and superior customer service.

Brand History

1890 Solomon Marshall starts to quarry in Southowram, Halifax and, in 1904, establishes S. Marshall & Sons Ltd in West Yorkshire.

1947 A second production site is opened, manufacturing lintels, steps and fence posts. In 1948 an engineering division is established.

1964 Marshalls becomes a plc with shares quoted on the London Stock Exchange.

1972 New product development sees the introduction of block paving and the famous 'Beany Block', which combines drain and kerb.

1988 Brick manufacturer George Armitage & Sons is acquired, becoming Marshalls Clay Products.

2004 Marshalls acquires Woodhouse, expanding its product offering to include design-led street furniture, lighting and signage.

2009 More than 2,000 of Marshalls' commercial products now have a Carbon Trust Carbon Reduction Label.

2011 Marshalls announces a European venture, Marshalls NV.

2012 Marshalls is an official supplier to the London 2012 Olympic Park. In addition, an office opens in Xiamen, China.

2013 Marshalls opens an office in North America and announces a three-year partnership with UNICEF.

2014 Marshalls is accredited by the Living Wage Foundation.

2015 UNICEF launches Marshalls funded research into child labour in the Indian Sandstone sector.

OVER THE LAST 15 YEARS MARSHALLS HAS SUPPLIED ENOUGH KERB TO CIRCLE AROUND THE WORLD TWICE

mercedes-benz.co.uk

Mercedes-Benz is synonymous with style, beauty and glamour and the guiding principles in the creation of every car remain the same. Combining tradition with cutting-edge innovation and advanced technology, Mercedes-Benz makes modern luxury attainable. Mercedes-Benz builds supercars; cars to take on and off road; family cars; and projects the future with cars that drive themselves.

The Mercedes-Benz S-Class Cabriolet

Market

In 2014, Mercedes-Benz achieved the highest sales in its history, selling 1,650,010 vehicles. After the US, the second-largest market for Mercedes-Benz is China, followed by Germany and the UK. The brand's global sales success was especially due to the range of compact models, the new C-Class, and the class-leading S-Class, which continued to be the world's best-selling luxury saloon, with sales last year of more than 100,000.

The sports car and performance brand Mercedes-AMG also achieved a new sales record of more than 47,500 in 2014. Meanwhile, at the microcar end of the product range, the extremely compact, agile and iconic smart is also an international success.

Product

Mercedes-Benz is one of the biggest producers of premium cars and the world's biggest manufacturer of commercial vehicles. The brand also provides financing, leasing, fleet management, insurance and innovative mobility services.

To meet customer needs, Mercedes-Benz Cars has steadily expanded its model range and occupied new niches in recent years. This continues and between now and 2020 Mercedes-Benz will launch at least 10 new models without predecessors. At the microcar end of the market, smart is setting standards for urban mobility with its new generation smart fortwo and smart forfour. Meanwhile, the SLS AMG and GT models have transformed the sports car and

performance brand Mercedes-AMG into a separate car manufacturer. To underscore its lead in the luxury segment, Mercedes-Benz has also created a new sub-brand: Mercedes-Maybach, which is geared towards status conscious customers and meets their needs for prestigious individuality and exclusivity. The Mercedes-Maybach S 500 and the Mercedes-Maybach S 600 are the first two models of the new sub-brand.

IN NOVEMBER 2015 SALES WERE ALREADY AHEAD OF 2014 AT

1.69 MILLION

Brand History

1886 Carl Benz completes his Patent Motor Car while, separately, Gottlieb Daimler and Wilhelm Maybach motorise a carriage.

1888 The first long distance drive in automotive history, approximately 100 kilometres, is undertaken by Bertha Benz, Carl's wife.

1926 The two rival companies, Daimler-Motoren-Gesellschaft and Benz & Cie, merge and the first brand name Mercedes-Benz vehicles are produced in manufacturing plants across Germany.

1934 Mercedes-Benz W25 750kg racing car debuts at the International Eiffel Race, winning in record time.

1950s The Mercedes-Benz 300 debuts at the first Frankfurt International Motor Show.

1962 The millionth Mercedes-Benz passenger car rolls of the assembly line.

1978 Mercedes-Benz develops a diesel version of the S-Class, to be more economical.

1994 Mercedes-Benz presents two studies of the Micro Compact Car, which comes onto the market as smart in 1998.

1999 All Mercedes-Benz cars are equipped with the Electronic Stability Program as standard resulting in far fewer driver-related accidents.

2004 BlueTec technology is introduced to reduce the emissions of diesel engines.

2009 Mercedes-Benz offers customers locally emission-free mobility with the B-Class Electric Drive, along with battery and fuel-cell-powered electric mobility ranges.

2013 The Mercedes-Benz S 500 INTELLIGENT DRIVE repeats Bertha Benz' historic drive without any intervention by a human driver.

2015 Continuing its Formula One legacy, Mercedes-Benz supplies engines to the Williams, Sahara Force India and Lotus F1 Teams.

Achievements

During 2015, the Mercedes-Benz S-Class was the recipient of many UK awards, including 'Best Luxury Car' in the Auto Express Awards; it was awarded 'Best Executive Car' in the Diesel Car Awards and Luxury Car of the Year at the What Car? Awards.

At the World Car Awards 2015, Mercedes-Benz C-Class was awarded World Car of the Year and the S-Class Coupé was voted World Luxury Car, while the Mercedes-AMG GT sports car was voted World Performance Car.

Mercedes-Benz was also recognised as the best in the Fleet Industry by winning the Fleet Manufacturer of the Year Award at the Fleet World Honours 2015.

Recent Developments

As a pioneer of automotive engineering, Mercedes-Benz continues to shape the future of mobility. The company focuses on innovative and green technologies with the long-term goal of emission-free driving: from hybrid vehicles to electric vehicles powered by battery or fuel cell. One of the key technologies for achieving zero-emission driving is the plug-in hybrid and the company plans to launch a total of 10 plug-in hybrid models on the market between now and 2017.

The company also follows a consistent path towards accident-free driving and intelligent connectivity with the ultimate goal of autonomous driving. Autonomous driving offers huge potential for mobility by the connection and interaction between vehicle, passengers and the outside world.

In early 2015, Mercedes-Benz presented the F 015 Luxury in Motion research vehicle in Las Vegas, Nevada, showing the company's vision of the future in which self-driving vehicles become more than just a means of transportation and evolve into a private place of refuge.

Promotion

Mercedes-Benz aims to be the best at everything, from products and technology to services. Its brand claim is to develop the safest, most comfortable and most efficient vehicles in the world for its customers and to manufacture them in top quality in its worldwide plants.

At the same time, Mercedes-Benz continues to conduct research that underpins its claim to leadership in the automotive industry with constantly new innovations. As the inventor of the car, Mercedes-Benz invests in the development of alternative drive systems such as electric vehicles or plug-in hybrid technology. In addition, it is significantly advancing the research into autonomous driving.

DID YOU KNOW?
More than 129,000 employees worldwide work in the Mercedes-Benz Cars Division.

Brand Values

Mercedes-Benz Cars is the passenger car division of Daimler AG and encompasses the brands Mercedes-Benz and smart. Together with its sub-brands Mercedes-AMG and Mercedes-Maybach, the premium manufacturer offers everything from compact to luxury cars for a wide variety of customer requirements.

The company adapts the design and specification of its vehicles to specific customer requirements in different markets around the world.

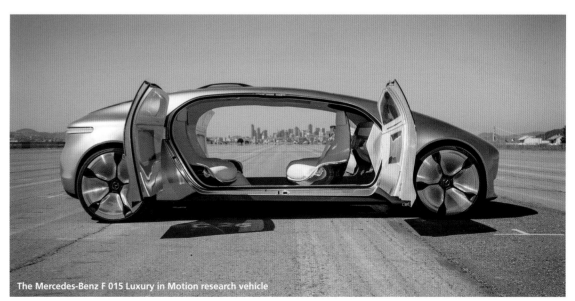

The Mercedes-Benz F 015 Luxury in Motion research vehicle

 Microsoft

microsoft.com/uk

With more than 110 million devices running Windows 10 and more than 1.5 billion people using its products daily, Microsoft is a world leader in software, services and solutions that help people and businesses grow. Building on this position by becoming the productivity and platform company for the mobile-first and cloud-first world, Microsoft aims to reinvent productivity to empower every person and every organisation on the planet to achieve more.

Market

In 2015, CEO Satya Nadella continued Microsoft's transformation into a mobile-first, cloud-first business, whilst also growing its revenue to US$93.58 billion. The company has subsidiaries in more than 120 countries and employs more than 115,000 people worldwide.

Microsoft has cemented its commitment to the cloud with the announcement of a data centre expansion programme in Europe. This includes new data centre regions in the UK and Germany, and the completion of data centre facilities in Ireland and the Netherlands, both of which serve as cloud computing hubs for European customers.

Microsoft's services are also leading innovation with more apps, social communication and collaboration tools driven by the cloud and Windows 10, launched in July 2015. There are more than 669,000 apps for phones, desktops and tablets in the Windows Store with hundreds more added every day.

Product

In 2015, significant launches included Windows 10, the Surface Book, Surface Pro 4, Office 2016 and new Lumia devices the 950 and 950 XL. With Windows 10, the Windows ecosystem has been unified across devices from phone to Xbox.

In order to extend its offerings to an even wider global audience, the company has expanded in the hardware sector with the launch of Surface Book and Surface Pro 4 as well as Windows Phones, with the launch of the 950 and 950XL Lumia devices. As well as launching services across multiple platforms, Microsoft makes 'anywhere, anytime communication' and sharing a reality in the home and at work. For example, Office 365 provides easy access to tools such as Microsoft Excel and Word, complemented by OneDrive's cloud storage for files. Office mobile has been downloaded over 200 million times. In addition, Skype, Lync and Yammer let people stay in touch wherever they are via PCs, mobiles, tablets and TVs.

DID YOU KNOW?
Microsoft is developing innovative technology in the UK to help the 246 million people in the world with sight loss (Source: Microsoft).

In addition, cloud services such as Microsoft Azure enable businesses to quickly build, deploy and manage applications in an intelligent and trusted ecosystem, whilst Dynamics CRM Online delivers a unified view across applications, making businesses more responsive to customer needs. Microsoft aims to reach an annualised commercial cloud revenue run rate of US$20 billion by 2018.

Achievements

Microsoft regularly receives plaudits from around the world, not only for its products but also for the responsible way in which it does business. Microsoft's YouthSpark programme has helped millions of young people in more than 100 countries since 2012. In addition, Microsoft has donated an average of US$2.6 million in software each day to more than 86,000 nonprofits around the world.

The company is also helping to keep people across the globe communicating and sharing with Outlook.com, which has over 400 million active users as the world's fastest-growing email service.

Brand History

1975 Microsoft is founded in Seattle by Paul Allen and Bill Gates.

1981 IBM introduces its PC with Microsoft's 16-bit MS-DOS 1.0.

1989 Microsoft launches the first version of its Office suite.

1990 With the launch of Windows 3.0, Microsoft is the first PC software company to exceed US$1 billion in annual sales.

1995 Bill Gates outlines his commitment to the internet. Windows 95 launches, selling over one million copies in four days.

2001 Office XP and Windows XP launch. Microsoft enters the gaming market with Xbox.

2008 Bill Gates steps down from the day-to-day running of the company.

2010 Xbox Kinect gets the Guinness World Record for being the fastest-selling consumer electronics device.

2011 Microsoft unveils Cloud Power and moves its business product suite to cloud-based services.

2012 Windows Server 2012, Windows 8, Windows Phone the Surface tablet, Office 365 and Yammer are launched.

2013 Microsoft launches Windows 8.1, Surface 2, Xbox One and Dynamics CRM 2013, and reorganises to focus more on devices and services.

2014 Microsoft launches Surface Pro 3, Office for iPad, Windows Phone 8.1, reorganises to focus on mobile and cloud first and announces Windows 10.

2015 Microsoft announces, Office 2016, Surface Book, Surface Pro 4, Microsoft Band 2, Lumia 950 and Lumia 950 XL and European data centre expansion programme.

Furthermore, Xbox One has been the most successful launch in the company's history, and is home to some of gaming's biggest franchises including 'Halo', 'Gears of War', 'Fable' and 'Forza Motorsport'. In addition, more than 84 million Xbox 360 consoles have been sold worldwide, while Xbox Live has 39 million active users globally.

Recent Developments

In 2015, Microsoft, the BBC and other partners announced an initiative designed to get a pocket-sized, codeable device, the BBC micro:bit, into the hands of nearly a million Year 7 students in the UK, to enable them to explore the possibilities of computer science, both in and out of the classroom.

In addition, to expand the reach of the BBC micro:bit even further, Microsoft has

DID YOU KNOW? 80 per cent of the Fortune 500 use Microsoft's cloud services.

committed to buy 15,000 additional devices once they become commercially available in 2016. These will be given to the 35 UK schools in its global Showcase Schools programme, designed to recognise schools that are leading the way with technology.

Promotion

Microsoft's single-minded marketing strategy reflects 'one company'. It is taking an integrated approach to ensure all communications are more brand than product-led. This new external, outward-facing approach is in harmony with the company's internal values of being 'personal, valued, inspired and forward-looking'.

Microsoft is a champion of reimagining the way people communicate and work together, believing that the correct use of technology can liberate the individual. That

is why Microsoft is reinventing productivity and embraces 'Anywhere Working', an initiative that offers advice to help people live and work smarter. Specifically, the company promotes remote working, which can increase productivity and well-being, protect the environment and encourage a positive work-life balance.

MORE THAN 1.2 BILLION PEOPLE USE MICROSOFT OFFICE

Brand Values

As Microsoft moves forward, its mission is to empower every person and organisation on the planet to do more and achieve more through digital technology.

The company will achieve its mission through three core ambitions. To offer a new generation of intelligent cloud solutions that give individuals and organisations new power and insight; to reinvent productivity to empower both individuals and organisations not just to survive, but to thrive and; to usher in a world of more personal computing with Windows 10 as one unified platform and experience that runs across all devices.

For Microsoft, this sense of mission and purpose drives transformation, for individuals and organisations. This starts with the company's ambition to reinvent productivity and the importance of cloud and analytics in beginning the era of intelligent and more personal computing.

misys.com

Established in 1979, Misys has been at the forefront of the financial software industry for more than 35 years. It is transforming the global financial services industry by making banks and financial institutions more resilient, more efficient and more competitive. It achieves this today by helping clients to expand their business, reduce their operational costs, decrease their financial risk exposure and improve their customer experience.

Market

Misys has the broadest portfolio of banking, capital markets, and investment management and risk solutions on the market. With more than 2,000 customers in 130 countries, its team of domain experts, combined with its partner eco-system, have an unparalleled ability to address industry requirements at both a global and local level. Misys solutions connect systems, collect data and create intelligent information to drive smarter business decisions.

Misys is a US$1 billion company operating within the financial services industry. It operates in over 50 countries with more than 4,700 employees. In the UK alone it works with seven of the eight Tier 1 banks.

In today's interconnected, global financial markets, Misys is committed to keeping its solutions compliant with new regulatory requirements to help its customers meet current and emerging regulations.

Product

Misys provides software solutions for retail and corporate banking, lending, treasury, capital markets, investment management and enterprise-wide risk management. Its open, integrated and componentised systems fit into any existing infrastructure, or provide a new platform. Misys builds its software to be flexible, so that it can adapt and change at the same pace as market conditions.

DID YOU KNOW?
Approximately 10 per cent of daily trade finance operations are managed through Misys solutions.

Achievements

Misys is a regular winner of industry awards for its software solutions – having won 30 awards in 2015. These included the 2015 Global Finance awards: Barclays and Misys named The Innovators 2015 – Transaction Services, as well as The Asian Banker Technology Implementation Awards: Best Treasury Management Project. Misys was also the recipient of three FStech Awards: Risk Management Software of the Year, Best Trading System and Online Technology Provider of the Year.

Misys was also named UK National Champion for the Award for Customer Focus at the European Business Awards. The award was given in recognition of Misys Connect, the client engagement model. Developed in 2014, the programme is designed to drive competitive advantage and maximise returns for customers on their technology investments.

Misys FusionBanking Essence is the company's flagship solution for retail and digital banking and was named a

MISYS SOFTWARE ENABLES
250 MILLION+ RETAIL ACCOUNTS

'Leader' in Gartner's Magic Quadrant for International Retail Core Banking Systems.

Recent Developments

For the second consecutive year, Misys will be sponsoring the Woman of Achievement Award – an accolade created by the Women in the City organisation based in London. The award recognises senior and partner-level women who actively support the progress of females in their organisations and the wider business world. Misys is sponsoring the Financial Services category award, demonstrating its long-term commitment of promoting diversity and the growth of female leadership talent within the financial sector and wider industry.

In 2015, Misys employees slept out overnight as part of Byte Night, an annual fundraiser for Action for Children. The team met its target and raised more than £10,000 for Action for Children, a sum that has been matched by Misys. The company also participated in the Royal Parks Half Marathon. Taking place in Hyde Park, 33 Misys employees joined more than 16,000 runners in the 13-mile route through central London, through the iconic sights of the capital and Royal Parks. All of the donations raised and matched went to support Action for Children, Byte Night and Starlight as Misys' chosen charities, contributing to the company's corporate social responsibility.

DID YOU KNOW?
Misys customers include 93 of the top 100 world banks.

Promotion

Misys launched its new brand in 2014. This changed the way the company categorised and consolidated its portfolio of financial software products. The brand communicated this internally across its main offices using the Misys Brand Game. The game was available via a downloadable app, enabling it to share content with its employees through video, PDFs and written text. Each element of content was triggered by a bluetooth iBeacon, meaning the player moved around the building to locate the next piece of information. A web version was also made available allowing all staff to participate, learn, understand and engage with the brand.

Before 2012, Misys had a siloed product structure operating across different vertical markets. The company was then acquired by private equity firm Vista Equity Partners and subsequently merged with Turaz, an offshoot of the Reuters business. Now with a larger product portfolio the company decided to rebrand, putting the customer firmly at the centre.

The new Fusion platform and Fusion product family was created to promote modern, scalable, cloud-ready technology from Misys, and its comprehensive set of solutions that work together to bring additional value to customers through next-generation user interfaces and integrated, front-to-back office approaches.

Brand Values

Connect: Misys enables clients to connect its systems quickly and easily, not only to other Misys solutions but also to in-house and third party systems and services.

Innovate: Misys re-energises existing solutions with global components that provide additional functionality; and help customers to develop new ways of doing business through shared components and state-of-the-art Fusion software.

Expand: Misys software enables clients to expand their business quickly and respond to the changing market place with agility, giving them a competitive edge and increasing profitability.

Brand History

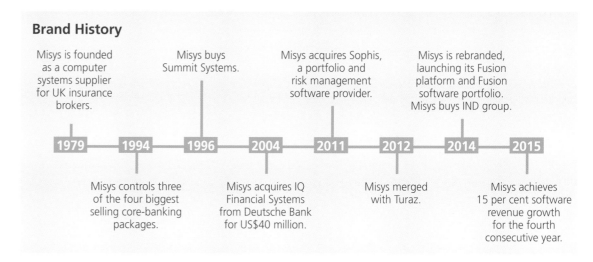

Misys is founded as a computer systems supplier for UK insurance brokers.

Misys buys Summit Systems.

Misys acquires Sophis, a portfolio and risk management software provider.

Misys is rebranded, launching its Fusion platform and Fusion software portfolio. Misys buys IND group.

1979 — **1994** — **1996** — **2004** — **2011** — **2012** — **2014** — **2015**

Misys controls three of the four biggest selling core-banking packages.

Misys acquires IQ Financial Systems from Deutsche Bank for US$40 million.

Misys merged with Turaz.

Misys achieves 15 per cent software revenue growth for the fourth consecutive year.

pandora.net

PANDORA is dedicated to offering luxury, hand-finished jewellery at affordable prices. Today, PANDORA is one of the largest and most loved global jewellery brands, inspiring women all over the world to share their unforgettable moments and express their individuality and inner values.

Market

PANDORA was founded in Copenhagen in 1982 by husband and wife duo, Per and Winnie Enevoldsen. Since starting out as a small Danish jeweller's, PANDORA is now one of the largest jewellery companies in the world. Available in more than 90 countries across six continents, PANDORA has a global presence everywhere from Vietnam to Venezuela. With a strong franchise model, it sells its products through approximately 1,500 concept stores worldwide.

After successful trading in key markets such as the USA and Australia, PANDORA first launched in the UK as a wholesale distributor in 2008, experiencing well-documented success ever since. Year-on-year growth has facilitated the brand's expansion from wholesale accounts to 180 concept stores in addition to more than 94 wholesale stores in just 7 years, with the company present on most major UK highstreets. With plans to open a 200th concept store in 2016, the UK is now PANDORA's largest European market.

Product

PANDORA's mission is to celebrate women by offering them the opportunity for personal expression through high-quality and contemporary jewellery at affordable prices. Renowned for its famous charm bracelet, which launched in 2000, PANDORA has begun to redefine itself as having a full jewellery offering, with other product categories such as rings, earrings and necklaces becoming increasingly popular.

With customers able to mix and match, layer and stack different designs, PANDORA operates an inclusive business model, meaning women with different backgrounds, tastes and ages can put together a collection unique to their style and story – all at an affordable cost. With seven product launches each year, the collections remain consistently fresh and tailored to the season.

Previously focusing on jewellery which would encourage women to celebrate life's 'Unforgettable Moments', in 2013 PANDORA unveiled the ESSENCE campaign; a unique collection of hand-finished, meaningful charms, alongside a slender sterling silver charm bracelet. Taking inspiration from its consumers, PANDORA created the collection after carrying out market research from 7,500 women across the globe. ESSENCE remains an ongoing focus for the brand and continues to be a popular alternative to the traditional charm bracelet.

With high quality jewellery at the heart of its strategy, PANDORA operates several production facilities in Bangkok, Thailand, where centuries old craftsmanship meets state-of-the-art technology to produce luxury jewellery that stands the test of time. Insisting on using the best materials available,

PANDORA incorporates sterling silver, 14ct gold and gemstones in each of its designs, shipping Murano glass from Venice to create some of its famous charms. With demand at an all-time high, PANDORA has plans to open a new factory in the Chiang Mai region in 2016.

Achievements

As a relative newcomer to the jewellery industry, PANDORA has experienced ongoing success since first entering the UK market. This growth supported the launch of the first PANDORA e-store, national marketing

campaigns and celebrity partnerships, with the brand experiencing a record turnover in 2014.

In addition to financial achievement, the brand has also gained industry recognition for its ethical initiatives. PANDORA's production facilities in Thailand won the Jewellery News Asia Employer of the Year award in 2014 and PANDORA UK was also awarded two stars from the Best Companies Accreditation in 2015, as a result of outstanding employee satisfaction.

Promotion
PANDORA is committed to delivering an aspirational and engaging promotional strategy. To appeal to existing and potential customers, the jeweller has partnered with a number of celebrities, including Girls

Aloud and, more recently, Tess Daly who was brand ambassador for PANDORA's SS15 and AW15 campaigns.

In addition to working with influencers for seasonal campaigns, PANDORA has more recently placed its customer at the heart of nationwide promotion. In 2014, PANDORA launched a user-generated content campaign called #MyRingsMyStyle, which encouraged consumers to share their ring stacks across social media using the campaign hashtag. The project was a huge success, illustrating PANDORA as a full jewellery brand with many styling opportunities. The financial results were also impressive, with ring sales increasingly significantly by the year end.

DID YOU KNOW?
Customers have over 1,000 design variations to choose from.

PANDORA launched a short film in the run-up to Mother's Day 2015, celebrating the bond between mother and child. The film became a viral sensation; with over 19 million views on Facebook and more than 590,000 shares. Its positioning on YouTube was equally high, with the film being watched more than 16.7 million times.

Brand Values
With ethics at the forefront of the business, PANDORA operates a vertically integrated value chain, which dictates that the brand has full visibility over its production processes, employee structure and materials selection. As a member of the Responsible Jewellery Council (RJC), PANDORA only works with ethical suppliers, meaning any materials entering the production facilities are conflict-free. In 2014, PANDORA anounced 99 per cent of all silver and 90 per cent of all gold was sourced from certified refineries, meaning minimal impact on the environment.

PANDORA ensures a fair and comfortable working environment across all territories. A Scandinavian mentality dictates employees around the world are provided with a healthy and nutritious lunch every day, and encouraged to socialise during breaks.

With corporate social responsibility at the top of the agenda, PANDORA supports charity initiatives each year. In the UK, it has partnered with Breakthrough Breast Cancer, ABF The Soldiers' Charity, the British Heart Foundation and BBC Children in Need, designing charms for each cause and pledging funds for research. In 2014, PANDORA donated just under £1 million to charity globally.

Recent Developments
In 2013, PANDORA launched an innovation centre in Thailand near its crafting facilities. The centre uses state-of-the-art technology alongside traditional craftsmanship to produce contemporary and high quality jewellery. The centre resulted in the invention of PANDORA Rose; a unique blend of metals that doesn't tarnish. The metal is the first of its kind in the industry and embodies the values of PANDORA, offering a high quality product at an affordable price.

91 MILLION
PIECES OF JEWELLERY WERE MANUFACTURED IN THAILAND LAST YEAR

Brand History

1982 PANDORA is founded by Per and Winnie Enevoldsen.

1989 PANDORA begins manufacturing in Thailand.

2000 The Charm Bracelet launches and PANDORA undergoes rapid expansion.

2003 PANDORA enters USA and Canada.

2004 PANDORA opens branches in Germany and Australia.

2005 The first fully owned PANDORA factory opens in Thailand.

2007 Creative Director, Lee Antony Gray, joins PANDORA and the first Concept Store opens in Hamburg, Germany.

2008 PANDORA UK launches.

2010 PANDORA's third and fourth factories in Thailand open and PANDORA launches on the stock exchange, entering new markets such as Russia and Italy.

2011 Stephen Fairchild, Chief Creative Officer, joins PANDORA.

2012 PANDORA becomes a member of the Responsible Jewellery Council.

2013 PANDORA ESSENCE Collection launches and an Innovation Centre in Bangkok is opened. PANDORA's 1,000th concept store opens in Paris.

2015 PANDORA Rose launches.

2016 PANDORA's 200th store in the UK opens and factories begin opening in Chiang Mai.

pilgrimschoice.com

Pilgrims Choice is here to shake up the cheddar category – it is not here to imitate, but here to differentiate. At Pilgrims Choice, only the very best cheese is hand-selected by experts, carefully chosen for its superior flavour, texture and aroma. As one of the UK's leading cheddar brands, Pilgrims Choice places emphasis on sourcing and grading only the tastiest, strongest cheddar. Consumers who love the taste of cheddar, love Pilgrims Choice.

Market

Pilgrims Choice takes pride in being the challenger to the market leader using disruptive and creative marketing to encourage consumer loyalty to a superior tasting cheddar brand. Pilgrims Choice appeals to a mind-set rather than a demographic, connecting with those that have a genuine passion for cheese – the cheese appreciator.

The UK branded cheddar market is in challenging times. Volume is being driven by ever increasing promotional investment, whilst at the same time, the majority of brands continue to convey messages in the same safe way.

Pilgrims Choice wants to inject excitement back into the category, moving the consumer mind-set away from simply selecting cheddar that is on offer, to selecting and then loving the best possible cheddar. Pilgrims Choice also wants to give consumers a reason to buy and remain loyal to branded cheddar through proving its difference. The company's 'well-chosen' role is more important than ever.

DID YOU KNOW? Pilgrims Choice Vintage cheddar is typically matured for 20 months – enough time for the rich, sweet and crunchy cheddar to develop.

Product

The Pilgrims Choice brand focus is on stronger tasting cheddar. Although mild and medium cheddar variants are available, the company's predominate emphasis is on strength, with the hero variant being Pilgrims Choice Extra Mature cheddar.

Consumers perceive Pilgrims Choice to have a stronger taste profile, and this is supported by the product range which champions a stronger cheddar.

As well as block cheddar, sliced, grated and deli, mini portion variants also feature in the range. In addition, lighter products that have the same distinctive taste as the full-fat equivalents. The larger 500g family packs appeal to those with higher consumption requirements.

All of Pilgrims Choice cheese is hand-selected for quality, with regular bench-marking to ensure the consistent high quality that consumers love. Each block of cheese is individually graded by experts to the highest specification, giving consumers the best cheddar, time after time.

Achievements

Adopting a new, quirky tone of voice that is unique in the cheese category has helped Pilgrims Choice to reach out and make an emotional connection with its 'cheese appreciator' audience.

37 MILLION+
PACKS OF PILGRIMS CHOICE WERE CONSUMED IN 2015

simple yet vibrant new look naturally reflects the Pilgrims Choice personality.

Promotion

Whilst the television campaign creates reach and generates popularity for Pilgrims Choice, in-store media and point of sale communication is used to drive the message home at point of purchase.

In store promotions are viewed as an essential part of the marketing mix, and the company is supported by retailers with appropriate aisle space and feature space for promotions.

The depth of distribution allows Pilgrims Choice to drive its penetration and frequency. Whilst its advertising campaign pushes consumers to stores, its job in-store is to convert these consumers to make a purchase.

DID YOU KNOW?
The penetration rate of cheddar is higher than toilet rolls, with more households buying more cheese than toilet rolls.

Brand Values

Pilgrims Choice has a strong desire to bring the excitement back to the cheddar category and show consumers that cheddar can be more than a standard dairy product. Pilgrims Choice lives by the mantra 'differentiate, don't imitate', practising what it preaches through an alternative approach to marketing.

The company's brand vision is to spread the word that not all cheese is made equal; at Pilgrims Choice only the very best cheddar is selected. Pilgrims Choice uses a disruptive tone of voice to champion a better choice of cheddar which appeals to those with a real love of cheese.

This consistency of taste is why more consumers are repeat purchasing Pilgrims Choice and why brand loyalty is growing by the day.

There is more to cheddar than a cheese sandwich and Pilgrims Choice wants consumers to fall in love again with this versatile ingredient.

Pilgrims Choice connects with its fans via social media platforms, priding itself on producing unique and engaging content with a share-ability factor. In return, consumers are regularly engaging with the company on social media, something that other cheddar brands could only aspire to. Pilgrims Choice Facebook fans have reached in excess of 75,000, a figure rising with each day. Its social media content has had a reach of 1.8 million in during 2015, with aims to increase this wide-reaching figure in the upcoming year.

After a highly effective stint on television, more customers are repeatedly purchasing Pilgrims Choice. The company's product penetration levels are higher than ever, and recently, sales volumes have increased by a massive 20 per cent, significantly out-performing the category.

Recent Developments

Creativity was the overriding theme in 2015, with a year-round integrated campaign. Stepping away from six-week television

campaigns, Pilgrims Choice refocused its vision on disrupting the category with a fresh approach to marketing cheddar.

It was the first to invite consumers to choose their own music for the television ad; the impact of which gave Pilgrims Choice a clear market lead when it came to social media.

Earlier in the year the brand launched a bold new packaging design, developed to stand out from the crowd when on shelf. This

Brand History

1985	1997	2013	2015
North Downs Dairy formed and the Pilgrims Choice brand is created.	North Downs Dairy, along with the Pilgrims Choice brand, is acquired by The Irish Dairy Board.	Pilgrims Choice hits television with the infamous cowboy ad. Pilgrims Choice becomes the primary challenger to the market leader.	A fully integrated, campaign including TV advertising, is launched and re-ignites the brand. A new black packaging design launches.

Polypipe

polypipe.com

Polypipe designs, develops and manufactures the UK's widest range of engineered piping systems and solutions for sustainable buildings. As a market leader, its primary focus is on developing and supporting pragmatic product systems through specific knowledge and understanding of the residential, commercial, civils and infrastructure market sectors. Polypipe's growth ahead of the market is driven by both its focus on delivering systems that meet the ever-changing demands of legislation and substitution of traditional legacy materials with innovative plastics.

Market
Polypipe operates primarily within the construction market, manufacturing and supplying products for a diverse range of applications including drainage, plumbing, heating, water management, ventilation, ducting and cable management. It ensures that customers, including professional installers, specifiers and engineers, can trust its unrivalled expertise to provide intelligently engineered, fit for purpose piping solutions for the growing diversity and complexity of the construction sector and the building technology challenges they face.

Product
The Polypipe range offers the most diverse choice of engineered piping systems and solutions available to the UK construction industry. They include above and below ground drainage, plastic plumbing, underfloor heating systems, ventilation solutions, water supply systems, sewer pipe, land drainage, surface water management systems, green/blue roof podium deck solutions and cable protection. All Polypipe products are manufactured to the appropriate British and European standards.

The success and diversity of Polypipe's range of product systems and solutions is the result of both a longstanding commitment to research and development, investment in new manufacturing methods and the versatility of plastic as a modern manufacturing material. Polypipe products have been designed to replace existing legacy materials such as concrete, clay and copper because they offer the same inherent strength. As these products are lighter in weight they reduce health and safety risks in handling and are easier to transport and subsequently install. They also have a high resistance to chemical attacks and at the end of their life are fully recyclable.

Achievements
In 2015 Polypipe won a range of awards, including 'Best Services Product' at the Housebuilder Product Awards for the Domus Radial Duct System, the Investors in People Silver Award and Good Housekeeping Reader Recommended status. In addition to this, Polypipe Terrain received BES 6001 accreditation from the BRE for a

DID YOU KNOW?
Polypipe's Permavoid has recently taken a starring role in the redevelopment of the new Coronation Street set in Manchester, helping to ensure that filming is never rained off.

framework standard for sustainable sourcing and Nuaire (acquired by Polypipe in 2015) won 'Best Product Launch', at the B2B Marketing Awards, for the DAVE product launch.

Recent Developments
Along with new government legislation and the increase in environmentally conscious customers, Polypipe continue to invest in

Brand History

1980 Polypipe is formed in Doncaster, Yorkshire.

1988 A full range of plastic drainage products become available for the residential construction market.

1996 Polypipe moves into the mainland European construction market with manufacturing facilities in France.

1997 Polypipe enters into the civils and infrastructure market.

1998 Plastic hot and cold water plumbing and heating systems are launched as a direct alternative to copper.

Polypipe enters the domestic ventilation systems market.

2000 Polypipe's underfloor heating system provides a sustainable alternative to wall hung radiators for the house builder market.

Polypipe enters the Italian market.

2004 Polypipe launches the new Polystorm range of sustainable urban water drainage system products and solutions.

2007 A specialist Water Management Solutions team is created to provide technical and legal advice on water management system design.

Polypipe enters into the commercial market.

Polypipe Gulf forms to develop a presence in the Middle Eastern market.

2008 Ridgistorm-XL large-scale pipe for the civils and infrastructure market launches in the UK, introducing bespoke engineered pipe wall stiffness construction.

2012 Polypipe Carbon Efficient Solutions launches.

2013 PolyMax launches to further enhance the UK's widest range of plastic plumbing systems.

2014 Polypipe Group plc is admitted to the London Stock Exchange.

2015 Polypipe Underfloor Heating makes its TV debut.

Polypipe acquires the Nuaire Business.

more carbon efficient products and systems that enable the collection, transmission, emission and control in heating, ventilation and cooling systems. These are helping to create a more comfortable environment for occupants of homes and commercial buildings, as well as helping to reduce the amount of energy required for heating. These efforts aim to reduce carbon emissions and heating costs as a result.

Polypipe's new polymer reprocessing plant has recycled 325,000,000 plastic bottles to date that would have otherwise gone into landfill. The investment in the technology to do this ensures that all Polypipe's recycled material meets the necessary quality standards.

One of Polypipe's latest projects includes its extensive involvement in the new £1.5 billion regeneration project at Elephant & Castle. This collaboration relied on the co-ordinated expertise and resource from across Polypipe's Building Products, Terrain and Civils' operations.

Using its combined expertise and experience, Polypipe ensured every solution was both effective and more carbon efficient.

One of the primary objectives for Polypipe was to provide a solution that would cope with the site's drainage requirements in the event of a 'one in 100 year' storm. To meet this challenge, approximately 2,000m^2 of Permavoid cells and 40m^2 of Permafoam irrigation systems were used to create the Permavoid Podium Deck. It replaced the need for 150mm depth of aggregate and dramatically reduced the number of vehicle deliveries to the site – a major factor in lowering the overall carbon footprint of the project.

Other solutions included Terrain Fuze HDPE Drainage, which is manufactured from high-density polyethylene and provides a high-performance solution with strong abrasion, chemical and temperature resistance. Prefabricated stacks were produced for One The Elephant, which considerably reduced installation time on site.

Polypipe also supplied its acoustic underfloor heating system across each apartment block, replacing the need for screeds to level the floor. The removal of wet screeds from the floor construction process significantly reduced vehicle movements on site and eliminated the screed drying time, thus improving both carbon efficiency and speed of construction.

Promotion

In 2015, Polypipe's underfloor heating took to TV with a campaign running on SkyPlus, supported by an intensive digital campaign. Polypipe also engaged the services of Kelly Hoppen in the role of brand ambassador. Other campaigns saw the company give away 50,000 product samples, attend a number of national and international exhibitions and launch Polypipe's new Technical Centre in Dubai, UAE.

POLYPIPE MANUFACTURES IN EXCESS OF 20,000 PRODUCTS

There's nothing more welcoming than a warm home

Brand Values

The core brand values within the business have been created from understanding the needs of customers and the key market drivers. These are deployed strategically throughout each and every project it undertakes. This ensures that Polypipe does not just meet but exceeds the global demands for better water management and carbon efficient solutions.

By combining all its strengths and capabilities, Polypipe continues to maintain its market-leading position for creating piping technology and sustainable products that are intelligently engineered for a fast developing world.

postoffice.co.uk

Founded in 1635, Post Office has since provided essential services to the UK through an unrivalled network of 11,500 branches – that's more than all of the country's retail banks and building societies combined. Today, the desire to better serve the needs of its customers is driving one of the largest retail transformations in history. And Post Office has a unique role in the UK as a commercial business with a social purpose.

Market

Providing the ultimate in convenience, Post Office network ensures 99.7 per cent of the population is within three miles of a branch, connecting customers to some of life's most essential products and services.

As one of the UK's most cherished and trusted brands, Post Office is a familiar part of the cultural fabric of the UK. From tiny villages to the largest cities, for almost 400 years, Post Office has inhabited a unique place in the heart of customers. So whether it's via a branch, over the phone or through an ever-growing digital footprint, Post Office provides the gateway to help customers get life's important things done.

Post Office also takes pride in its commitment to communities. It is one of BBC Children in Need's leading corporate partners raising over £1.2 million last year alone.

Product

Serving the ever-changing needs of UK customers in a commercially sustainable way is at the heart of Post Office's strategy. Building on its enviable position as the UK's leading mails and parcels retailer, Post Office also has a rapidly growing financial services and telecoms business.

In fact, some 170 products and services are now available through three main channels: in branch, call centers and online via Post Office's website.

Achievements

The aim of Post Office is to continue to be a trusted partner, helping customers fulfill their needs, both traditional and new.

It is proud to provide its customers with award-winning products and services; from CIM Marketing team of the year 2015, Best Exchange/Travel Money Retailer from 2007-2014

17M
PEOPLE VISIT A POST OFFICE EVERY WEEK

and Best Travel Insurance Provider from 2006-2014 at the British Travel Awards and Best Home & Contents Insurance Provider by Your Money. This continued recognition reinforces Post Office's position as a trusted and respected business by both customers and industry experts alike.

Recent Developments

Put simply, Post Office isn't the type of organisation to rest on past achievements. In fact, Post Office is currently implementing the largest investment and modernisation programme in its history, which includes new-style Post Office branches that open for longer, and over 3,000 branches now open on Sundays.

DID YOU KNOW?

A Post Office branch is within one mile of more than 97 per cent of the UK population and three miles of more than 99 per cent of the population.

95% OF THE UK ADULT POPULATION VISIT IN A YEAR

New open-plan retail environments are one of the signature features of many modernised branches, giving a more personal customer experience. This also allows many smaller branches, housed within larger retail businesses, to seamlessly provide Post Office services at its retail counters.

Flagship Post Office branches have also benefited from the introduction of new self-service options and dedicated mails drop-off counters, fast-tracking many mail and retail transactions and reducing queue times.

Around 8,000 branches will be modernised within the coming years, with half of these already live. Feedback from customers has been positive, with satisfaction scores consistently over 95 per cent, according to independent research.

It has also successfully launched a same day click and collect service in selected branches for Travel Money, reinforcing its digital capability and enviable number one market share position.

Post Office now also has the largest contactless network in the UK, making it easier for customers to pay.

Post Office identified an opportunity to create a small pool of 'Concept Stores' where it could concentrate efforts on live testing.

One concept store, in Kennington Park has allowed Post Office to hothouse innovation and renovation of technology and customer journey improvements in a controlled, low cost and efficient way, allowing it to evaluate benefits to the business before undertaking a larger scale roll out.

Finally, Post Office was one of the first to launch an Apple iWatch app, bringing to life its Travel Money offering in a relevant, simple way.

Promotion

Post Office is reinventing itself, putting customers' needs at the heart of everything it does.

Brand identity is also being refreshed with communications de-cluttering to strike a positive and sunny tone and leave customers smiling. Post Office aims to connect emotionally as well as rationally with its

DID YOU KNOW?
Ten Post Office branches are modernised every day.

customers. It is also enhancing the digital experience, to spread a good feeling to a much wider audience. Post Office was recognised by Twitter for its #holidayfeeling campaign with Simon Bird, offering behind the scenes moments from its TV ad.

Brand Values
Post Office is here to help customers get life's important things done.

Purposeful – keeping customers trust by helping them get their jobs done quickly and easily.

Uplifting – so customers feel good about choosing Post Office – and want to come back again.

Positively Surprising – Post Office does things in a way that changes perceptions.

Brand History

1635 Charles I opens up his private mail service to the general public. For the next 350 years, the General Post Office (from 1969 The Post Office Corporation) is a national institution, holding the monopoly in communication services.

1914 Post Office Rifles are remembered for their involvement as infantry on the Western Front in World War I.

1965 Post Office Tower opens.

1981 British Telecom is created as a separate public company.

1986 Post Office Corporation is reorganised into separate market-facing businesses – Royal Mail Letters, Royal Mail Parcels (later to become Parcelforce Worldwide), and Post Office Counters Ltd – creating, for the first time, a separate business "to manage the nationwide network "of Post Office branches.

2000 The Postal Services Act 2000 creates Royal Mail Group out of the old Post Office Corporation.

2001 Post Office Counters Ltd is renamed as Post Office Ltd, remaining a wholly-owned subsidiary of Royal Mail Group.

2004 Financial Services product range launches.

2005 The launch of Homephone marks the Post Office's re-entry into the telecommunications market after almost a 25-year absence.

2012 Post Office Ltd becomes an independent company.

2014 The modernisation of its network and the large scale rebrand continues.

radissonblu-edwardian.com

Exuberant. Exquisite. Exceptional. Radisson Blu Edwardian, London is a collection of individual hotels inspired by London, and rooted in the neighbourhoods they inhabit.

From stylish boutique to luxury of the grandest scale, each hotel boasts design that doesn't compromise on comfort, complimentary Wi-Fi, with chic bars and concept restaurants. Complimented by the brand's service ethos, Radisson Blu Edwardian, London creates unforgettable experiences.

Market
Radisson Blu Edwardian, London stands out from the crowd with stunning four-and five-star properties in illustrious locations. What helps the brand stay ahead of other key players is individuality. Where competitors offer indistinguishable service and interiors, Radisson Blu Edwardian, London offers hotels with quirky idiosyncrasies, unique design and excellent guest relationships from start to finish.

Radisson Blu Edwardian, London is part of Edwardian Hotels London (EHL), which has been developing luxury hotel premises since it was founded by Jasminder Singh OBE

in 1977. EHL is intrinsically linked to the capital, with 12 of its 14 owned and managed properties in London. EHL has been committed to establishing upscale hotels in the city for decades and is inimitably embedded within the landscape.

Product
Known for its presence in London's most desirable locations, the brand invests heavily in its properties and technology. Designed for comfort and convenience, with tactile furnishings and original art throughout, each hotel is unique in look and feel.

Staying with Radisson Blu Edwardian, London is an experience that never feels formulaic – from Kensington to Covent Garden – a real sense of place is evident.

Achievements
Radisson Blu Edwardian, London has been ranked among the best hotel groups in the UK in the Which? Travel consumer magazine. This standard is evident across regional hotels including Guildford, winner

DID YOU KNOW?
In 2016 Edwardian will relaunch the brand to consumers with a new logo, design and brand ethos.

of The Experience Guildford Customer Service Awards, and The Beautiful South Gold award, as well as Manchester Tourism's Hotel of the Year for the Manchester hotel. Futhermore, in 2015 the riverside hotel in New Providence Wharf won Visit England's coveted Rose Award.

Sustainability is high on the agenda, with awards recognising the brand's reputation as one of the UK's greenest hotel groups, including a Green Tourism Business Scheme Gold Award, Best Carbon Reduction in a Hotel Chain, and a Sustainable Restaurant Association two star badge.

Last year was the first in a five-year partnership with The Francis Crick Institute, a Cancer Research UK initiative. Throughout 2015, Radisson Blu Edwardian, London ran a calendar of fundraising events to raise money for the Institute, to show support for a cause close to its heart.

Recent Developments
Radisson Blu Edwardian, London is part of one of the world's fastest growing upscale

hotel groups, while retaining individuality as a privately-owned hotel collection. The company remains confident and continues to expand its food and beverage offerings.

Last year, Scoff & Banter welcomed a new addition to its family in Scoff & Banter Tea Rooms, on Oxford Street. While its popular

DID YOU KNOW?
The Radisson Blu Edwardian, Vanderbilt takes its name from the influential American family, the Vanderbilts, who converted it from 10 19th century town houses into a single hotel in the 1920s.

THE FIRST PUBLIC MEETING FOR SUFFRAGETTES OCCURRED AT THE FREE TRADE HALL IN 1905. THE 5* RADISSON BLU EDWARDIAN MANCHESTER IS LOCATED THERE TODAY.

Brand Values
At the heart of Edwardian Hotels London is a simple founding belief – that from back of house to the boardroom each employee is a Host. Everything Edwardian Hotels does is driven by a desire to exceed guests', clients' and partners' expectations so that even the shortest stay will last long in the memory.

Steak & Lobster restaurant chain expanded to Heathrow and Marble Arch.

Promotion
Despite belonging to a larger parent company, the group's brand communications remain distinctive. Through cherry-picked partnerships and a cross-channel calendar, every hotel continues to weave itself into the fabric of the community in which it resides.

In London, Radisson Blu Edwardian demonstrates its affinity with the arts through long-standing partnerships with the National Theatre, Royal Albert Hall and the Royal Shakespeare Company.

Every January and June, Radisson Blu Edwardian Bloomsbury Street demonstrates its links with fashion as the official hotel of London Collections Men. Brands such as Topman, Penhaligon's and Warsteiner have joined forces to turn the lobby into a stylish men's grooming lounge, abuzz with male models and bloggers.

Radisson Blu Edwardian Manchester continues to cement its place in the heart of Manchester through its title as official hotel of Manchester Pride. In 2015, celebrities and customers were invited to join their social media campaign, which called for people to show support with a selfie on #showusyourpride.

Brand History

1977 Edwardian Hotels is established by Jasminder Singh, OBE.

1992 A marketing agreement with Carlson is signed to increase global reach, and the brand becomes Radisson Edwardian Hotels.

2004 The first hotel outside London opens in Manchester, a five star hotel at the city's iconic Free Trade Hall.

2007 The company opens a brand new hotel opposite The O2 at New Providence Wharf.

2011 The second hotel outside London opens in the heart of Guildford.

2012 An agreement is signed with Carlson Rezidor Hotel Group to become part of the global Radisson Blu brand portfolio, and the brand becomes Radisson Blu Edwardian, London.

2013 Radisson Blu Edwardian, London launches Steak & Lobster and Scoff & Banter.

2014 Radisson Blu Edwardian launches two new Steak & Lobster restaurants, Great British Fish Company and the extensively refurbished Scoff & Banter Kensington.

2015 Two more Steak & Lobster restaurants are launched, along with the opening of Scoff & Banter Tea Rooms.

RICOH ARENA

Business | Entertainment | Sport

ricoharena.com

A versatile pioneer in the world of sport, business and entertainment the Ricoh Arena integrates top-class corporate event offerings with inspiring leisure activities. The venue's ability to create events tailored to meet clients' needs sets it apart from other arena venues. Ricoh Arena, the home of Wasps rugby, attracts the world's biggest names in sport, business and entertainment as it continues to evolve and expand its business, while helping to power the ambitions of the local community.

Market

The requests placed on conference and exhibition venues by event organisers are becoming increasingly stringent and complex. In today's competitive market, the size of space offered by venues is no longer a key differentiator.

Being able to adapt and change to meet specific needs is incredibly important. Since its opening in 2005, the Ricoh Arena has attracted 17 million visitors and hosted over 12,000 events. From sell-out musical performances featuring global icons to Olympic and European sporting events, alongside international conferences and exhibitions, from the launch of the Jaguar F-TYPE to the British Tarantula Society.

The Ricoh Arena is a firm favourite with music promoters for large-scale outdoor concerts and arena-style gigs for 10,000 to 40,000 music fans. Sports organisations have also hosted high profile events including the Football at the 2012 Olympic Games, the Davis Cup, European Rugby, football internationals and Champion of Champions Snooker.

Product

Located in the heart of the UK, the 20,000sq m Ricoh Arena prides itself on offering versatility, attracting large audiences who wish to attend a wide variety of events ranging from intimate to epic.

DID YOU KNOW?
Rihanna will open the UK leg of her Anti World Tour at the Ricoh Arena on 14 June 2016.

The site features a 32,602-seater stadium bowl – home of AVIVA Premiership rugby team Wasps and where Coventry City football club also play. World famous acts such as Take That, Coldplay and Bruce Springsteen have also performed at the venue.

Combining business with leisure, the venue's purpose-built conference centre has the flexibility to host conferences for up to 4,000 delegates with a range of lounges and halls for breakout sessions and meetings. The Ricoh Arena also has two on-site restaurants and one of the largest casinos in the UK.

The venue is one of the most accessible venues in the UK, located near the M6, M1, M40 and M42 and situated within a two-hour drive for 75 per cent of the UK's population.

With three train stations within a seven-mile radius, London only 55 minutes away by rail and Birmingham International Airport a 20-minute drive, access is easy for local, national and international visitors. The Ricoh Arena is set to further improve its connections with a new railway station onsite, scheduled to open imminently.

32,019 PEOPLE
WATCHED WASPS VS LEICESTER TIGERS
IN A NEW AVIVA PREMIERSHIP RECORD ATTENDANCE IN 2015

Achievements

Over 638 events took place at the Ricoh Arena in 2014 across its range of locations, which include the Jaguar Exhibition Hall, Halls 3-5, E.ON Lounge and Club Jaguar.

With a total of 21 international and national award wins since its inception, including the recent Global Icon at the Coventry and Warwickshire Tourism and Culture Awards, the venue's management team has picked up honours including Best Venue Salesperson at the Exhibition News Awards and The Networker Award at the Stadium Business Awards.

Global recognition was achieved during the Olympic Games in 2012 when the Ricoh Arena hosted 12 football matches, helping to generate in excess of over £80 million for the local economy.

The Olympic legacy has also led to bookings from UK governing sporting bodies and interest from the planners of new stadiums in New Zealand, China, Sweden and Japan, keen to use the Ricoh Arena as a template for a successful multi-purpose stadium.

Recent Developments

Due to the large volumes of visitors, a separate hotel and second atrium entrance have been constructed to improve the flow of people using the building. The hotel has recently been refurbished and opened as a DoubleTree by Hilton; including a new bar and brasserie called The Mill, which also houses a coffee shop and bakery.

The Ricoh Arena and Wasps have a strong portfolio of partners that will further develop the arena's ambition to become a leader in innovation and stadium experience. The brand family includes partners such as RICOH, Land Rover, E.ON, EMC2, Under Armour, Heineken, Purity Brewing Co, Majestic, Pins & Stripes, DS Smith and Causeway.

A new on-site Club Store was recently launched, selling Wasps, Under Armour and Pins & Stripes tailored products. Event ticketing has been brought in-house with the development of a new ticket office, providing improved customer service and the opportunity to sell through a multitude of channels.

Infrastructure work has enabled up to 4,500 delegates to use Wi-Fi simultaneously. Additionally, a £3 million renovation project involved installing energy saving equipment to ensure efficient use of utilities. Furthermore, achieving category C status in the Government's energy performance ratings is helping to support a long-term, sustainable future for the venue.

Catering is a vital element for the venue and, recently, the Ricoh Arena has introduced multi-national 'Street Food' catering, offering a range of cuisines for visitors whether they are attending a concert, trade show or exhibition. Re-iterating the strong focus on

social responsibility, Ricoh Arena staff raised £200,000 for charities including Guide Dogs for the Blind, Macmillan, Memusi, NSPCC and Different Strokes.

Promotion

The Ricoh Arena has built relationships with organisations in Coventry to promote and strengthen the region as a whole, and has access to a 500,000 strong database to publicise its events and increase its brand exposure.

Staff at the Ricoh Arena work closely with each organiser to ensure their event is the best it possibly can be. This hands-on, friendly approach is reflected in the venue's large number of repeat bookings.

Brand History

2005 The Ricoh Arena opens when Coventry City faces Queen Park Rangers in the Championship.

2006 The on-site hotel and one of the largest subterranean casinos in the UK open.

2007 Rugby fans watch Heineken Cup action at the Ricoh Arena for the first time.

2008 Highest sporting attendance to date is 31,407 for Coventry City's FA Cup quarter-final tie against Chelsea.

2009 Fans enjoy three sell-out nights during Take That's Circus Tour.

2012 The Ricoh Arena is the only Midlands venue for live sporting action during London 2012, hosting 12 Olympic football matches in eight days.

2013 The Co-operative Group brings 4,100 delegates to its annual conference – the largest conference the venue has held.

2014 Wasps rugby purchase the Ricoh Arena, bringing top-class rugby to the West Midlands.

Brand Values

The Ricoh Arena strives to stand out from the crowd in terms of innovation and hospitality, delivering exciting and entertaining events in sport, business and entertainment to offer great experiences.

rolls-royce.com

Rolls-Royce designs, develops, manufactures and services integrated power systems for use in the air, on land and at sea. It is one of the world's leading producers of aero engines for large civil aircraft and corporate jets. Rolls-Royce is the second largest provider of defence aero engines and services in the world. In land and sea markets, reciprocating engines and systems from Rolls-Royce are in marine, distributed energy, oil and gas, rail, as well as off-highway vehicle applications. In nuclear, it has strong instrumentation, product and service capability in both civil power and submarine propulsion.

Market

The markets Rolls-Royce address have a number of similar characteristics: they have very high barriers to entry; they offer the opportunity for organic growth; and they feature extraordinarily long programme lives, usually measured in decades. The size of these markets is generally related to world gross domestic product growth or, in the case of the defence markets, global security and the scale of defence budgets. Rolls-Royce annual revenues are more than £14.6 billion, half of

which comes from services. The Group's order book in 2015 stood at just over £76 billion.

Product

Rolls-Royce is probably best known for aero engines that power many of the world's most advanced passenger jets. The Trent family of engines is a leader in power for modern widebody aircraft. In civil aerospace, Rolls-Royce powers commercial aircraft, from business jets to the largest airliners. A fleet of 13,000 engines is currently in service on 35 types of aircraft.

In defence there are 16,000 engines currently in the service. These engines power aircraft in every major sector including: transport; combat; patrol; trainers; helicopters; and unmanned aerial vehicles.

In the marine market, products include established names such as Kamewa, Ulstein and Aquamaster, which, together with a strong focus on research and development, have made Rolls-Royce a pioneer of many important technologies, including aero-derivative marine gas turbines, controllable pitch propellers and water jets. The company is also

DID YOU KNOW?
Through MTU diesel engines, Rolls-Royce now powers trains.

ROLLS-ROYCE POWERS NEARLY
30,000 ✈
COMMERCIAL AND DEFENCE AIRCRAFT

a world leader in the design of offshore support vessels.

In the power systems market, Rolls-Royce produces high-speed reciprocating engines, propulsion and distributed energy systems through its MTU product family.

Achievements

Rolls-Royce is recognised as a leading sustainable business, achieving Industry Leader in the Aerospace and Defence sector in the Dow Jones Sustainability Index (DJSI) 2015. It increased the total company score by 17 per cent from 2014, as measured in the DJSI, the world's leading benchmark indicator of sustainable business. Rolls-Royce is listed in both the DJSI World and DJSI Europe index.

Recent Developments

Rolls-Royce now produces the MTU diesel engine range as a result of a major acquisition in Germany. The acquisition combined Rolls-Royce's medium-speed diesel

and gas engines business with MTU's high-speed reciprocating engines. The acquisition significantly enhanced Rolls-Royce's core diesel and gas engine product, systems portfolio and its global network of sales and service facilities.

As part of its commitment to supporting STEM projects in the community, Rolls-Royce is a sponsor of the Bloodhound SSC adventure. This project aims to enthuse young people about engineering by building a car capable of beating the land speed record – achieving over 1,000mph using the EJ200 engine as part of its propulsion system. The speed record attempt is scheduled for 2016.

DID YOU KNOW?
In 2014 Rolls-Royce employed 354 graduates and 357 apprentices through worldwide training programmes.

The Trent XWB is the latest Rolls-Royce engine to enter service, powering the Airbus A350 XWB airliner. It is the sixth member of the Trent family and the world's most efficient large aero engine.

Promotion

The company vision is to create 'better power for a changing world'. Rolls-Royce invests more than £1.2 billion annually in research and development. The Group is determined to give an effective response to climate change and other environmental concerns.

Similarly, it is committed to research and development in order to provide leading-edge technologies that reduce fuel burn, emissions and noise across all products. It is also at the forefront of research into advanced technologies, such as nuclear power, that provide new approaches to low-carbon energy.

Brand History

1904 Henry Royce meets Charles Rolls, whose company sells high quality cars in London.

1914 At the start of World War I, Royce designs his first aero engine, the Eagle, which goes on to provide half of the total horsepower used in the air by the allies.

1940 Royce's Merlin powers the Hawker Hurricane and Supermarine Spitfire in the Battle of Britain. Four years later, development begins on the aero gas turbine.

1953 Rolls-Royce enters the civil aviation market with the Dart in the Vickers Viscount. It becomes the cornerstone of universal acceptance of the gas turbine by the airline industry.

1976 Concorde, powered by the Rolls-Royce Snecma Olympus 593, becomes the first and only supersonic airliner to enter service.

1987 Rolls-Royce returned to the private sector becoming the only company in Britain capable of delivering power to use in the air, at sea and on land.

1999 Rolls-Royce acquires Vickers for £576 million, transforming Rolls-Royce into the global leader in marine power systems.

2003 BMW takes over the responsibility for Rolls-Royce cars.

2011 Trent 1000 engines power the new Boeing 787 Dreamliner into service.

2012 Rolls-Royce opens a new 154,000m^2 aero engine build facility in Singapore.

2013 Rolls-Royce announces its involvement in the Bloodhound SSC adventure: a project that aims to build a car capable of beating the land speed record.

2014 The world's most fuel-efficient aero engine, the new Rolls-Royce Trent XWB, enters service on the Airbus A350 XWB.

Brand Values

Rolls-Royce is one of the most famous brands in the world. The company brand promise is 'trusted to deliver excellence'. The Rolls-Royce brand means more than standards of engineering – it is about the reputation of the company across all its activities.

ROTARY

Established in Switzerland 1895

rotarywatches.com

Rotary is a 121-year-old Swiss watch brand offering ladies' and gents' dress watches in the mid-market price bracket. Established in La Chaux-de-Fonds, Switzerland in 1895 by Moise Dreyfuss, Rotary is proud of its reputation as a trusted brand known for high quality, design-led, Swiss timepieces at an affordable price. In the UK, Rotary is a brand leader in the midmarket sector, defined as 'watches that retail for between £100 and £400'.

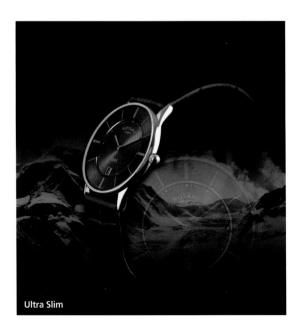

Ultra Slim

Market

The UK watch market is worth an estimated £1.22 billion (Source: GfK 2015). The market has grown in value as consumers are becoming more aware of the benefits of investing in a classic watch that will last a lifetime. Similarly, the market is showing the enduring appeal of classic, traditional brands and styling.

Consumers are extremely discerning when making considered purchases such as a new watch and clearly prefer to invest in trusted and established brands. Rotary has been a respected brand for 121 years and offers strong consumer assurances such as

the waterproof standard and the lifetime guarantee. Rotary is part of The Dreyfuss Group and is exported worldwide. The brand has expanded internationally into major markets such as China, America and Russia whilst also achieving strong growth in recent years within the travel retail sector.

Product

Rotary offers consumers an extensive choice of dress watches with a range of more than 200 models – all designed to the highest specification, guaranteeing longevity and reliability.

Rotary's most popular range of watches for ladies and gentlemen is the Rotary Les Originales collecion. A classic, elegant, accessibly-priced Swiss-made proposition of the highest quality, which is not only affordable but an investment to be treasured forever.

The innovative Rotary Revelation models feature two watch faces that can be reversed to track two different time zones. Differentiated dials to suit daywear or evening wear with scratch proof sapphire glass make these watches a popular choice for Business travellers. Meanwhile, the Revelation family

DID YOU KNOW?
In the 1940s, Rotary's wartime ad campaigns featured non-magnetic watches.

Revelation

has dual style as well as dual purpose features with luxury leather straps and either PVD plated or stainless steel cases. These exceptional reversible timepieces are ideal for the busy traveller.

The Ultra Slim collection of dress watches underlines Rotary's dedication to its reputation as a superior supplier of premium quality and elegant timepieces. Both the ladies and gentlemen's models have sleek

Brand History

1895 M.Dreyfuss begins making timepieces in a small workshop in the Swiss town of La Chaux-de-Fonds.

1907 Georges and Sylvain Dreyfuss, two of M.Dreyfuss three sons, open a UK office to import watches.

1920 The company introduces its 'Winged Wheel' logo.

1940 Rotary is appointed as official watch supplier to the British army.

1987 Robert Dreyfuss succeeds his father, Teddy Dreyfuss, as Chairman, becoming the fourth generation of the family to run the business.

2006 The patented Rotary Round Revelation™ is launched.

2009 Rotary introduces two significant initiatives: the Waterproof standard and the Lifetime guarantee.

2011 Rotary sponsors Clipper Around The World yacht race.

2012 Rotary announces the launch of its own proprietary movement.

2013 Rotary announces its partnership with Chelsea FC as the Official Global Timekeeper.

2014 China Haidian Holdings LTD acquires a 100 per cent share of the Dreyfuss Group and becomes the parent company.

China Haidian Holdings LTD are renamed as City Champ Watch & Jewellery Group Ltd on 7th July.

The Dreyfuss Group is awarded the Queen's award for International trade.

2015 Rotary celebrates 120 years in business.

4.85mm side profiles and stunning two-step dial designs that complement the classic appeal of the collection as a whole.

Achievements
In 2014, The Dreyfuss Group was honoured with Britain's most coveted commercial prize, the Queen's Award for International Trade, which it will carry for the next five years.

The Dreyfuss Group has a brand portfolio that includes; Rotary, Dreyfuss & Co and J & T Windmills. The group is committed to achieving sustained growth through profitability and innovation. The belief in international trade is central to the company's yearly business strategy.

Recent Developments
The launch of the waterproof standard marked one of the most important technological breakthroughs in watch making in the last decade. For consumers, this offers peace of mind, thanks to a simple 'waterproof' promise. It is unique for two key reasons, the most notable being the fact that the standard marks a move away from the complex and confusing numeric system of water resistance to which the rest of the industry subscribes.

Secondly, Rotary also applied the waterproof standard to virtually its entire range, including delicate ladies' models.

Rotary has been a family watch making business until the recent acquisition in April 2014 by City Champ Watches & Jewellery Ltd. Rotary's rich family heritage offers an unrivalled ability to produce classic, traditional

Monaco

DID YOU KNOW? In 1920 Rotary launched the winged wheel logo. Whilst on a train journey Moise Dreyfuss was inspired by the train's motion and wheels, it reminded him of the balance wheel within a watch movement. The wings signified the company's growth.

timepieces. Building a lasting home in the hearts and minds of watch enthusiasts who recognise that the knowhow and care that goes into the design and manufacture of a Rotary timepiece imbue them with intrinsic value, to be enjoyed and appreciated by all.

Promotion
Since the launch of Rotary's fully transactional website in 2013 it has enjoyed many successes. The website aims to combine timeless charm with outstanding functionality. Consumers are able to discover Rotary's fascinating rich heritage along with all the latest watch launches that Rotary are proud to offer.

Lucerne

Specific design features offer the consumer an easy navigation process and detailed information on the collections, along with a quick and easy search engine which directs consumers to their Rotary purchase.

 SWISS MADE  WATERPROOF SWIM & DIVE ALL DAY

 ROTARY IS EXPORTED TO MORE THAN 60 COUNTRIES

Brand Values
For 121 years, Rotary has preserved its Swiss heritage, crafting watches with the same quality materials and testing each watch to ensure it can withstand the rigours of everyday life. Rotary builds on this heritage by investing in new product development, staff training and leading information technology to ensure it meets the needs of the modern consumer.

Royal Albert Hall

royalalberthall.com

The Royal Albert Hall is the world's most famous stage. Since 1871, the Hall has been held in trust for the nation's benefit to promote purposes connected with the arts and sciences. The world's greatest musicians, dancers, sportsmen and statesmen have appeared on its stage. In 2015, more than 1.7 million people enjoyed a live performance at the Hall and millions more experienced events through broadcasts and recordings.

Market

The Royal Albert Hall is one of the most instantly recognisable international brands in the highly competitive entertainment, leisure and tourism sectors. It is a registered charity and receives no public revenue funding. A leading player in the London arts and entertainment market, it is also highly renowned and respected throughout the UK as well as overseas.

Product

Built to fulfil Prince Albert's vision of a central venue to celebrate the arts and sciences, the Hall was opened in 1871. Almost 400 events were held in the venue's iconic 5,200-seat auditorium in 2015. The diverse range of events included music, sport, circus, charity events, award ceremonies, the BBC Proms and the Royal British Legion's Festival of Remembrance. In addition, the Hall presented 400 shows in other spaces, offered daytime tours of the building, free exhibitions and performances in its public spaces, and inspired creativity in more than 100,000 children through its extensive Education & Outreach programme.

Achievements

Highlights of the main auditorium programme in 2015 included Interstellar Live, for which Professor Brian Cox hosted a pre-film talk with Hans Zimmer, Christopher Nolan and Professor Stephen Hawking; the World Premiere of the new Bond film, Spectre; and the Royal Variety Performance. The Hall hosted multi-night residencies from David Gilmour, Cliff Richard, Bob Dylan on the 50th anniversary of his first appearance, and Eric Clapton celebrating his 50th anniversary, 70th birthday and 200th appearance at the Hall.

The year also featured two nights from pianist Lang Lang, six weeks of Cirque du Soleil's Kooza, 22 performances of Puccini's Madame Butterfly, and the expansion of the Hall's series of film with live score including the 30th anniversary of Back to the Future and the World Premiere of Frozen in Concert. The summer season of BBC Proms concerts saw more than 300,000 people attending 88 concerts and over half of all concerts in the Royal Albert Hall sold out.

The ever-expanding programme of events beyond the main stage in 2015 included Lulu Gainsbourg, a series of Late Night Laughs including five-star shows from the Edinburgh Fringe, exhibitions by Noel Fielding and Miles Davis, Miss Behave's Cabaret Cornucopia, a new silent film strand and weekend Live Music Brunches, as well as the regular Late Night Jazz and Classical Coffee Mornings.

The charity 'free let' for 2015 was The Salvation Army, celebrating 150 years as an organisation and 120 years at the Hall.

DID YOU KNOW?
It took 6,000,000 bricks and 80,000 terracotta bricks to build the Royal Albert Hall.

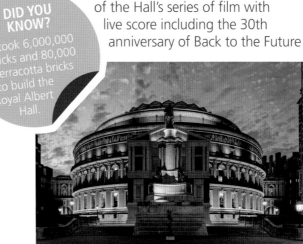

DID YOU KNOW?
There are 9,999 pipes in the Grand Organ – which total nine miles.

Throughout 2015, the Hall hosted 40 charity performances including a series of shows and workshops in aid of Teenage Cancer Trust, the WI's centenary meeting, Tony Bennett and Lady Gaga in support of WellChild, Music For Youth, the Help Nepal Network as well as the Rays of Sunshine Children's Charity.

The Hall's Education & Outreach programme continued with a wide range of activities including a special concert with the Tri-borough music hub, Seven Seeds, written with the input of children and performed by 1,200 young singers alongside an orchestra made up of professional musicians and students from the Royal College of Music and the Royal Academy of Music. It also included a cross-generational multi-location project based on Madame Butterfly, the introduction of Family Storytelling and Music sessions, Primary Proms, Events Management workshops and Songbook – free, interactive concerts for elderly people in care homes, hospitals, day centres and hospices.

With the support of the Lord Leonard and Lady Estelle Wolfson Foundation, the Hall joined forces with renowned charity Nordoff Robbins in a new music therapy programme, designed to inspire and transform the lives of children and adults of all ages who have a range of disabilities and Special Educational Needs.

Recent Developments

The new, responsive website was launched in July 2015, with the objectives of selling more tickets with less waiting and telling the full story of the Hall. A vast wealth of archive material became available to the public for the first time through a searchable online database and there is a curated time machine which gives a glimpse of the Hall's history since 1871.

In 2015 the Hall invested over £6 million in the building and completed a new heating and cooling system throughout the building that is more efficient and effective in controlling the environment. In addition, the West Arena Foyer was completely refurbished as the Heineken Green Room.

The expansion of tours has seen the introduction of the Secret History Tour, which reveals the untold story of the venue, from Allen Ginsberg's Poetry Incantation to John Lennon's Bagism, as well as a séance, a funeral and an appearance by three up-and-coming boxers with the surname Kray. Afternoon Tea Tours were also launched to sit alongside the Grand Tour; Story of the Proms Tour; Victorian Interactive Tour and Inside Out Tour; and Christmas 2015 saw Father Christmas's first residence at the Hall in a magical Christmas grotto.

Promotion

The Hall has continued to develop its profile through digital media, with more than 70 per cent of tickets now sold online. The Hall undertook a visual refresh in February 2015, introducing a new logo and design system befitting of one of the Top 20 CoolBrands for 2015/16.

The Royal Albert Hall works with promoters to maximise sales of the performances and events they stage at the Hall and, in addition, markets its own activity, including events in the main auditorium, performances in other spaces, tours of the building, corporate hospitality opportunities, as well as food and drink.

IN 2015, THE HALL'S ICONIC 5,200 SEAT AUDITORIUM HOSTED 1.7 MILLION PEOPLE

Brand History

1871	The Royal Albert Hall is opened by Queen Victoria in March.
1941	The first BBC Proms season at the Hall takes place.
1963	The Beatles and The Rolling Stones appear on the same bill.
2006	President Bill Clinton speaks at the Hall about his vision for leadership in the 21st century.
2012	100th Royal Variety Performance in aid of the Entertainment Artistes' Benevolent Fund takes place.
2015	The Hall hosts the World Premiere of Spectre.

Brand Values

The Royal Albert Hall is breath-taking and unforgettable – there is nothing like it. Its mission is to promote the arts and sciences and to preserve and enhance the Grade I listed building, which is held in trust for the nation.

The Hall's vision is to inspire artists and audiences worldwide with the magic of the iconic building; creating life-enriching, unforgettable experiences for everyone.

The Royal Albert Hall is more than just a building. It is one team, passionate and open to all. Together, artists, audiences and staff are writing the story of the Royal Albert Hall, inspiring as many people as possible with unforgettable experiences.

the Luxury Included® holiday

sandals.co.uk

Since opening its first resort in 1981, Sandals Resorts has been at the forefront of the Caribbean all-inclusive travel sector by offering luxury, innovation and choice. In an industry brimming with new contenders, the combined knowledge and experience of Sandals' management team and resort staff is the reason the company keeps setting the Gold Standard in the expanding all-inclusive market. After all, it was Sandals that introduced the Luxury Included® concept.

Market

In recent years the concept of luxury travel has steered away from conservative, off-the-shelf five-star packages towards tailor-made individualism. Sandals Resorts sets itself apart by placing an emphasis on personal choice, always aiming to offer more for the price of the holiday.

Sandals Resorts' prices cover gourmet specialty restaurants, premium brand drinks, tips and taxes, in addition to land and water sports such as golf and scuba diving. Currently there are 15 Sandals resorts aimed at 'two people in love' located in Jamaica, Saint Lucia, Antigua, the Bahamas, Grenada and, most recently, Barbados. Its sister brand, Beaches Resorts,

currently comprises three resorts in Jamaica and Turks and Caicos. Beaches Resorts caters for families, groups, couples and singles.

Product

Sandals was the first all-inclusive resort company to offer à la carte dining with a range of culinary experiences reaching far beyond its Caribbean roots. To expand this approach, Sandals introduced Gourmet Discovery Dining; an extensive programme which encompasses every element of the dining experience from speciality restaurants, à la carte menus, innovative design and first-class service, to culinary creations that allow customers to dine around the world without leaving the resort.

Sandals latest innovation stems from the design of its Love Nest Suites. These suites each offer privacy and elegance, from custom furnishings to the added touches provided by dedicated staff who strive to make each holiday a unique experience. At Sandals LaSource Grenada, innovation was delivered in the form of Skypool Butler Suites. Perched atop the Italian Village, the Love Nest Suites have direct access to a private cantilevered, solar heated plunge pool with an infinity edge and ocean views. The suite's living room also has an indoor dining table, sofa area, smart television, a butler pantry, and fully stocked wet bar with premium brand spirits. The living area leads to a balcony and a Tranquility Soaking Tub. This is accompanied by the service of Sandals' elite Butlers.

Sandals are experts when it comes to destination weddings and honeymoons, and the 'Your Wedding. Your Style.' concept allows couples to customise and execute their dream wedding at any one of Sandals and Beaches' 18 Caribbean resorts, complete with an exclusive online Destination Wedding Designer tool.

DID YOU KNOW?
Sandals has been voted the world's leading all-inclusive resort for the past 19 years, with more inclusions than any other resort on the planet.

EACH RESORT HAS UP TO

16 RESTAURANTS WITH

21 INTERNATIONAL CUISINES

Achievements

Sandals has strived to perfect the all-inclusive concept since its inception. For over three decades, it has won many industry accolades. Last year it received an array of awards including Hotel & Resort Operator of the Year at the TTG Travel Awards, Best All Inclusive Resort Operator at the Travel Weekly Globe Travel Awards, Travel Agent Choice Award for Best Resort for Wedding and Honeymoons and Best Family Hotel (Outside of Europe) at the Junior Design Awards.

In addition to these industry events, the company has won an array of consumer awards. Most recently being voted the Best All-Inclusive Hotel & Resort Brand at the British Travel Awards.

Recent Developments

One of Sandals Resorts® biggest developments in 2015 was the opening of the newly renovated Sandals Barbados; Barbados' only five star Luxury Included® resort. Located on Dover Beach, the 280-room resort features a beachfront whirlpool, fire pits, a new swim-up pool bar, land and water sports, as well as 11 gourmet

restaurants, including Bombay Club Sandals® first ever Indian restaurant.

Following a multi-million dollar renovation project, Sandals' largest resort, Sandals Grande Riviera Beach & Villa Golf Resort was relaunched as Sandals Ochi Beach Resort. The resort features a fresh, modern design with seven new dining options, a fresh Ochi Beach Club, reinvented resort entertainment and upgraded luxurious accommodation.

In 2015, work commenced on five stunning Maldivian-style over-the-water suites built onto the private offshore island at Sandals Royal Caribbean Spa Resort & Offshore

Island. Each of the suites features a private outdoor Jacuzzi tub and shower, interior spaces extending over 1,600sq ft, and glass flooring in the living area.

Promotion

Sandals Resorts' advertising campaign supports the efforts of travel agents and tour operators to market the Sandals Resorts and Beaches Resorts brands. Sandals' visual brand identity is evolving to suit global markets, in particular its expansion into Europe, ensuring the brand is more sophisticated and lifestyle-focused. Sandals Resorts and Beaches Resorts operate a sophisticated customer relationship management programme, which includes a loyalty scheme, Sandals Select.

Brand History

1981 Gordon 'Butch' Stewart opens Sandals Montego Bay, the flagship resort.

1985 Sandals opens Carlyle in Montego Bay, now called Sandals Carlyle.

1986 Sandals Royal Caribbean opens becoming the only resort in Jamaica with a private island.

1989 Sandals Ocho Rios, now Sandals Grande Riviera makes its debut in 'Butch' Stewart's hometown.

1991 The chain welcomes Sandals Grande Antigua – the first destination outside of Jamaica to have a Sandals presence.

1994 Sandals introduces Sandals Halcyon in Castries, Saint Lucia.

1996 Sandals Royal Bahamian opens in Nassau, Bahamas.

1997 Sandals introduces its first family resort in Jamaica, as Beaches Negril opens its doors. Beaches Turks and Caicos opens in Providenciales, becoming the second family resort.

2002 Both Sandals Grande St. Lucian, Saint Lucia and Beaches Ocho Rios, Jamaica open.

2005 Sandals Whitehouse European Village & Spa – the first resort development on the unchartered south coast region of Jamaica – opens.

2008 Grand Pineapple Beach Resorts open in Jamaica and Antigua.

2009 The Sandals Foundation is announced.

2010 Sandals Emerald Bay, Great Exuma, Bahamas opens.

2013 Sandals LaSource Grenada Resort & Spa opens.

Sandals Barbados is acquired.

2015 Sandals Barbados opens following an extensive renovation project.

Sandals Grande Riviera relaunches as Sandals Ochi Beach Resort.

Brand Values

Sandals continues to build on its strong position in the Caribbean hotel industry with innovations such as the Luxury Included® concept, and being able to offer more quality inclusions than any other resorts on the planet.

Sandals Resorts International has a philanthropic arm, The Sandals Foundation. Since its inception in 2009, the Sandals Foundation has aimed to unite the region with one common goal: to elevate its people and protect its delicate ecosystem under the pillars of community, education, and the environment. Six years on, the Sandals Foundation has implemented projects and programmes worth over US$21.1 million including training over 1,000 teachers and impacting more than 190,000 people through healthcare initiatives.

savills.co.uk

savills

Savills plc is a global real estate services provider listed on the London Stock Exchange. The firm has an international network of more than 700 offices and associates throughout the Americas, the UK, continental Europe, Asia Pacific, Africa and the Middle East, offering a broad range of specialist advisory, management and transactional services to clients globally.

Its 30,000-strong workforce combines entrepreneurial spirit and a deep understanding of specialist property sectors with high standards of client care.

Market

Savills is the largest multi-service property advisory business in the UK, providing more sector specialisms than any of its competitors across the commercial, residential, rural and energy sectors. In 2015, Savills completed its largest ever UK acquisition, the merger of Smiths Gore, to create one of the market's leading business offers in the sector. Collier & Madge also joined the Savills business in 2015, enhancing the firm's property management offer. Savills now has the largest UK national footprint to rival its competitors and operates from a total of 137 offices across the UK and Ireland.

In 2015, Savills was recognised for its exceptional achievement at the 13th Annual Managing Partners Forum Awards for outstanding contribution to the property profession.

Savills is the largest sales agent of new build homes and apartments in the UK and one of the only UK advisers providing an end-to-end service from inception and site identification through to sales and lettings of completed schemes. Its strong market presence increased in London with the opening of six new residential branches in the last 12 months. It continues to dominate the London prime residential market with more than 30 per cent market share on sales of properties over £5 million.

The strength and breadth of the firm's commercial offer was demonstrated in its advice to the Peel Group in welcoming Legal & General Capital as a 50 per cent JV partner in its landmark MediaCityUK scheme in Manchester.

WITH A NETWORK OF

137 OFFICES

SAVILLS HAS THE LARGEST UK NATIONAL FOOTPRINT TO RIVAL ITS COMPETITORS

Brand History

1855 Savill & Son is founded by Alfred Savill.

1972 The firm rebrands as Savills and moves to Mayfair.

1988 Savills is listed on the London Stock Exchange and begins trading as a plc.

1997 A 20 per cent share of Savills is sold to First Pacific Davies – one of Asia's foremost property companies – and the subsidiary is rebranded FPDSavills.

2000 Savills plc is listed in the FTSE 250 and acquires First Pacific Davies in April.

2004 To coincide with the company's 150th anniversary in 2005, the decision is made to drop 'FPD' from FPDSavills. The rebrand brings all the subsidiaries back under the Savills umbrella.

2013 Commercial Chairman, Mark Ridley, is named CEO of Savills UK.

2014 Savills announces its biggest ever acquisition of US firm Studley at £154 million.

CEO of Savills UK, Mark Ridley, takes on the additional role of European CEO.

2015 Savills completes its largest ever UK acquisition, the merger of Smiths Gore.

Other highlights across commercial markets throughout 2015 include its retail team acting on 50 per cent of all deals transacted on Oxford Street, its industrial leasing team advising on 18 million sq ft including a 400,000 sq ft pre-let to Nice-Pak at Westwood Park, Wigan. The firm has been at the forefront of driving capital into London and was involved in 25 per cent of all City transactions over £100 million and 19 per cent of all West End transactions, advising clients from over 14 different countries.

Product

During its 159-year history, Savills has grown from a family firm of chartered surveyors

into an international property real estate group. Spanning the breadth and depth of the residential and commercial property markets, Savills continues to adapt its offer to cater for its diverse client base. The significant boost to its Corporate Real Estate team in the US is expected to spark further growth across the globe.

Achievements

Savills was the Times Graduate Employer of Choice for the ninth consecutive year in 2015. The firm won Estates Gazette's UK Industrial and Logistics Advisor of the Year, Property Week's Leisure and Professional Services (valuation) Advisor of the Year, UK Sales Agency of the Year and Residential Consultancy Practice of the Year at the RESI Awards. The firm's Edinburgh and West End business space agency teams were both awarded best in class at the CoStar Agency Awards in terms of top agent by disposal sq ft. In addition, Savills has received accolades for Business Energy,

Excellence in Learning and Development and Commercial Agency of the Year at Ireland's Property Industry Awards.

Recent Developments

Savills remains a leading UK international property service with a total turnover topping £1 billion. The UK business now accounts for 46 per cent of its turnover, with a third generated by its Asia business. In Europe, Savills has opened new offices in Stuttgart and

DID YOU KNOW? Savills completed its largest ever UK acquisition, the merger of Smiths Gore, in 2015.

Barcelona, and secured new office leasing teams in Frankfurt, Stockholm, Gothenburg, Amsterdam and Paris. It is also developing its Building and Project Management Consultancy services with the acquisition of Tagis in the Netherlands and a new team in Paris. In 2015, Savills extended its global network with a new office in Colombia and associates in Cambodia, while Savills Studley opened the firm's first office in Canada.

Promotion

The company continues to be at the cutting-edge of research and thought leadership, demonstrating its understanding of key trends in all market sectors. In 2015 it launched two major campaigns through social media: 'Tech cities' launched through The Wall Street Journal with the article shared by 3,800 Facebook users; and the award-winning Savills 'Love London' social media marketing campaign, which utilised online networks to share video and blog content with an audience of prospective home buyers, sellers, landlords and tenants across London. The campaign had more than one million video views and was awarded 'Best Professional Services Content Marketing Strategy/Campaign' at The Drum Content Awards 2015.

Brand Values

Savills attracts the best individuals within its market, and through careful selection and the preservation of a unique culture, provides a global platform from which its talents and expertise can not only benefit clients but also the wider community. The firm's vision is to be the real estate adviser of choice in the markets it serves. Savills does not wish to be the biggest, just the best (as judged by its clients). Its values capture commitment not only to ethical, professional and responsible conduct but also to the essence of real estate success; an entrepreneurial, value-embracing approach.

SEARCYS
REDEFINING DINING

searcys.co.uk

Founded in 1847 by John Searcy, the pastry chef to the Duke of Northumberland, Searcys is one of the most reputable hospitality companies in Great Britain. Searcys currently operates at 29 iconic venues. With its long and illustrious catering heritage, there are two fundamentals which have remained constant – innovation and quality. Searcys is committed to delivering a luxurious experience through its inspiring settings, exceptionally high standard of product and engaging service.

Market

Searcys operates across a wide mix of sectors within a broad range of venues including hotels, restaurants, bars, visitor attractions and iconic venues, stately homes, museums, shopping centres and hotels. This rich collection allows Searcys to apply key learnings between venues, creating high impact campaigns at the forefront of the industry.

The common thread across these diverse offerings is utmost commitment to high standards and maintaining the unique identity and voice of each site. Searcys focuses on celebrating every

DID YOU KNOW?
1,101 bottles and 4,778 glasses of champagne were sold during National Champagne week 2015.

venue's personality, while implementing a bespoke approach within the framework of quality standards and accessible luxury.

Product

Searcys' commitment to delivering first class food and beverages is driven by pristine execution and innovation, the end result being outstanding experiences which last a lifetime. From intimate events in a Knightsbridge townhouse, VIP dinners overlooking Tech City, to a spontaneous bottle of Champagne in the travel hub at St Pancras International, every single experience is meticulously planned by an expert in their field.

Achievements

Searcys established National Champagne Week in 2010, now the most successful trade champagne campaign in the UK. The campaign generates strong sales and considerable press interest across each of its venues at events held throughout the week. Searcys Champagne Bars are considered industry leaders for the range of champagnes offered, the variety of events run and the expertise of the team.

Searcys restaurants enjoyed a range of accolades and awards throughout 2015. Its restaurant, Sixtyone in Marlyebone, maintained three AA rosettes and its latest venture, Urban Coterie, was included in the exclusive list of 'Top 25 new restaurants of 2015' by The Times.

Searcys events venue, 30 Euston Square, was recognised in two categories at the inaugural London Venue Awards 2015. The venue won Best Conference Venue for up to 300 delegates, and Best Board Room, Meeting or AGM Venue.

In 2015 Searcys I The Gherkin hosted a six-week 'Moroccan Sky Riad' Summer Pop-up,

#CHAMPAGNEWEEK GENERATED
265,297 IMPRESSIONS
REACHING 193,781 ACCOUNTS

Brand History

1847 Searcys is created by the Duke of Northumberland's pastry chef.

1956 On behalf of the Duke and Duchess of Norfolk, Searcys is responsible for the first ball at St James's Palace since the 16th century.

1963 Searcys opens 30 Pavilion Road in Knightsbridge, the company's spiritual home.

1990 Searcys is appointed caterer to the Barbican Centre.

1996 Having served his private functions for the previous five years, Searcys is granted the Prince of Wales' Royal Warrant.

2004 Searcys starts at the newly opened 30 St Mary Axe (The Gherkin).

2008 Searcys Champagne Bar at St Pancras International becomes the longest Champagne Bar in Europe.

2010 Searcys undergoes an MBO led by CEO Douglas Tetley.

2011 Searcys is appointed caterer at Blenheim Palace.

2013 Searcys opens the Balcony Bar & Brasserie in Selfridges Birmingham.

2014 Searcys is purchased by WSH.

2015 Searcys opens restaurants Tonic & Remedy, Urban Coterie and Bonfire.

which sold out within a week of opening and saw around 100,000 consumers experience the food, cocktails, teas and environment. The reviews were favourable and Searcys is planning for another Pop-up this summer.

Recent Developments

Operating under parent company Westbury Street Holdings (WSH), Searcys has enjoyed incredible success in 2015. With Managing Director Chris Maddison at the helm, the executive team has focused on further diversifying the portfolio, as well as strengthening the offering across the existing estate.

Last year saw three new retail openings for Searcys. Tonic & Remedy showcases cutting-edge cocktails and contemporary dishes in the M by Montcalm hotel in Shoreditch, with a focus on creating a neighbourhood vibe in the heart of Tech City.

Sky bar, kitchen and members club Urban Coterie marked the start of a long-term collaboration with Anthony Demetre; with the menu inspired by the bistromony movement which lets striking ingredients do the talking.

Searcys has faith in its heritage and people to explore new culinary aspects, cue the opening of the brand's first 'street food' chicken and burger joint, Bonfire, where guests order from clipboards sitting on the communal tables.

Leading on all things champagne and wine, Searcys produced its own champagne, 'Searcys' cuvee, which had positive reviews in industry press. In November 2015, Searcys also launched its new range of wines, Vin Occitan, which were blended in the Languedoc region, in the South of France, by two of its best sommeliers.

Promotion

Searcys was created by a chef, so it is no surprise that quality of food is at the heart of the company ethos. A team of executive chefs headed by Arnaud Stevens (formally of Maze Grill and La Tante Claire) concentrate on developing original, innovative and exciting menus for weddings, dinners and conferences.

Over the last decade, Searcys has developed a core competency in the marketing and selling of venues, often on behalf of its clients. Paramount to this is the understanding of a venue's unique attributes and how this can be brought to market in a commercial way.

At venues as wide ranging as Searcys | The Gherkin, Vintners' Hall and Inner Temple, Searcys leads the on-site marketing. There is no better example of this than Searcys | The Gherkin, which opened in 2004, as the London offices of Swiss Re. When the building moved to a mixed tenancy basis in 2007, Searcys utilised the available space in a variety of ways, which led to the creation of one of London's most desirable event spaces.

In 2010, Searcys opened up an exclusive private members' club on the 38th floor of The Gherkin, which has once again redefined this incredible building and offers unparalleled luxury to its 500 members.

In 2015, Searcys | The Gherkin hosted over 1,000 events in its private dining rooms and stunning event space at the top of the building for clients including Bentley Motors and Patek Philippe, with celebrity guests including Olivia Colman, Tony Blair, George R.R. Martin, and Ranulph Fiennes.

Brand Values

Searcys brand values are Heritage, Innovation and Quality. It consistently demonstrates intent to lead and innovate in line with client values and commercial objectives. Every single location in which Searcys operates has seen evidence of evolving and innovative offerings to make it operationally, emotionally and commercially better off. With Searcys every location is nurtured, cherished and grown.

Shredded Wheat

shreddedwheat.co.uk

Back in 1893, Henry Perky invented a machine to make a revolutionary type of breakfast cereal, the one consumers now know and love as Shredded Wheat®. Made from 100 per cent whole grain wheat, with no added salt or sugar, Shredded Wheat remains one of the UK's most popular breakfast cereals.

Market

Breakfast is often referred to as the most important meal of the day, and this is reflected in annual cereal sales of £1.4 billion (Source: IRI w/e 5th December 2015). Cereals are a breakfast staple in the UK, featuring in 57 per cent of in-home breakfast occasions (Source: Kantar Usage Panel 52 weeks to August 2015).

Shredded Wheat is one of the UK's top 10 breakfast cereals, with annual sales of more than £35 million (Source: IRI w/e 5th December 2015). As consumer demand for healthier foods has increased, Shredded Wheat's naturally healthy offering has become ever more relevant.

Product

Shredded Wheat was first produced by Henry Perky, a lawyer from Denver who,

at the time, was suffering from chronic indigestion and was recommended a diet of thoroughly cooked wheat by his doctor. Not only did it work, he argued that such an excellent food should be made more palatable.

From its creation, the secret of Shredded Wheat's ongoing success is in its simplicity. The original product still contains nothing but 100 per cent whole grain wheat, with no added salt or sugar. While the production process is simplicity itself – the wheat is farmed, cleaned, cooked, shredded, then formed into biscuits and baked.

Achievements

Shredded Wheat's greatest achievement is its longevity; few brands have remained in the UK consumers' hearts for so long. Shredded Wheat has been a British breakfast favourite for well over a century.

What made Shredded Wheat so popular back in 1893, its simple, natural healthiness, is what keeps it on breakfast tables to this day. Today, over 282 million

DID YOU KNOW?
The tall cereal silos that form part of the original Welwyn Garden City factory are a local landmark and are listed structures. The smoke stacks were used as landmarks for visiting German bomber pilots in WWII.

bowls of Shredded Wheat are consumed each year, that is the equivalent of nine bowls every second (Source: Kantar Usage Panel 52 weeks to August 2015).

OVER 282 MILLION BOWLS OF SHREDDED WHEAT ARE CONSUMED EACH YEAR

Promotion

Shredded Wheat has been a part of UK life through the years with iconic ad campaigns.

The 'Bet You Can't Eat Three campaign' in the 1970s and 1980s is so well known, that during the 2015 UK election, when asked if he'd consider a third term, David Cameron said, "Like Shredded Wheat, two are wonderful, but three might be just too many."

Over the years, Shredded Wheat campaigns have featured iconic sports stars such as Ian Botham, Brian Clough, Jack Charlton and Kevin Keegan.

Last year saw a new direction for the brand, with the D&AD award winning 'Live from the Heart' campaign. The campaign used real people following their passions, to bring to life the message that 'Shredded Wheat looks after your heart, so you're free to follow it'.

In addition to memorable advertising campaigns, Shredded Wheat is also currently engaged in a partnership with Heart UK – The Cholesterol Charity, highlighting the product's heart-healthy credentials*.

Brand History

1893 Henry Perky develops a machine to press whole grains of wheat into strips which, when baked, become the whole grain Shredded Wheat biscuits.

1908 The Canadian Shredded Wheat company establishes its UK headquarters in Aldwych, London.

1924 Sales grow so rapidly it becomes necessary to build a factory in England.

1926 The UK factory, based in Welwyn Garden City, is officially opened by The Marquis of Sailsbury. In the week following, 19 year old Katy Potter hand-packs 32,400 Shredded Wheat biscuits in one day, earning the title of 'First Champion'.

1929 The National Biscuit Co. acquires The Shredded Wheat Company including the site in Welwyn Garden City.

1945 Welgar (after Welwyn Garden City) becomes a registered name and is used on packs until the 1960s. The Welgar boy becomes a popular sight on packs and sales posters.

1950s Shredded Wheat 'Bitesize' is launched.

1962 The last hand-packed box of Shredded Wheat is produced on 20th May.

1980s In 1985, RJ Reynolds purchases the business from Nabisco Inc., which in turn is then bought out by Rank Hovis McDougall in 1988.

1990 Cereal Partners Worldwide is formed as a 50:50 joint venture between Nestlé S.A and American food giant General Mills Inc.. Welwyn Garden City is today the head office of Cereal Partners UK.

1997 Honey Nut Shredded Wheat is launched.

2008 The Welwyn Garden City factory closes and production moves to Staverton, Wiltshire.

2014 Shredded Wheat forms a partnership with Heart UK The Cholesterol Charity.

2015 Apple Crumble and Cherry Bakewell Shredded Wheat are launched.

Recent Developments

While Shredded Wheat's success has, in part, rested on an unswerving commitment to retaining the simple integrity of its original offering, no brand survives for a long time without innovating.

The original 'Shredded Wheat Big Biscuit', created by Henry Perky, remains at the heart of the range but over the years the franchise has developed to meet consumer needs.

In the 1950s, Shredded Wheat Bitesize was introduced to meet the needs of consumers who were looking for something smaller.

In more recent years, versions of Shredded Wheat with various flavours have arrived in the cereal aisles. Honey Nut Shredded Wheat was introduced in 1997, and is still a firm favourite with consumers. While in the last year, Shredded Wheat Apple Crumble and Shredded Wheat Cherry Bakewell have been launched, combining a real fruit filling with a crunchy topping, to bring popular British flavours to the breakfast table.

All these new varieties remain true to Shredded Wheat's commitment to providing healthier breakfasts, being made with whole grain wheat and low in saturated fat.

Brand values:

Shredded Wheat believes in simplicity, integrity and the important role that healthy eating can play in helping people live their lives to the full.

® Reg Tradmark of Société des Produits Nestlé S.A * Reducing consumption of saturated fat contributes to the maintenance of normal blood cholesterol levels. Shredded Wheat is low in saturated fat.

The secret to a great night's sleep

silentnight.co.uk

Silentnight is the UK's largest manufacturer of branded beds, mattresses and sleep accessories. With a wide consumer profile, Silentnight's mission is to use its passion, product knowledge, exceptional quality and sleep expertise to provide sleep solutions for all the family. As one of the UK's most recognised bed brands, Silentnight is constantly developing its proposition to build on its core bed and mattress offerings, launching more technologically advanced products but also providing a comprehensive range of sleep-related solutions.

Market

The UK retail bed and mattress market is worth over £1 billion. Silentnight is the UK's favourite bed and mattress manufacturer (Source: GfK data) and remains well known, with strong brand recall and consideration from consumers, in particular the brand's iconic Hippo & Duck characters.

Product

Founded in North Yorkshire in 1946, Silentnight's factory and offices have remained in the heart of Lancashire. Over the years it has developed a strong core product offering to cater for the mass market, with families being the key target audience. Products

include a wide selection of mattresses using its exclusive Miracoil® and Mirapocket® advanced spring system technologies, bases with different storage options and a comprehensive children's proposition.

Working with a large selection of multi-channel retailers is at the heart of Silentnight's approach, ensuring the product meets the needs of specific channels and retailers. Silentnight also sells bed frames and accessories, such as pillows and duvets, in the UK as well as a range of heating and cooling products.

As the UK's leading bed and mattress manufacturer, Silentnight is committed to working to the highest quality standards for its customers. All products and raw materials are rigorously tested in its in-house SATRA-approved testing lab, which was established in 1980. Experienced staff, proficient in materials testing, structural testing of finished products and flammability testing, ensure customers can sleep safe in the knowledge that their bed or mattress meets all safety, quality and flammability standards.

Achievements

Silentnight has been awarded a Which? Best Buy accreditation for three consecutive

years for its mattress-now® Memory 3 Zone rolled mattress. In June 2015, the 1200 Mirapocket® mattress was also recognised by Which? as being 'one of the best value mattresses tested'.

Silentnight is a full member of The National Bed Federation, the recognised trade association representing UK manufacturers of beds and mattresses and is also a member of the Furniture Industry Sustainability Programme, having shown commitment to social, economic and environmental sustainability across its business.

Silentnight has worked hard to make its bed manufacturing process more sustainable

Brand History

1946 In Skipton, North Yorkshire, Tom and Joan Clarke form a new company under the name Clarke's Mattresses Limited.

1948 Tom and Joan register the company Clarke's Mattresses Limited and rent their first shop.

1949 Clarke's mattresses are in demand and operations move to a bigger site.

1951 The company name changes from Clarke's Mattresses to Silentnight Limited.

1961 The business continues to expand and moves to its current premises in Barnoldswick.

1979 The big 'shed' exhibition centre in Salterforth is built.

1986 Silentnight launches its 'Ultimate Spring System'. To demonstrate its no-roll-together properties, Hippo & Duck are introduced.

1990s The unique spring system is improved and renamed the 'Miracoil® Spring System'.

2001 Hippo & Duck debut in an animated TV commercial, set to a reworked version of Hot Chocolate's 'You Sexy Thing' (I Believe In Miracoils).

2003 Silentnight begins production of beds and mattresses for the children's market. Its 'My first bed' wins Bed of the Year at the Furniture Awards.

2006 The company celebrates its 60-year anniversary.

2008 Mattress-now® – the first Silentnight 'convenience' rolled mattress is launched.

2010 Silentnight returns to television screens with sponsorship of American Idol. It also launches its Best for Bedsteads range.

2012 The Safe Nights and Healthy Growth ranges launch.

2013 The next generation sleep technology, Geltex® inside, collection launches.

2014 The first triple decker sprung mattress from Silentnight, the Diamond 4000 launches.

2015 Miraform® launches, along with developments in the rolled mattress range.

and, in 2011, achieved Forest Stewardship Council certification for all the timber used in the production of its divans and headboards.

Recent Developments

Silentnight continues to invest in developing its range and point of sale solutions for the brand's various retail channels.

It is committed to new product innovation in its drive to give consumers the best sleep experience possible and to remain at the forefront of the market place. In 2015, Silentnight launched new products including the innovative spring-free mattress technology Miraform, as well as collaborating with a leading UK designer on a contemporary bedframe collection.

The new Studio by Silentnight is another development for the brand, offering customers a modern sleeping experience with style and storage at the heart. Silentnight are catering for the whole family with the launch of their new luxury Pet Bed range.

Promotion

Silentnight's new advertising campaign focuses on the benefits of quality sleep using the concept – 'it's amazing what you can achieve after a great night's sleep'. The campaign uses photography showing different members of the family waking refreshed and ready to begin the day. The bed manufacturer signed Olympic athlete Jo Pavey to front the campaign.

Silentnight continues to offer strong annual promotions. The 'With our compliments' campaign ran throughout 2015 enabling the brand to collaborate

DID YOU KNOW?
Since 1961 Silentnight's factory and offices have remained in the heart of Lancashire.

with key retail partners to offer bespoke promotions with above-the-line and digital display advertising.

The brand's social media channels have promoted competitions, PR activity using Hippo & Duck, and customer reviews that have lead to a marked increase in customer engagement.

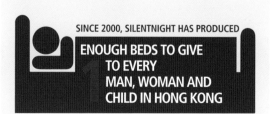

SINCE 2000, SILENTNIGHT HAS PRODUCED
ENOUGH BEDS TO GIVE TO EVERY MAN, WOMAN AND CHILD IN HONG KONG

Brand Values

Silentnight's mission is to help everyone in the family find their perfect sleep solution. To ensure Silentnight remains an authority in sleep expertise, it invests in continuous research into sleeping habits, building the latest scientific developments and technical innovations into its products. The past year has seen collaboration with The University of Leeds to conduct a national sleep survey on the UK's sleeping issues with research supported by Sleep Tips from Silentnight's in-house Sleep Expert, Dr Nerina Ramlakhan.

THE BEST START IN LIFE

silvercrossbaby.com

Founded in 1877, Silver Cross is one of the world's leading nursery brands. Loved and trusted by parents across the globe, it produces an array of award-winning products for newborns, babies and toddlers. Nearly 140 years after its birth, Silver Cross still stands for the same principles of innovative design and high quality manufacturing that have given more than 10 million babies the best start in life.

Market

Silver Cross is a leading name in the competitive baby and nursery market. Its product range is unrivalled, with traditional coach prams, sophisticated travel systems, innovative pushchairs and handcrafted nursery furniture. The company continues to expand globally, with its products now selling in more than 70 countries worldwide. As well as its UK headquarters, the company has offices in Hong Kong, Shanghai, Melbourne and Barcelona.

Product

The key to every Silver Cross product is excellent design and premium quality. The company has an expert team of in-house designers and product development specialists based at its UK head office.

Thanks to its long heritage of quality, the Silver Cross product range is unique. It continues to produce iconic coach prams, a masterpiece of design and engineering, and the only prams that are still handcrafted exclusively in the UK.

Silver Cross has an outstanding collection of innovative and modern pram systems, pushchairs and car seats. Combining the latest advances in technology with contemporary and stylish design, it is at the forefront of the baby travel market.

A second collaboration with Aston Martin, uniting two iconic British brands, produced the new and ultra-exclusive Surf Aston Martin Edition – the ultimate luxury pram system.

A more recent addition to the range are the home and nursery products which, thanks to the brand's trusted name and reputation for quality, have proved a huge success. Following two new launches in 2015, Silver Cross now offers eight collections of beautiful handcrafted nursery furniture.

DID YOU KNOW?
Founded in 1877, Silver Cross is credited with invention of the baby pram concept.

Achievements

Silver Cross products continue to impress industry experts and parents alike, winning an array of awards from parenting websites and magazines.

A strong, evolving product range means the brand's success continues apace and globally it goes from strength to strength. Following the success of its flagship stores in Hong Kong and Shanghai, Silver Cross opened a third global store in Moscow.

In 2015, Silver Cross unveiled a world first – the show-stopping Rose Gold Balmoral. The pram features 18-carat rose gold plating and attracted overwhelming international interest at the Kind und Jugend baby show, showcasing the artisan pram building skills unique to Silver Cross.

Recent Developments

Silver Cross strives to develop and drive forward its range of products to meet the demands of modern families, with more exciting launches planned for 2016.

The Special Edition collections continue to grow in popularity with the Eton and the new Henley collection, both displaying exceptional attention to detail with beautiful textiles and features, which set new standards in the industry for couture fine finish.

In addition, the nursery furniture collections have continued to evolve with the addition of the new Soho space saver collection, which has unique design innovations, allowing for a concealed baby changing station within existing bedroom furniture.

DID YOU KNOW?

A piece of history returned to Silver Cross in 2015, when one of the first prams produced by founder William Wilson in 1878 was purchased from a private collector at auction.

Promotion

Silver Cross communications reflect its values of being authentic and open – a theme that runs through all of the brand's consumer touch-points. Silver Cross' strong brand values of Quality, Innovation, Design and Heritage remain at the forefront of the brand's appeal. The brand's strongest marketing tool however has always been word-of-mouth and endorsement from those who have first-hand experience of Silver Cross products.

Online activity remains a key tool to communicate and engage with consumers around the world. Silver Cross has a global website, while social media channels allow the brand to hold direct conversations with its consumers and increase engagement.

MORE THAN
10 MILLION
PARENTS WORLDWIDE CHOOSE SILVER CROSS FOR THEIR BABIES

Brand Values

Silver Cross is proud to say millions of parents all over the world have trusted its products to give their baby the best start in life. Almost 140 years after it was founded, it continues to develop the most innovative products, with a focus on design excellence and premium quality. Silver Cross' 138-year heritage shapes its future. Its mission is to be loved by parents and babies alike.

Brand History

1877 Silver Cross is founded by William Wilson, a prolific inventor credited with inventing the first ever baby carriage.

1900-1950s Silver Cross becomes incorporated and is crowned the number one baby carriage for royals, supplying its first baby carriage to King George VI for Princess Elizabeth.

1950-1970s Silver Cross launches numerous innovative coach built prams and becomes Britain's favourite baby carriage.

1977 Silver Cross celebrates its centenary by flying customers around the world in its centenary aircraft and presents a baby carriage to Princess Anne.

1980s Silver Cross develops innovative lightweight pushchair manufacturing techniques to complement the Heritage Collection and the first product, The Wayfarer, is launched and becomes Britain's best-selling pushchair.

2002 Entrepreneur and businessman Alan Halsall acquires Silver Cross and CEO Nick Paxton launches a new approach to innovation and product development from the headquarters in North Yorkshire, England.

2006 Silver Cross goes global, forging partnerships with distributors and opens development offices in Hong Kong and China to complement the UK manufacturing and design facilities.

2010 Silver Cross becomes Britain's favourite nursery brand and develops a new and innovative nursery furniture collection.

2012 The brand expands online with a new transactional website and develops social media channels to support customer service and consumer interaction. Silver Cross' first flagship store opens in Hong Kong, followed by Shanghai.

2014 Silver Cross collaborates with Aston Martin to create the Surf Aston Martin Edition pram. It captures the world's imagination utilising air sprung suspension, a natural leather finish and super lightweight aluminium.

2015 Silver Cross continues its growth in the UK, Asia, Middle East and Europe.

stobartgroup.com

Stobart Group is the leading and best-known infrastructure and support services businesses in the UK. It operates within the biomass energy, aviation and railway maintenance sectors as well as having investments in a national property and logistics portfolio, including the Eddie Stobart business and brand. The Group aims to continue delivering on its strategy of realising value and building sustainable return from its growth businesses, while maintaining its dividend policy.

Market

In a competitive market, Stobart Group aims to stand out using its business development capabilities, logistics heritage, capital and the respect and following of the brand. Group revenue for the year ending 28th February 2015 was £116.6 million, up 17.6 per cent on 2014.

Product

Stobart Group is made up of five key divisions: Stobart Energy – with a focus on green and renewable energy, this part of the business transports and supplies biomass fuel; Stobart Aviation – owns and operates London Southend Airport

and Carlisle Lake District Airport; Stobart Rail – focuses on third party rail contracts and supports Stobart Energy with its green energy investment plans; Stobart Infrastructure – comprises a wide range of properties including airports, investment/operational and green energy; and Stobart Investments – encompasses logistics specialist, Eddie Stobart, and aircraft leasing company, Propius.

Achievements

Volumes of biomass supplied through Stobart Group's

DID YOU KNOW?
Stobart Group sponsors the Flat and Jump Jockeys' Championships and 12 of its fleet of iconic trucks feature imagery of the UK's leading jockeys.

Energy division are up 29 per cent, with new site locations coming on stream as the division continues to grow and increase its operational efficiency.

Stobart Aviation's passenger numbers have increased by nine per cent to 1.09 million and, for the third year running, London Southend Airport

THE SIZE OF THE CARLISLE LAKE DISTRICT AIRPORT DISTRIBUTION CENTRE IS EQUIVALENT TO FOUR FOOTBALL PITCHES

Brand History

1960s	Founder Eddie Stobart goes into business as an agricultural contractor.
1970s	The business incorporates, becoming Eddie Stobart Limited.
1980s	The business expands, opening depots across the UK. Andrew Tinkler forms WA Tinkler Building Contractor.
1990s	WA Tinkler Building Contractor becomes WA Developments, growing its turnover to over £20 million a year.
2001	William Stobart leaves Eddie Stobart Limited to become a shareholding Director in WA Developments.
2004	WA Developments International acquires Eddie Stobart Limited.
2005	Eddie Stobart wins its first Tesco Distribution Centre contract and introduces a new livery for the fleet.
2006	The first Stobart-Rail freight service is launched.
2007	The LSE-listed Stobart Group is formed.
2008	Stobart Group acquires London Southend Airport.
2009	An Iberian rail freight service is launched.
	Stobart Group enters the FTSE 250 category of leading businesses.
2010	Stobart Biomass Products is formed to source and transport sustainable biomass. 'Eddie Stobart: Trucks & Trailers' airs on Channel 5.
2011	Stobart Group takes full control of Stobart Biomass.
2012	Stobart acquires Autologic Holdings, the UK's leading vehicle logistics company.
2013	Stobart Fest attracts 20,000 people.
2014	Stobart sells 51 per cent of its Transport and Distribution division.
2015	Stobart Energy secures its target of supplying over two million tonnes per annum with new long-term contracts.

DID YOU KNOW?
2014/15 saw a 29 per cent growth in the supply of responsibly sourced, recycled and renewable virgin material, with over 555,000 tonnes of arboricultural arising-derived product delivered in the year.

was rated best UK airport in the Which? customer satisfaction survey.

Within the rail sector, external revenue has increased 35 per cent, delivering healthy margins for the Group.

Realisations from the Stobart Infrastructure property portfolio generated more than £27 million in 2015.

Recent Developments

Stobart Energy has secured its position as the number one supplier of biomass in the UK. It has sourced and supplied fuel to biomass plants under long-term contracts, which has delivered a 29 per cent growth in tonnages in 2015 with the target of two million tonnes per annum by 2017/18 well secured.

Stobart Rail continues to underline its place as one of the UK's leading names in rail network maintenance, repair and improvement with a 35 per cent increase in external revenue during the year, a coveted accident frequency rate (AFR) of zero and an innovative new, proprietary ballast replacement machine successfully developed by the division.

Stobart Aviation's passenger numbers broke through the one million barrier for the first time in 2015, with nine per cent growth to 1.09 million passengers. A new air and road freight distribution centre, pictured above, at Carlisle Lake District Airport has been built. The Stobart Air partnership with Flybe continues with a total of four new destinations launched.

Promotion

Promotion is at the heart of the Stobart brand's strength, and is conducted across all its divisions – Stobart Energy, Stobart Aviation, Stobart Rail, Stobart Infrastructure and Stobart Investments. Highlights from 2015 included an integrated campaign across the aviation offering, which focused on London Southend Airport and its place as the capital's fifth air travel hub, with its proximity and ease of transfer into the City and vibrant East End. Social media also plays its part across the Group, and Stobart Fest was another huge success in 2015 both at the event and among online communities of fans and supporters.

Brand Values

Quality, service, performance and sustainability are values inherent to the Stobart Group brand, which also counts exemplary employment and environmental practices among its core principles.

tassimo.co.uk

Tassimo wants people to enjoy the lighter side of life in their coffee moments. It offers an unmatched variety of branded drinks and a range of machines to ensure they are perfectly served, every time. Its hot beverage range offers consumers single-serve coffee systems that prepare one-cup servings of espresso, regular coffee, tea, hot chocolate, and various other coffee drinks, notably those including milk such as lattes and cappuccinos, as well as other specialties, for a full coffee shop experience in the comfort of the consumers' home.

Market

Tassimo believe that the real joy in life is found in the moments and experiences shared with others, where nothing else matters except having a little fun together. The Tassimo range is made for those moments and those with more time to socialise and relax spontaneously, from empty nesters to escaping nesters who enjoy sharing time with others.

Product

Tassimo is the only in-home coffee machine in partnership with the nation's biggest, most recognised and favourite coffee shop brand, Costa. It offers a range of nine machines, made by Bosch, each offering features which are tailored to consumers needs, from relaxed social occasions to individuals on the move.

The range welcomes consumers to a whole new way of enjoying perfect barista style coffee, tea or hot chocolate, any time a consumer chooses. Each Tassimo machine automatically scans the barcode on each T DISC to obtain the information it needs to prepare a selected drink, including the amount of water, the brewing time, plus the optimum temperature. The self-cleaning programme and removable water tank make light work of maintenance. An adjustable, removable cup stand means large or small beverages can be chosen depending on the situation or need. The brewing process for each drink takes between 30-60 seconds and all machines feature Intellibrew™ technology, which ensures each beverage is made perfectly each time.

The Tassimo Fidelia+ is ideal for group scenarios, it has an extra large water tank and an LED display, whereas the Tassimo Vivy is a compact brewer and creates drinks at

DID YOU KNOW?

Tassimo is available worldwide, from Europe and the USA to South Korea.

the touch of a button – ideal for a quick coffee. In addition to all the standard Tassimo features, Tassimo Charmy offers an advanced water filtration system and a unique strength adjustment setting for the ultimate in drinking pleasure. The Tassimo Joy machine is reliable, innovative and designed for ease of use.

Due to the popularity generated by the Costa partnership, 2014 saw the Tassimo brand reach the broadest base of appeal in terms of relevance and familiarity when compared with other market leaders (Source: Brands Live 2015). The strong appeal of the Tassimo product range is enhanced by its partnerships with some of the most loved brands in the UK and around the world. These include the top UK coffee brands Costa and Kenco as well as the Cadbury and Oreo ranges. In 2014 the highest grossing products were the Costa, Carte Noire and Cadbury brands, with three quarters of Tassimo shoppers buying into Tassimo Costa.

As further proof of Tassimo's leveraging of brand familiarity and brand love, last year saw Tassimo T DISC sales producing £71.6 million (Source: Tassimo 52 w/e August 2015) leading the market in terms of penetration and sales.

Recent Developments
The UK's on-demand pod market is growing and has continued to expand rapidly over the past few years, with a turnover of £112.4 million in 2014 (Source: Nielson). In order to maintain a leading place in the market, Tassimo developed the new Tassimo Caddy. In addition to providing all of the existing Tassimo features, the Caddy is designed to hold all of the T DISC flavours exactly where they should be – neatly stacked, right next to the machine.

Promotion
Spontaneity is at the heart of the Tassimo brand, which prides itself on going with the flow and bringing out the fun in everyone and everything in does. This fun-loving side to the brand extending into its

2014 TV advert, showcasing Tassimo's range. The campaign 'Be Indecisive' featured the 40-plus T DISCS, all strong consumer favourites, demonstrating the wide variety of options to choose from – one of life's little luxuries.

Tassimo also showcases its variety of recipes on YouTube, all featuring T DISCs. The recipes range from cappuccino waffles to espresso biscotti, to iced coffee and affogatto, all with a Tassimo beverage at the centre.

Brand Values
The Tassimo brand aims to offer a world of colour in the otherwise black and white offerings of the on-demand pod market. Tassimo has a playful spirit, is charismatic and welcoming, with products that know how to make people feel at home. It is insightful, perceptive and able to cater to any situation. Tassimo, through its range, is the entertaining host, using an instinctive and uncomplicated approach.

Brand History

In addition to the diverse range of machines, Tassimo offers over 40 varieties of unique T DISC pods, including Cadbury, Twinings, Milka, Kenco, Carte Noire, Oreo, Costa and Jacobs. In addition to the coffee classics, Tassimo has a heavy focus on milky drinks.

Achievements
In 2012, an international jury of experts awarded Tassimo Charmy with the IF Product Design Award for design and innovation. The judges noted the machine's unique design and efficiency.

1.7 MILLION
HOUSEHOLDS HAVE A TASSIMO COFFEE MACHINE

TATA CONSULTANCY SERVICES

tcs.com

A global IT services company, Tata Consultancy Services (TCS) was the fastest growing brand in its industry worldwide in 2015, with a brand value of US$8.7 billion. It ranks in the topmost tier in terms of market capitalisation and employees, and leads the industry in customer satisfaction. Its 21-country European operations account for 25 per cent of global revenues, with more than 50,000 employees serving 350 clients – including 44 of the FT Europe 100 companies.

Market
Business never stands still, but today's technology is accelerating the pace of change as never before. TCS is reimagining how business is being done across every sector, leading to a transformation of enterprises both in the UK and globally. As the fastest growing IT services brand in the world, it is at the forefront of the current digital revolution.

Product
Celebrating its 40th year in the UK, TCS is a trusted IT services, consulting and business solutions organisation. This means that it is assisting leading banks in their digital transformation, helping airlines redefine their business processes and even making

the UK General Election more socially connected. TCS takes pride in delivering a service that is highly tailored to the needs of its customers, with a flexible and relationship-based approach that resonates with customers in the UK and globally. A testament to this is that TCS has been consistently ranked number one in customer satisfaction both in the UK and across Europe by more than 1,470 CXOs from Europe's leading companies. This is an accolade that means more for the TCS team than any other metric it measures itself on.

Achievements
Strong financials with a compounded annual growth rate of more than 20 per

cent over the past decade, combined with heavy investments in the brand, has paid dividends for TCS. In 2012 London-based Brand Finance rated it as a global Big Four IT services brand. In 2013 it became the world's second largest IT services employer. Furthermore, as of September 2014, TCS is second among the world's most valuable IT firms with a market cap in excess of US$80 billion. The same year, the company entered the Superbrands list for the first time. In 2015, Brand Finance recognised TCS as the fastest growing IT services brand in the world over the last five years.

Recent Developments
The IT sector is the new backbone of Europe's economy. However, as the number of digital jobs is growing, the number of new IT graduates is shrinking. The European Commission estimates that Europe faces up to 900,000 unfilled IT jobs, leading to declining competitiveness. Through its involvement with over 200 schools in Europe and initiatives such as the Queen Elizabeth Prize for Engineering, TCS is committed to addressing the growing digital skills gap by engaging young people and encouraging careers in STEM (Science,

DID YOU KNOW?
Forbes rated TCS as one of the world's most innovative companies in 2015.

Designed, built and delivered by TCS, ElectUK was created to engage UK General Election voters by turning their smartphone into a Big Data social media analytics tool.

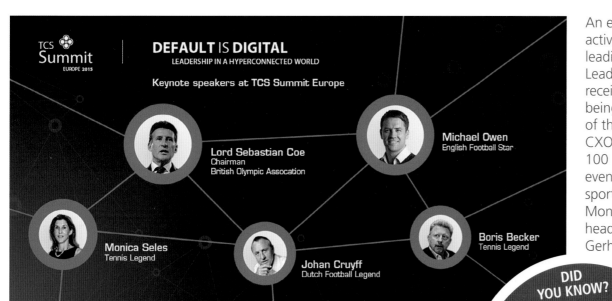

DEFAULT IS DIGITAL
LEADERSHIP IN A HYPERCONNECTED WORLD

Keynote speakers at TCS Summit Europe

Lord Sebastian Coe
Chairman
British Olympic Assocation

Michael Owen
English Football Star

Monica Seles
Tennis Legend

Johan Cruyff
Dutch Football Legend

Boris Becker
Tennis Legend

Technology, Engineering and Mathematics) subjects. Its strong commitment to the communities it operates in, combined with a forward-thinking HR environment, saw TCS ranked as the number one employer both in the UK and across Europe by the Top Employers Institute in 2015.

As a Strategic Partner to the World Economic Forum (WEF), TCS is engaged in its mission of improving the state of the world. Its CEO, Natarajan Chandrasekaran, serves as the chair of the IT Governors steering committee of the WEF. In this capacity, he works with WEF and CEOs of other global IT companies in defining an agenda of priorities for the

industry, as they help other industries navigate an era of transformational change.

Promotion

TCS' recent brand building and communications activities have been widely recognised and have won more than 30 awards. These include a Gold Corporate Engagement Award for its initiative: 'The digital skills gap: bringing the voice of 90 million European youth to boardrooms and policy makers' and a Gold Digital Impact Award for the running campaign #TCSsuperheroes.

An example of a successful brand building activity is the annual TCS Summit – a leading forum for CXOs and Senior Leaders in Europe. TCS Summit has received several top accolades including being awarded International Conference of the Year by the C&IT Awards. With CXOs of more than 50 per cent of Top 100 FT Europe companies present, recent events have seen keynote addresses by sports stars such as Michael Owen and Monica Seles, as well as seven former heads of state including Nicolas Sarkozy, Gerhard Schröder and Mario Monti.

Award juries have recognised the event for its strong strategy to engage senior leaders, rich conference content and highly effective branding and communications strategy.

DID YOU KNOW?
TCS has major focus on wellness and community development through sports, both in the UK and globally. As part of its internal Fit4Life challenge TCS UK employees ran 57,000km in 2015. Globally, TCS has partnerships with seven of the world's leading marathons including the title sponsorships of the TCS Amsterdam Marathon and the TCS New York Marathon.

Brand Values
The TCS brand promise is captured by two words: Experience certainty. In a nutshell, Experience certainty means that clients can count on TCS to reliably deliver business results, provide leadership to drive transformation and work in partnership to provide success for clients.

Brand History

1968 TCS is founded as India's first software services company.

1975 The first UK office opens.

2004 TCS goes public in the largest private sector initial public offering (IPO) in the Indian market.

2005 TCS is awarded a Special Recognition Award for Outstanding Contribution to the UK Knowledge Economy by Tony Blair.

2006 TCS acquires the life and pensions operations of the Pearl Group to set up its BPO unit Diligenta.

2009 TCS becomes a top 10 player in the global IT software and services industry.

2010 TCS wins the largest Government deal in Europe to date from Personal Accounts Delivery Authority (PADA), UK. It becomes official partner to World Economic Forum.

2012 TCS is recognised as a global 'Big Four' IT Services brand by Brand Finance.

2013 TCS wins over a dozen accolades for brand excellence and is awarded the Platinum Big Tick – the highest ranking in Business in the Community's Corporate Responsibility Index.

It becomes the largest software consultancy in UK to qualify for Investors in People – Gold standard.

2014 TCS becomes the world's second-most valuable IT services firm and is recognised as the world's fastest growing global IT Services brand by Brand Finance.

TCS launches an award-winning thought leadership study on The Digital Skills Gap with an aim to bring the voice of Europe's 90 million youth to senior policy makers.

2015 TCS is recognised as a Superbrand in the UK and is ranked number one in Customer Satisfaction across Europe by Whitelane Research, for the second consecutive year.

TCS launches the ElectUK app, built to engage voters in the UK General Elections. ElectUK wins several top accolades at the Drum Social Buzz Awards and the PRCA Awards amongst others.

BLOG

thomascook.com

Thomas Cook was the pioneer of travel, organising a successful one-day rail excursion from Leicester to Loughborough in 1841. That was 175 years ago and today, Thomas Cook Group is one of the world's leading leisure travel providers. The company uses its wealth of experience and knowledge in travel to inspire personal journeys while ensuring it always has the customer at the heart of everything it does.

Market

Thomas Cook operates in a growing industry. As a leading international travel company, its business is split into four main areas – UK and Ireland, Continental Europe, Northern Europe and Airlines. These sectors work closely together as one Thomas Cook, sharing innovative ideas across all of the countries in which it operates.

DID YOU KNOW?

Thomas Cook was the official passenger agent for the first modern Olympics in Athens in 1896.

Product

Building on the strong market reaction to its profitable growth strategy, Thomas Cook has an expanding portfolio of new products and services. Its commitment is to be there for its customers however, whenever and wherever they are in the world, offering a wide range of differentiated and exclusive products.

An integral part of Thomas Cook's product offering is its six hotel brands, which provide exclusive benefits to Thomas Cook customers.

The SENTIDO Hotels & Resorts brand continues to grow, offering Thomas Cook customers top quality service, varied cuisine and extensive fitness and entertainment facilities to provide them with a truly memorable holiday experience.

The smartline Hotel brand is perfect for customers looking for both a great deal and a fresh approach to their holiday. They're located in popular holiday destinations, with free Wi-Fi in the lobby areas and free fresh fruit and ice cream served from the Smartline ice cream trolley.

Sunwing Family Resorts offer great flexibility for families with different size rooms and a wide range of restaurants to choose from. They're also the home of the Thomas Cook Kid's Clubs and favourite children's characters Lollo & Bernie.

Sunprime Hotels are adult-only, offering four star service in a quiet and relaxing atmosphere with comfortable modern décor and beautiful surroundings.

SunConnect Resorts are the perfect place for a relaxing holiday with family and friends. Customers can look forward to entertainment for everyone, spacious pool areas, water slides and relaxed evenings with newfound friends at the pool bar.

Casa Cook is Thomas Cook's brand new hotel concept launching in 2016. These individually designed hotels create a sophisticated and inviting feeling where customers can unwind, enrich and relax. Casa Cook celebrates good food, shares a love for local products and has a deep appreciation of culture, style and trends.

holidaymakers on TripAdvisor, can book excursions and also find all the contact information they may need.

In July 2015, Thomas Cook launched a new strategic, three year partnership with Club Med, which will deepen the existing collaboration between the two companies. The partnership will give Thomas Cook customers access to more All Inclusive, upmarket holidays and will enable Thomas Cook to benefit from Club Med's brand appeal and high profile across a wide geographical area.

Thomas Cook's Retail Apprenticeship Programme, launched in 2011, was ranked outstanding by Ofsted in 2015. More than 300 Apprentices were introduced into the business over the year, and the programme is a key talent initiative. The 'outstanding' grades were achieved in all areas including; learner outcomes; quality of teaching; and effectiveness of leadership and management. This is an unprecedented result for a travel company, putting Thomas Cook at the forefront of UK businesses with successful Apprenticeship Programmes.

Promotion
The UK brand and communication strategy reflects Thomas Cook's commitment to its customers and features a wide range of exclusive products and services.

Brand History

1841 Thomas Cook organises his first excursion, a 12-mile rail journey from Leicester to a temperance meeting in Loughborough.

1855 Thomas Cook's first continental tour. He personally conducts two parties from Harwich to Antwerp, then on to Brussels, Cologne, Frankfurt, Heidelberg, Strasbourg and Paris.

1865 Thomas Cook opens his first high-street shop in Fleet Street, London, the upper floor of which is used as a Temperance Boarding House.

1872 Thomas Cook organises and leads the first round-the-world tour. He travels 29,000 miles in 222 days.

1919 Thomas Cook is the first travel agent in the UK to advertise pleasure trips by air.

1939 Holidays by air on specially chartered aircraft are included in Cook's main summer brochure for the first time.

1995 Thomas Cook launches its first website.

2003 Thomas Cook Airlines is officially launched in the UK.

2007 Thomas Cook and MyTravel Group plc merge to form Thomas Cook Group plc, which quickly becomes a FTSE 100 company.

2011 Thomas Cook and the Co-operative Group merge their high-street travel businesses to create the UK's largest retail travel network.

2013 Thomas Cook unveils its new group logo – the 'Sunny Heart' – to unify the brand identity across all markets.

THE THOMAS COOK GROUP

TAKES OVER 20 MILLION CUSTOMERS ON HOLIDAY EACH YEAR

HAS 27,000 EMPLOYEES AND

A FLEET OF 85 AIRCRAFT

Achievements
Thomas Cook UK won several awards in 2015 including the airline category in the Customer Service of the Year awards and Europe's Leading Charter Airline at the World Travel Awards. It also won the Consumer Award for Best Holiday Company voted for by readers of The Sun newspaper at the Travolution Awards.

As well as recognition from outside the business, Thomas Cook launched its own Sunny Heart awards in 2015 which recognise hotels that have gone the extra mile, received the highest customer satisfaction scores and recommendations from travel agents.

Recent Developments
Thomas Cook created exciting new initiatives in 2015. These include the My Holiday app designed to help customers manage their booking and plan every aspect of their holiday, straight from their mobile phone. Customers can see all their booking information, read detailed descriptions of their hotel's facilities, points of interest and reviews from other

DID YOU KNOW?
Before becoming an excursion manager, Thomas Cook worked as a gardener, a cabinet-maker and a Baptist missionary.

Brand Values
Thomas Cook's promise to its customers is to be personal, trusted and innovative, placing them at the heart of everything it does.

tommeetippee.com

Millions of families have grown up with Tommee Tippee® over the last 50 years. Traditionally known for cups and tableware, the brand's leading position was reinforced in 2006 with the launch of Closer to Nature®, a newborn feeding range now credited with revolutionising the bottle feeding category.

In 2015 Tommee Tippee launched its new Masterbrand and the brand's first ever global brand campaign #ParentOn. Tommee Tippee continues to be the number one selling newborn baby accessories brand in the UK (Source: IRI September 2015).

Market
In the UK, the baby accessories market is estimated to be worth almost £180 million (Source: IRI 2015 and Company Data) and encompasses a wide range of products from bibs and bottles to monitors and harnesses. The market does not include nappies, wipes, toiletries, formula milk, baby food or nursery furniture. Tommee Tippee has been identified as number one in seven out of the top 10 categories in the baby accessories market (Source: IRI September 2015).

Tommee Tippee has more than one-third of the total market share by value (Source: IRI October 2015). Internationally, it is sold in more than 70 countries.

Product
Tommee Tippee prides itself on its lasting commitment to innovation. Its product range is enhanced by a promise of quality, safety, simplicity, convenience and value.

The brand was the first to design a non-spill cup in the 1980s (Sip 'n' Seal), a groundbreaking bottle babies could hold themselves (the Nipper Gripper), and a teether filled with purified water that could be cooled for effective pain relief.

In recent years the product portfolio has grown to include the Closer to Nature, Sangenic® Tec and Express and Go™ ranges. Closer to Nature feeding bottles have been designed to mimic the natural flex, feel and movement of a mum's breast, making it easier to combine breast and bottle feeding. The Sangenic® Tec range helps to ensure hygienic nappy disposal both in and out of the home, by wrapping dirty nappies in antibacterial film. The Express and Go System makes life easier by using a single pouch to express, store, warm and feed breastmilk.

TOMMEE TIPPEE SELL
ONE PERFECT PREP EVERY
5 MINUTES
IN THE UK
+1

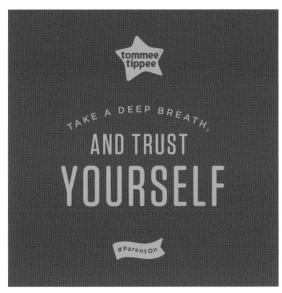

Achievements

In 2015, Tommee Tippee was awarded several accolades. It swept the board in the Mums' Choice Awards Feeding Equipment category – with UK mums voting Tommee Tippee top of the category for all five products – baby bottles, breast pumps, weaning accessories, electric sterilisers and non-electric sterilisers. The Tesco Mums' Choice Awards are free to enter and are voted for independently by Mums.

Throughout last year, consumers also voted Tommee Tippee the winner of nine Loved by Parents awards. The awards included two GOLD's for the Perfect Prep and the Black Tommee Tippee Closer to Nature Essentials Set. The Express and Go Bottle and Pouch Warmer also won a global innovation award from the Kind and Jugend trade show – the leading global fair for the baby and toddler outfitting sector. Tommee Tippee was also named UK Most Innovative Brand at the Corporate LiveWire Innovation & Excellence Awards 2015.

Recent Developments

In 2015 the innovative new Express and Go™ system was launched. The new system enables a mother who is expressing to feed baby in fewer steps. By using a single pouch to express, store, warm and feed, there is no need to transfer milk at any stage, so a mother will never lose a drop of breastmilk.

In 2015 the Sangenic® nappy disposal range was re-launched into a two system range, Sangenic® Tec with the unique anti-bacterial twist and lock system and Simplee Sangenic® the multi-purpose nursery bin with a simple smart seal lid.

The award-winning Tommee Tippee cups range was also relaunched during 2015 with a new one-piece valve and a simple, fun rebrand.

The award-winning Perfect Prep Machine and Essentials Kit have also both seen recent developments with the introduction of Black and Red special editions that enable parents to co-ordinate their baby accessories with their home furnishings.

Promotion

Tommee Tippee is one of the key exhibitors of the UK baby shows, which attract more than 75,000 parents and pregnant women every year. The one-on-one interaction the brand provides when exhibiting ensures that Tommee Tippee is closer to mum, engaging her with product demonstrations and answering feeding questions. Tommee Tippee has also invested in a dynamic digital programme including social media marketing and creating online retailer brand shops. Additionally, the brand receives a substantial amount of PR and editorial endorsement from the parenting press and online and also has a strong relationship with the parenting blog community.

In 2014, Tommee Tippee introduced a Mumbassador programme, which saw the brand work more closely than ever before with parent bloggers to drive parent to parent recommendation.

DID YOU KNOW?
The Tommee Tippee® name comes from the Tippee cup with its rounded weight base which made it impossible to tip over.

Brand History

1965	Manufacturing rights are acquired for Tommee Tippee baby products in the UK and Europe.
1986	Tommee Tippee introduces Pur™, the first silicone teat, to the market.
1988	Sip 'n' Seal, the first non-spill baby cup, is launched.
1997	Tommee Tippee buys Sangenic – a patented nappy disposal system.
2001	Easiflow becomes the first baby cup to be accredited by the British Dental Health Foundation.
2006	The launch of Closer to Nature changes the face of newborn feeding.
2009	Tommee Tippee's new 'star' brand identity is introduced.
2010	The brand launches in the US and Canada.
2011	The Explora toddler range is relaunched.
2012	The Closer to Nature Digital Video Monitor is launched.
2013	The Closer to Nature Perfect Prep Machine is launched.
2015	The Express and Go system is launched.
	Tommee Tippee #ParentOn launched.

Brand Values

For 50 years, Tommee Tippee has been designing and producing innovative, intuitive and stylish products to help parents on the rollercoaster ride of bringing up baby.

Now Tommee Tippee has created a new global platform that unites, encourages and empowers parents to trust their instincts and #ParentOn.

Tommee Tippee has brought the campaign to life with the engaging global microsite parent-on.com and encouraging parents all over the world to share their 'Parent On Moments' using the hashtag #ParentOn.

TONI&GUY™

toniandguy.com

TONI&GUY has long been renowned as an innovator within the hairdressing industry, bridging the gap between high fashion and hairdressing. Toni Mascolo OBE's franchise model has maintained the company's high education and creative standards, protected the brand and made successes of thousands of TONI&GUY hairdressing entrepreneurs worldwide.

Market

In the years since the birth of TONI&GUY, hairdressing has become a sophisticated industry worth billions, spawning some of the most influential and creative artists in the beauty and fashion sector. From individual salons to global chains, competition is fierce with consumers demanding the highest quality and service.

Having helped to change the face of the industry on an international level, today TONI&GUY has 211 salons in the UK and a further 265 salons in 46 countries, whilst essensuals has 23 salons in the UK and 72 international salons in 16 countries worldwide.

Product

TONI&GUY salons aim to offer a consistent level of service, guaranteed quality, exceptional cutting and innovative colour – in simple but well-designed salons at an affordable price. All techniques practised by the stylists are taught by highly trained and experienced educators in 18 academies around the world.

A client's in-salon experience is enhanced by extras such as TONI&GUY.TV, the TONI&GUY Magazine and luxury take away samples. Products from the professional label.m range – created and endorsed by Sacha Mascolo-Tarbuck, Global Creative Director, and her International Artistic Team – can be purchased in salons, so clients can replicate fashion-inspired styling at home.

Achievements

TONI&GUY has a worldwide brand presence and is recognised for its strong education network. It currently operates 23 teaching academies globally – two in the UK and 21 internationally.

An average of 100,000 hairdressers are trained each year, with more than 5,500 employees in the UK and a further 3,500 worldwide. This philosophy of motivation, inspiration and education are key to the brand's success.

Co-founder and CEO, Toni Mascolo OBE, former winner of London Entrepreneur of the Year, received an honorary OBE for his

label.m
PROFESSIONAL HAIRCARE

www.labelm.com

services to the British hairdressing industry in 2008. He has also been honoured with an International Achievement Award from the Fellowship for British Hairdressers and an International Legend Award from the Association Internationale Presse Professionelle Coiffure Awards.

Brand History

1963 TONI&GUY is launched from a single unit in Clapham, south London by Toni Mascolo and his brother Guy.

1982 The TONI&GUY Academy launches.

1985 TONI&GUY's first international salon opens in Tokyo, Japan.

1987 TONI&GUY's first franchise salon opens in Brighton.

2001 The TONI&GUY signature haircare range is launched. The following year, Toni and Pauline Mascolo launch the TONI&GUY Charitable Foundation.

2003 TONI&GUY Magazine and TONI&GUY.TV are launched in the UK. The brand also expands into different markets, opening an opticians and a deli-café.

2004 TONI&GUY becomes the Official Sponsor of London Fashion Week.

2005 label.m Professional Haircare by TONI&GUY launches, growing to include nearly 60 products distributed in over 50 countries.

2008 Toni Mascolo receives an OBE for his services to the British Hairdressing industry.

2010 Sacha Mascolo-Tarbuck and James Tarbuck join the British Fashion Council/Vogue Designer Fashion Fund.

2011 TONI&GUY becomes Official Sponsor of the British Fashion Awards.

2013 TONI&GUY celebrates 50 years of hairdressing success with a festival for over 5,000 staff.

2014 TONI&GUY celebrates 10 years as Official Sponsor of London Fashion Week and label.m becomes the Official Haircare Product.

2015 TONI&GUY launches its first dedicated barber shop in Shoreditch London and label.m celebrates 10 years of success.

TONI&GUY EDUCATES MORE HAIRDRESSERS THAN ANY OTHER COMPANY IN THE WORLD

Toni's daughter, Global Creative Director Sacha Mascolo-Tarbuck, was the youngest ever winner of Newcomer of the Year at just 19 years old. Additional awards since include London Hairdresser of the Year, Hair Magazine's Hairdresser of the Year, Creative Head's Most Wanted Look of the Year, and its Most Wanted Hair Icon in 2009, and Fashion Focused Image of the Year from the Fellowship for British Hairdressing, in addition to Hairdresser of the Year.

The label.m Professional Haircare range, created by Toni and Sacha Mascolo, has received multiple awards and recognition through numerous magazines including Hair Magazine, GQ, Pure Beauty, Men's Health, and Beauty Bible, to name but a few. Additionally, the company was the first ever winner of Hair Magazine's Readers' Choice Award for Best UK Salon Group in 2006, a title it has since won from both Reveal and Your Hair Magazine.

Recent Developments
The legendary Artistic Team, under the direction of Sacha Mascolo-Tarbuck, has won in excess of 60 British Hairdressing Awards;

most recently London Hairdresser of the Year 2015 and Newcomer of the Year 2015.

Promotion
As a brand, TONI&GUY juggles the need for consistency, the desire to be fashionable and the reassurance of solid service values, with the excitement of the avant-garde, supported by its philosophy of continual education.

DID YOU KNOW?
TONI&GUY Co-Founder and Chief Executive, Toni Mascolo OBE, still cuts hair once a week, alternating between London's Sloane Square and Marylebone salons.

TONI&GUY.TV launched in 2003 to enhance clients' in-salon experience. Containing up-to-the-minute content, from music to fashion and travel, it receives more than 90,000 views per week in the UK.

TONI&GUY Magazine was also launched in 2003 to echo and communicate the brand's heritage and philosophy, focusing on key trends in fashion, the arts, beauty, grooming and travel. Distributed in salons across Europe and globally, the magazine promotes an inspirational yet accessible face of the company to customers, employees and franchisees alike. In November 2004, it was named Launch of the Year at the APA

Awards, and in 2010 and 2011 won Best Consumer Publication.

Fashion has always been a major pillar of the brand. In 2004, the link grew even stronger with the sponsorship of London Fashion Week. Over 10 years on, the partnership continues to grow as demonstrated by the endorsement of its professional haircare range, label.m, which is the first product line that London Fashion Week has lent its name to.

The TONI&GUY Session Team works on more than 80 shows per year in London, New York, Paris, Milan, Tokyo and Shanghai, and offers support to key British design talent including Giles Deacon and House of Holland. In addition, the 10-times awarded Consumer Superbrand is proud to further support the industry as a leading sponsor of the British Fashion Awards.

Brand Values
TONI&GUY's reputation has been built on an impeccable pedigree and foundation of education, fashion focus and friendly, professional service. TONI&GUY aims to encompass the importance of local and individually tailored, customer-led service, promoting an authoritative, cohesive and – most importantly – inspiring voice.

TONI&GUY is one of the most powerful hairdressing brands in the world, offering some of the best education and guaranteeing innovative cutting and colour. It aims to be fashionable but friendly to provide the ultimate link between fashion and hair – pioneering, passionate and inspirational.

TRESemmé

tresemme.co.uk

TRESemmé was created in a US salon in 1948 by Edna Emmé – a leading stylist and opinion-former in the hair and beauty world. She understood the emotional relationship women have with their hair and developed a salon professional brand that was able to tap into the latest trends to enable women to have gorgeous looking hair with great colour and style.

"If a woman is feeling low in her mind, a trip to the beauty shop will pep her up every time." – Edna Emmé

Market
TRESemmé was the first brand to bring salon-grade products and innovation to women for use at home. Professional stylists around the world have used it for more than 60 years and today it is a key sponsor of New York Fashion Week.

Launched in the UK mass hair care market in 2004, TRESemmé quickly established itself as a key player in the market with its salon-standard technology and accessible prices. Now one of the UK's leading hair care brands, TRESemmé offers high quality, salon-style products across wash and care, post-wash and styling categories.

Despite a crowded UK market, TRESemmé has become the UK's most popular hair care brand (Source: Kantar Worldpanel, w/e 1st Feb 2015), with more than 10.5 million consumers. A by-word for affordable, transformative results, its three-tiered product system provides accessible solutions for every consumer, from value-conscious shoppers and trend-led buyers to those looking for specialist, targeted innovations.

Product
Bottling over 60 years of professional salon expertise, TRESemmé provides cutting-edge products and the latest trends know-how direct to consumers' fingertips.

With products developed by Unilever's research and development (R&D) department at the historical Port Sunlight, the wash and care portfolio provides solutions across every key look and consumer need, from the award-winning 7-Day Smooth range that offers lasting defence against frizzy hair, to the Moisture Rich line, launched 11 years ago, which remains a bestseller at the heart of the brand's offerings today.

DID YOU KNOW?
One TRESemmé product is sold every 2 seconds in the UK. *

As a trusted leader in R&D, TRESemme's styling ranges have been an integral part of hair kits backstage at shows by leading fashion designers at Mercedes-Benz New York Fashion Week for more than 13 seasons. Its partnership for nine shows during SS16 revealed a 59 per cent drive of TRESemmé conversations as a direct result of sponsorship. Such an endorsement by professionals means consumers are able to experience its high performing, salon quality products and recreate fashion-inspired styling in the comfort of their own home.

Achievements

With a strong brand presence in the UK, TRESemmé has won several magazine awards, recognising its standing as a leader in market innovation. Recent awards include Glamour Beauty Power List 2014 for 7-Day Smooth Heat Activated Treatment and recognition from the Fabulous Beauty Awards 2015 for TRESemmé Youth Boost Correcting Essence.

Recent Developments

Recognised for its contribution to thoughtful product design, TRESemmé has been responsible for bringing market innovation to the fore. Building on the success of the 7-Day Smooth and Perfectly (un)Done ranges, the brand constantly aims to create products for the mass market that tap into both salon trends and wide-reaching consumer needs. This is exemplified by the recent Runway Collection Creation Hairsprays launch and the specially formulated Beauty-Full Volume reverse wash system.

The Beauty-Full volume range was developed from an emerging trend spotted amongst beauty and industry influencers who were reversing their shampoo and conditioner routine to achieve volume and softness. Once this new beauty routine was discovered, TRESemmé R&D worked to formulate products that would perfect an intuitive method and provide volume seekers with professional products and salon-quality ingredients specifically designed for their volume needs, creating a completely new beauty regime. The pre-wash conditioner in the range is applied first and uses Fibre Polishing Actives to cover the surface of the hair fibres, leaving hair touchably soft.

The Beauty-Full Volume Shampoo, in a twist on the usual routine, follows this by using a bespoke formula to gently cleanse the hair to remove excess ingredients and weight whilst retaining body and bounce. In addition, the Hair Maximiser uses patented Fleximax Volumisers to create all the volume consumers need, while leaving hair noticeably softer.

Chris Barron, Global Brand Vice President, TRESemmé says: "This reverse haircare system is a TRESemmé first and represents a revolution in the way products come to market. The brand is truly integrating the new and innovative ways beauty influencers use products and providing the professional quality women have come to expect from TRESemmé."

Promotion

Becoming the official hair sponsor of The X Factor has cemented the brand's standing as a key figure in the mass hair care market in the UK, while its partnership with Mercedes-Benz New York Fashion Week allows its consumers to indulge in an at-home hair care experience with a leading fashion edge.

While creating large-scale awareness through traditional media channels, TRESemmé is also able to deliver engaging content to consumers on new media platforms. TRESemmé is aiming to evolve and strengthen the use of digital and social strategies to ensure a consistent flow of product advice goes directly to the consumers when they need it most.

USED BY OVER
10.5 MILLION
CONSUMERS IN THE UK

Brand History

1948	Leading hair stylist and influencer, Edna Emmé creates the TRESemmé brand in a US salon.
1959	Alberto-Culver purchases TRESemmé.
1992	TRESemmé launches into mass retail in the US.
2004	The salon-exclusive brand is launched in the UK in 2004 with the arrival of large 900ml black and white bottles.
2008	TRESemmé begins sponsorship of Mercedes-Benz New York Fashion Week, now in its 15th season.
2009	The 24-Hour Body range is launched with the iconic tagline 'Hair that won't fall flat'.
2010	Unilever acquires TRESemmé as part of the Alberto-Culver takeover.
2014	TRESemmé launches the award-winning 7-Day Smooth range, offering unique frizz resistance for up to seven days.
2016	Beauty-Full Volume launches, the reverse wash and care system for soft, touchable volume.

Brand Values

TRESemmé offers leading, salon-quality hair care that aims to make its consumers walk two inches taller every day. Understanding that when hair works, everything clicks, TRESemmé's ethos of professional, affordable product resonates with consumers everywhere.

* Source: Nielsen, Unit Sales, MAT 07.11.2015

VISA

visa.co.uk

With more than 2.4 billion cardholders worldwide, Visa is one of the world's leading consumer payment brands. In Europe alone there are more than 500 million Visa-branded cards. By providing consumers with a convenient, secure and globally accepted electronic payment solution, Visa's goal is to be the preferred alternative to cash and cheques. Through partnering with today's innovators and providing them with the technology and infrastructure needed to build the payment system of tomorrow, Visa remains at the heart of payment innovation.

Market
Visa Europe operates in 38 countries and, through its partnership with Visa Inc., cardholders can use their cards in millions of locations globally. Across Europe, there are more Visa cards than there are adults and €1 in every €6 spent in is on a Visa card.

Each of Visa Europe's member financial institutions has access to the same powerful brand, products and services, marketing, and other support including advanced systems to authorise, secure and process Visa transactions.

Product
Visa has led the evolution of payments for more than 50 years, from the creation of the credit card in 1958 to the move to magnetic stripe, the shift to chip and PIN, to the introduction of contactless and mobile payments. In 2015, Visa rolled out tokenisation in Europe, which is the technology that allows for secure and convenient contactless payments and is paving the way for mobile and wearable devices.

Today, Visa offers three cashless payment models to suit individual needs: pay now (debit cards); pay later (credit, charge and deferred debit cards); and pay in advance (prepaid cards). These are delivered through physical and virtual channels; chip and PIN and contactless cards, mobile contactless payments and other new forms of digital payment, such as wearables.

Achievements
Visa drives both the present and the future of payments – giving consumers the confidence to pay anywhere, any time and on any device, whatever their preference.

In Europe alone this has resulted in €1.4 trillion point of sale spending on Visa cards, a 283 per cent increase in contactless transactions and €16.1 billion in transactions being cleared and settled in 2014 (Source: Visa Annual Report, 2015).

In 2015, the use of Visa cards continued to grow, while the value of the brand increased further. Visa rose two places to fifth in BrandZ's Top 100 Most Valuable Global Brands Index, with an estimated 16 per cent increase in brand value. This marked Visa's third straight year in the top ten.

DID YOU KNOW?
Between November 2014 and October 2015, £148 billion was spent online with UK-issued Visa cards, equivalent to £4,693 per second.

Recent Developments
In November 2015 Visa Inc. announced a definitive agreement to acquire Visa Europe, bringing together the two organisations. On closing of the deal, European financial institutions will gain greater access to Visa Inc.'s scale, resources and technology investments, while global clients will enjoy a more seamless experience.

35 CONTACTLESS PAYMENTS ARE MADE EVERY SECOND ACROSS THE UK

DID YOU KNOW?
Friday is the busiest day of the week for contactless transactions.

Brand History

1958	Bank of America launches BankAmericard, the first successful general purpose credit card.
1976	BankAmericard changes its name to Visa.
1979	Visa introduces the first point-of-sale electronic terminal.
1983	Visa launches the world's first 24-hour ATM network. The following year the 'dove' hologram is introduced to cards for the first time.
1986	Visa becomes the first card payment system to offer multiple currency clearing and settlement, and begins sponsorship of the Olympic Games.
1993	Visa issues the first smart card to accrue loyalty points, plus corporate business and purchasing cards.
1999	Visa conducts the world's first Euro transaction using a payment card.
2000	A world first, Visa issues its one billionth card.
2002	Visa becomes the first global sponsor of the Paralympic Games.
2007	Visa introduces Visa payWave, a contactless payment solution.
2012	London 2012 is the first 'contactless' Olympic Games.
2015	Over one billion Visa contactless payments are made in a 12 month period across Europe for the first time.

The announcement of the acquisition came at the end of another significant year for Visa Europe, with advances made in contactless, mobile, online and wearable payments. These reflected continued developments in technology and changing consumer behaviour. In the UK for example, more than half of payments were made without cash for the first time in 2015.

Also in 2015, usage of contactless, which enables consumers to pay for low value goods and services without inserting their card into a terminal, continued to accelerate. The number of Visa contactless transactions in Europe passed one billion over a 12 month period for the first time. By 31st October, 1.3 billion contactless transactions had taken place across Europe during 2015 and €12.7 billion had been spent.

In the UK, there were around 50 million Visa contactless cards in circulation by the middle of 2015 and 410,000 places accepting them. In March, Transport for London was named Visa's fastest growing contactless user with over 200 million journeys to date. Meanwhile in September, the spending limit increased to £30 per transaction signaling that the technology is fast becoming the new normal when paying for everyday items.

Visa also furthered the development of mobile contactless payments, in partnership with banks, handset manufacturers and mobile network providers. Notable launches in 2015 included Apple Pay, with other mobile payment solutions to follow. Separately, Visa launched a partnership for a 'pay by the wrist' watch with Swatch, which is going on sale in selected markets in 2016.

Promotion

Visa continues to evolve its communications under the 'Always On' tagline, launching several campaigns in 2015. In the UK, Visa championed the ubiquity of contactless payments with its 'Everyday Britons' campaign, demonstrating how people from all walks of life are using contactless.

In November 2015, Visa launched its 'Ready' campaign. Featuring a central theme of anticipation, it used imagery to draw analogies to the speed, ease and reliability of using a Visa card on Apple Pay.

Finally, Visa Europe announced a sponsorship deal, mirroring the brand's commitment to innovation, by supporting the FIA Formula E Championship – the world's first fully-electric racing series. In addition, Visa will again be supporting the Rio 2016 Olympic and Paralympic Games.

Brand Values

The Visa brand is an intrinsic part of a global, integrated system of banks, merchants and the consumers as well as businesses they serve.

The world is increasingly complex, demanding and fast-paced. Visa's brand, and the technology that powers its systems, ensures customers feel confident in responding to these changes with confidence and certainty. Visa is one of life's constants and this has shaped its brand promise: 'Wherever you are, anytime, Visa gives you certainty'.

By combining the reliability of Visa's network, which in Europe has gone 3,000 days without interruption, its innovations and the power of its partnerships, Visa brings certainty, new thinking and possibilities to everyone, everywhere.

engaging, always.

BLOG

webershandwick.co.uk

Weber Shandwick is a full service global communications agency. Its communications experts and creative teams work for some of the most innovative brands and biggest organisations in the private, public and not-for-profit sectors. The agency creates public relations campaigns for clients around the world, from single-market activations to multi-country programmes.

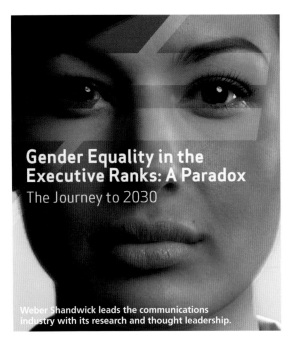

Gender Equality in the Executive Ranks: A Paradox
The Journey to 2030

Weber Shandwick leads the communications industry with its research and thought leadership.

Market

Weber Shandwick is one of the world's leading PR networks. With a core of 75 owned offices in 34 countries and affiliates and partners that expand the network to 123 offices in 81 countries, Weber Shandwick operates in virtually every major media, government and business centre on six continents.

The EMEA region spans 61 markets, from Stockholm to Johannesburg, Dublin to Dubai, with a network of 30 offices and 44 affiliates. Weber Shandwick is one of the leading players in the UK, EMEA and global PR markets, with growth that outperforms most of its peers.

With offices in London, Manchester, Aberdeen, Belfast, Edinburgh and Glasgow, the firm also offers a strong UK network.

Product

Weber Shandwick's practice groups include consumer marketing, corporate communications, crisis communications and issues management, digital, financial communications, health communications, public affairs, sports marketing, sustainability and technology communications. The firm has specialists in all industry sectors across the UK and the EMEA region, from energy and cleantech, to travel and tourism.

Achievements

Weber Shandwick EMEA remains the most awarded agency in the region with 439 wins in 12 years across 15 markets. The Weber Shandwick network was awarded a Bronze PR Lion and a Bronze Media Lion at the 2015 Cannes International Festival of Creativity. To date, in 2015 it has won 80 awards in EMEA; 28 awards for UK campaigns.

In 2015, Weber Shandwick was named Global Agency of the Year by PRWeek and The Holmes Report and was the only PR firm on the Advertising Age Agency A-List for two years running, based on creativity, innovation and performance.

For the fourth year running, Weber Shandwick in the UK was listed by The Sunday Times in its prestigious '100 Best Companies to Work For' review. It was also named as one of the top companies to work for in the UAE by the Great Place to Work® Institute.

Recent Developments

As part of Weber Shandwick's continued focus on digital communications, it launched three content creation studios across EMEA. The company now has 600 people globally working in digital communications. Blurring the lines of traditional PR, Weber Shandwick also became advertising agency-of-record for a number of major clients.

In 2014, Weber Shandwick acquired Swedish PR agency Prime and its business intelligence arm, United Minds. Prime is one

DID YOU KNOW?
Weber Shandwick EMEA remains the most awarded agency in the region with 439 wins in 12 years across 15 markets.

WEBER SHANDWICK IS THE ONLY PR AGENCY TO BE AWARDED 4 CANNES LIONS FOR UK CAMPAIGNS

Weber Shandwick helped Nespresso to communicate its commitment to re-establishing the coffee industry in South Sudan.

DID YOU KNOW?

Weber Shandwick operates one of the largest social media agency networks in the world.

Brand History

1974 Shandwick International is established in London with a single client and a global vision.

1987 The Weber Group is founded in Cambridge, Massachusetts, USA as a communications agency for emerging technology companies. In less than a decade it becomes a top 10 PR firm.

1998 Shandwick International is acquired by the Interpublic Group.

2000 Shandwick International merges with The Weber Group and becomes Weber Shandwick.

2001 BSMG Worldwide merges with Weber Shandwick.

2014 Weber Shandwick acquires global creative powerhouse Prime, adding 130 employees based in Stockholm.

of Europe's most awarded communications agencies with expertise ranging from marketing communications, public affairs and sustainability to public sector, change management and issues management.

In 2015, United Minds opened in London. It is a multi-sector strategy and planning division that brings together strategists spanning political polling, management consulting, market analysis, statistics, trend analysis, consumer behaviour and communications consulting.

In 2014, Weber Shandwick launched Mediaco, a content creation and distribution unit that enables every company to become a media company. Mediaco offers a comprehensive approach to content planning, creation, production and distribution, from audience mapping and

developing a distinctive editorial voice, to creating an ecosystem of owned and shared channels, and evaluation.

Weber Shandwick continued its network development and extension with its first standalone branded PR service in South Africa, the first full year of operation in Turkey, and new offices in Brasilia and Mexico.

Weber Shandwick is committed to being an active and responsible corporate citizen, and recently produced its third annual corporate citizenship report. The company works with a number of organisations on pro-bono, volunteering and corporate fundraising projects. In London, for instance, Weber Shandwick has supported War Child for more than 10 years.

Promotion

Since launching its 'Science of Engagement' research in 2012, a ground-breaking initiative working with leading experts in the fields of neuroscience, psychology and anthropology to understand what drives human engagement, Weber Shandwick has helped clients – from global development organisations to brands targeting millennials – tackle PR in a more sophisticated manner and advise what activity is most likely to drive purchase across the entire marketing mix.

The 'Science of Engagement' has been used as the basis of other projects including 'The Science of Ingagement' report, which captured the dynamics of how UK employers engage employees.

Other recent high-profile original research has included: 'The CEO Reputation Premium: Gaining Advantage in the Engagement Era'; 'The Female CEO Reputation Premium?

Differences and Similarities', and the second and third iterations of the company's 'Socialising Your CEO' report.

Weber Shandwick is committed to diversity, inclusion and gender equality, and recently launched its 'Gender Equality in the Executive Ranks' research, including the Weber Shandwick GFP Index, which measures gender balance in the Fortune Global 100 companies.

In 2015, Weber Shandwick launched its EMEA blog, a platform for thought leadership from its communications experts across the region, a London-based politics and public affairs blog, The Debate, and the global Media Decoded platform, which looks at media, business, marketing, creativity, and technology.

Brand Values
Five core values shape Weber Shandwick's company culture and support its overall vision:

Integrity: it demands the highest levels of professionalism.

Collaboration: the company believes it serves clients best when they all work together.

Learning: knowing more about clients, the profession and the places where it operates is essential.

Innovation: Weber Shandwick believes that creative thinking is the key to excellence, enduring growth and success.

Quality: the firm's constant quest for improvement helps it deliver high-quality service.

whirlpool.co.uk

SENSING THE DIFFERENCE

Whirlpool is the world's number one household appliance brand and a leading manufacturer and marketer in Europe.

Its emphasis is on giving people the luxury of more time, so they can focus on what really matters. Whirlpool's mission is to sustain its commitment to make each experience an extraordinary one, with continued investment in superior performance, intuitive technology and cutting-edge design.

Market
Whirlpool is a leading producer and marketer of home appliances worldwide; a Whirlpool appliance is purchased every second. In the UK, Whirlpool sells a range of home appliances online and in-store, through a variety of well-known multiple and independent retailers where it is experiencing growth in the premium brand segment. Globally the company employs more than 100,000 people and has 70 manufacturing, technical research and development centres.

Product
Characterised by ergonomic design and high-quality materials, the range of appliances offer intelligent functionality via Whirlpool 6th Sense® technology.

The built-in range has premium specification, offering consumers a selection of products for the kitchen. Each product has an easy to maintain and long-lasting stainless steel finish protected by a nanotechnology coating called iXelium™. To complement the design and innovation-led built-in range are the freestanding appliances that include features such as the quietest spin cycle in washing, technology to preserve food for longer in the fridge, and a quick drying feature for plastics in dishwashing.

Achievements
Whirlpool is a world leader in environmental protection through innovation. Forty-five years ago, the company began research

dedicated to eco-efficiency. In 1998, Whirlpool invented 6th Sense® intelligent electronic sensor control, energy and resource saving technology that is one of the key elements in all the company's appliances today.

In 2003 Whirlpool became the first major appliance manufacturer to sign up to the Kyoto Protocol and agreed to the reduction of CO_2 emissions of 6.6 per cent.

In 2014 the company gained the Quiet Mark accreditation for its award-winning, Supreme Care washing machines.

In addition, Whirlpool won the Gold Award for Innovation in Technology for its Supreme Care product at the 2015 Designer Awards.

The US Environmental Protection Agency (EPA) recognised the Whirlpool Corporation, with a 2015 ENERGY STAR® Partner of

Brand History

1911 Upton Machine Corporation is founded in Michigan, to produce electric motor-driven wringer washers. It subsequently merges with the Nineteen Hundred Washer Co. in 1929.

1919 Gottlob Bauknecht starts a small electric workshop in Germany, establishing his first factory in 1933. Philips acquires the Bauknecht business in 1982.

1941 The company becomes the world's number one washing machine manufacturer.

1950 Nineteen Hundred Corporation changes its name to the Whirlpool Corporation and adds washers, dryers and refrigerators to the range.

1970 The corporate office for environmental control is established.

1989 Whirlpool Corporation and Philips form a European joint venture.

1993 The Philips Whirlpool brand becomes Whirlpool.

1998 Whirlpool launches the first appliances with 6th Sense® intelligent technology.

2003 Whirlpool becomes the world's first appliance manufacturer to announce a global greenhouse gas reduction target.

2006 Whirlpool acquires the Maytag brand.

2010 The Green Generation washer, dishwasher and fridge freezer are launched.

2012 The Green Kitchen launches, offering energy savings of up to 70 per cent compared to conventional kitchen appliances.

2014 Whirlpool's groundbreaking dishwasher that uses just six litres of water is launched.

2014 Indesit Company S.p.A is acquired and is the world's largest manufacturer of home appliances.

2016 Whirlpool launches a range of appliances with connectivity.

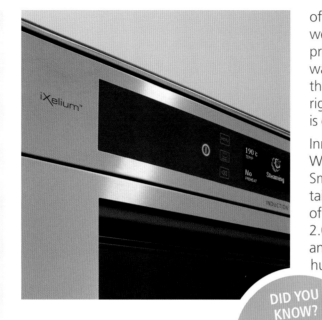

the Year award. The company received the award for its outstanding contribution to reducing greenhouse gas emissions by manufacturing energy-efficient products and educating consumers about energy efficiency. Whirlpool has received the ENERGY STAR Award 25 times.

Recent Developments
In 2015, the company showcased a robust selection of new appliances and introduced a visionary concept of the kitchen of the future.

The focus was on a range of smart appliances that communicate directly with consumers and interact with each other. They incorporate innovative 6th Sense® LIVE technology designed to control an appliance from anywhere, at any time, with the utmost ease, via an app on both iOS and Android devices. Aiming for simplicity and making consumer's lives easier, it sends reminders

of food expiry dates and a shopping list, as well as tips on where to store food for best preservation. The intelligent Supreme Care washing machine is interlinked and 'talks' to the matching tumble dryer so it is set to the right programme when the wash cycle is complete.

Innovating the cooking space further, Whirlpool has created a fully flexible Smart Cook induction hob, featuring tailor-made cooking programmes as part of 'The Interactive Kitchen of the Future 2.0' – a concept cooking environment and fully connected social media hub that synchronises devices with kitchen appliances.

DID YOU KNOW?
One Whirlpool home appliance is sold, somewhere in the world, every second.

Promotion
Whirlpool pursues its business objectives, while contributing to improve the lives of people in the communities where it operates. The most important project supported by Whirlpool is its partnership with Habitat for Humanity, which is committed to providing simple, decent, affordable

housing for families in need in more than 100 countries. Whirlpool has supported this global, non-profit organisation, dedicated to eliminating poverty housing worldwide, not only providing products but, in 2013, nearly 50 per cent of Whirlpool Corporation's salaried employees worldwide donated 423,729 hours of volunteer work.

WHIRLPOOL APPLIANCES ARE IN MORE THAN
200 MILLION
HOMES WORLDWIDE

Brand Values
Throughout its history, Whirlpool has strived to make intelligent appliances that provide an intuitive experience through technology and design. Whirlpool is determined to make lives easier with simplicity of use, superior performance and cutting-edge design. The Whirlpool brand is relentless about innovation, consistently producing industry-leading design and technological solutions for freedom and consumer empowerment.

How to Become a Permanent Fixture

What brands can do to ensure longevity in the Superbrands Top 20

Chris Walmsley

Co-Founder, Cubo

Eleven years ago, Superbrands introduced its first Top 20 consumer vote. Since then, plenty has changed, but an elite handful of 'Premier League' Superbrands have stayed remarkably consistent, ranking repeatedly every year. The question every brand wants to know the answer to is why have some stars stuck around while others have drifted away? And what can brands that are just beginning to make their ascent learn from them?

Only three brands have consistently sat in the top tier since 2008 – Coca-Cola, Google and Mercedes-Benz. Close behind them, Microsoft, the BBC, British Airways and Apple hit the Top 20 in eight of those nine years, while LEGO, BMW, M&S and Rolex appear seven times. Conversely, some ostensibly similar big brands like Sony, Amazon, BP and the AA have only cropped up twice.

It's no surprise that the permanent 'Premier League' Superbrands are a highly exclusive group; nestled in the nation's subconscious. Just like football, where the same teams fluctuate between the top two tiers, the Superbrands have invested significant time and energy into retaining their top spots.

So what's the difference between the premier elite and the rest of the Superbrands alumni? On first glance there isn't a great deal to differentiate the permanent fixtures from those that have only appeared, say, three times in the Top 20, like Cadbury, Hilton, Guinness and Gillette. However, when considering what makes a brand 'super' this isn't surprising.

All of the brands that appear in the Top 20 are built around strong products people want and need in their lives. By definition, if they lead in a public vote, they are likely to be established brands that have captured a large share of mind; which implies they are distinctive, recognisable and widely available. These criteria are the base level to expect of any Superbrand.

Notably, the top 'Premier League' brands have eschewed the familiar promise of short-term commercial returns, having instead built up significant value over years of work. They are backed by histories of award-winning creative campaigns, which have earned them enduring emotional connections in people's minds.

Similarly, these top tier brands have settled upon the optimal 'contributions' they can make to people's lives, rewarding people's interest through being informative, useful or just entertaining. Coca-Cola define themselves as being in the business of spreading global happiness, while Google and Apple achieved much the same through products that contribute to our lives and culture. Mercedes-Benz delivers aesthetically desirable contributions that speak to us individually, while the BBC has contributed societally for nearly a century.

Establishing the most appropriate contribution approach for a particular brand is one of the best ways to reinforce positive feelings towards it, a strong basis for being 'super'. Our brains find it easier to recall good times and strong feelings towards brands outlast memories of facts and figures. Combine these facts and it is clear why delivering memorably positive

CREATIVE BRAND ENGAGEMENT

Inform Entertain & Be useful

brand engagements is ultimately self-reinforcing.

Much has been written about the declining mental space that people are prepared to give to brands and how marketing tools are relatively weak in terms of affecting the totality of brand experience. So it is no surprise the 'Premier League' Superbrands are some of the most adept at maximising limited influence – using their budgets to do things that people actually want, even if they don't know it yet.

Herein lies the killer difference amongst the very strongest Superbrands.

True Superbrands are institutions in their own right. The totality of the brand experience offered by the likes of Google, Coca-Cola, the BBC and Apple goes far beyond their marketing efforts. They are built around iconic products that contribute across society through being genuinely useful. Their branding runs seamlessly throughout every possible engagement with their products and business, providing textbook examples of the salient memory associations advocated by Professor Byron Sharp.

The staying power of these truly monumental brands comes from their unwavering investment to ensure absolute consistency of their products, the scale of their relevance, and the contributions they make as brands. Their familiarity provokes trust, meaning from LEGO to M&S they have become part of the wider fabric of culture, and, in the case of brands like Mercedes-Benz, people turn to them to gain or reinforce social status.

There's no one route to Superbrands stardom and arguably they have all reached this position in different ways; Google and the BBC through products that became fixtures in our day-to-day lives, Coca-Cola via iconic advertising and unparalleled distribution, and Apple through sustained innovation.

So which current contenders have the potential to join this top league for good?

Both Dyson (ranked four times) and Amazon (twice) have potential, but do they have what it takes to stay at the top? They offer alluringly effective new ways of doing things, but maintaining a place in people's minds alongside offerings from Google or the BBC is still a big ask.

The Top 20 is a difficult enough bullseye to hit, never mind stay in. Becoming the next 'institution' is out of reach for most brands, as their products are not iconic or significant enough. Brands like Airbnb and Uber are exciting, innovatory products of the digital revolution, but none are close to becoming cultural institutions yet.

Realistically-speaking, it would require a market changing, cultural shift to create the conditions for a new brand to become monumental in people's lives. It's not impossible, as Google's swift rise has shown, but this kind of shift will not happen through communications alone. To earn a lasting place at the front of people's minds, a brand would need to offer a unique way of doing things.

Perhaps the forthcoming revolution in self-driving eco-cars might hand a brand like Tesla a top spot in the 'Premier League'? Maybe Oculus Rift and their Virtual Reality peers will alter the way we consume and engage with media forever? The appeal of AI, Robotics and Human Augmentation all have potential to change the way we live and create monumental 'institution' brands in the process.

These changes are accelerating but all of this will take some time. Until then, the same 20 or 30 Superbrands will continue to drop in and out of the Top 20 as their contributions to people's lives fluctuate. But for now it looks like their status will remain largely unchallenged.

Cubo's approach centers on finding creative ways for brands to engage with people, by making a contribution to their lives through their communications.

cubo.com

Marketing Technology Infrastructure

As technology advances rapidly, B2B needs to step up the pace

Mark Lethbridge
CEO, Gravity Global and President of MAGNET (Marketing and Advertising Global Network)

Technology is making today's buying process more complex and putting more control in the hands of prospects. The new buzzword 'martech' is starting to become commonplace, but are B2B marketeers really taking full advantage of these new tools and do they fully understand what is possible?

Some businesses have already adopted very sophisticated marketing technology infrastructures to support business growth. However, most B2B businesses have not yet gone beyond search, marketing automation and customer relationship management infrastructures to support their initiatives.

For some, this has been seen as the 'saviour' of marketing. The challenging relationship between Chief Marketing Officers and their CEOs is familiar given reported concerns that marketing cannot be relied on to deliver growth. Then technology comes along and demonstrates the effectiveness of marketing investment.

Technology has much more to offer but it is not easy to navigate. This is unsurprising, bearing in mind the plethora of marketing technology available.

B2B companies that were early adopters of technology tools have moved on. They are now using marketing technology to define business strategy, discover the best business opportunities, measure brand sentiment in real time and identify the real drivers for accelerated growth.

Technology can validate how you go to market

When developing new messaging, identity, imagery and describing value proposition, how can brands ensure effectiveness? Conventional research tests address these questions via focus groups or in-depth interviews using stimulus boards, both very much removed from how target audiences might see a brand in real life. The alternative is online, quantitative research that puts brands in a digital context, but this only allows closed questions to be asked – lacking the insight of qualitative research.

Now technology exists to deliver testing environments that are more true to life. This allows brands to put messaging into context – on the screen of the target audience – depicted as web pages, advertising, emails, or brochures. The survey is all online but enables brands to gain qualitative responses. By responding electronically and dropping the digital equivalent of a post-it note onto their screen, respondents identify issues and the exact location of those issues.

This type of research should be called 'mass qualitative' – it has all the advantages of qualitative research but, because the survey is online, it is possible to mass sample a target audience quickly and cost effectively. Once the electronic responses are aggregated, it shows hot spots on the materials tested – where respondents have commented most. It gives an overall assessment identifying modifications and enhancements, and can dive into specific areas to reveal individual verbatim comments.

Technology reduces the risk of launching brand positioning and messaging that is unclear or misinterpreted by a target audience. It enables fine-tuning of a brand's proposition and message to improve engagement prior to investment and market collateral. This, in turn, puts a brand in a more real life context and minimises 'research effects', giving greater insight than conventional quantitative research through a larger sample size.

Technology enriches the customer experience

Technology exists that helps strengthen the brand experience for B2B customers. Net Promoter Score (NPS) is said to be the strongest overall measurer of brand experience, reflecting B2B customers' approval of their experience and their intention to recommend it to others.

But what is the next step after measuring NPS? How can a brand ensure next year's score will be higher? The issue with the single score is that it doesn't identify issues an organisation needs to address to enrich the experience and shift the score.

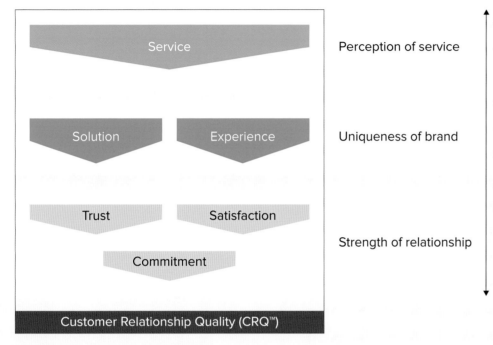

The building blocks of the brand experience.

The technology is a customer relationship assessment tool that considers B2B customers' end-to-end brand experience, getting their feedback not just as an overall NPS score – customers are also asked to score each aspect of their experience at a granular level. Armed with this set of measures, it highlights with accuracy which parts of a brand experience should be enhanced to make a positive difference on customers' perceptions.

In addition to providing an NPS, it details where improvements could be made to improve that score and the relationship strength with each B2B customer. It scores the strength of the customer relationship, indicates how likely that customer is to desert, and identifies what needs to be done to retain that customer's business. The technology provides clarity on where to spend resources to improve the brand experience and how to improve the relationship with key accounts. Over time, brands can track their performance in specific aspects and identify brand and operational strengths and weaknesses contributing to brand perceptions.

Technology to help drive brand performance

How healthy is your brand? How do you compare with your competition from capturing the interest of a prospect to turning them into a customer? What

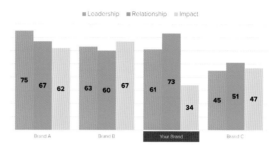

Benchmarking brands against the key attributes for competitive success.

competitive attributes are market buyers using to make their provider selection choices? Is your brand best positioned to attract the largest market opportunities, and if not, how should it be repositioned? Most brands can respond anecdotally to these questions, but few have hard evidence or tracking data as a key business metric.

Using a range of measures the tool is able to connect a brand directly to its business strategy and prove that continued brand investment will enhance the commercial performance and potential of the business.

There are three distinct elements to the performance modelling platform; a brand strength tracking index, an assessment of marcomms effectiveness in driving prospects to and through the purchasing funnel, and a map of competing brands, their relationship to these attributes and to the market segments missed.

As each of the above elements positions a brand amongst those of its main competitors, it's possible to relate a brand directly to commercial opportunity. It will identify, with great accuracy, how brands can capture market share from competitors by strengthening or transforming aspects of itself. It provides ongoing tracking metrics

to validate investments in the brand and evidence the impact a brand has had on the success of the business.

As a minimum, it will help you track brand health. Used to its full, this is a platform from which it's possible to capture unseen business growth opportunities and to connect the brand with the business development strategy of the organisation.

The benefits of this technology demonstrate to a business the existing and potential performance of a brand to generate sales and profit opportunities, while putting brand investment at the top of the boardroom agenda. The analysis provides an ongoing tracking of key brand performance metrics of an individual brand and competing brands through a benchmark set of metrics prior to change and the measures that validate change and investment.

These are just three of the many technology tools that go beyond the norm. Imagine the added value to a brand and business if B2B marketers unleashed the full potential technology now provides.

gravity
GLOBAL

Gravity is an award-winning, full-service global B2B agency network. It is integrated across all channels from strategic consultation to implementation.

gravityglobal.com

An Organic Regeneration

As creativity abounds in the business world, is originality suffering?

Sam Oxley

With innovative approaches to business springing up almost daily, it's harder to find something truly original. Today's consumers are on a search for the new.

We're all magpies really. Looking for the next new shiny thing to spark our interest and get our attention. Be it a new social network, a new phone, a new brand – new ideas are the oil for the engine of business, entrepreneurialism and brands. But these days, it's getting harder and harder to find 'new'.

Previously new was sourced in the metropolitan, hip, melting pot city centre, where minds meet, collaborate and create. But in the modern, hyper-connected world order, 'new' feels like it's becoming a bit of a formula. In theory, it's easier than ever to be inspired, but harder than ever to be original because we've seen so much before.

From coffee shops to pop-ups, selfie campaigns to experiential engagement, the formula for 'new' is found and shared everywhere. We share so much that we get to taste the nectar of new every day. It's like being trapped in a sweet shop, nibbling sugary pleasures but feeling hollow and unsatisfied afterwards. It's over in a fleeting six-second vine or periscope live stream before we're onto the next thing. In an age of tech hubs, identikit city 'villages' and social media, we're at risk of sharing so much and being emulated on such a grand scale that we've got to be careful we don't lose the quirks and creativity that used to make brands 'cool'. Which raises the question – where and how are those people who are truly making new, creative and original work finding their inspiration?

About five years ago, I attended a Guardian conference and sat in the audience eager to hear Arianna Huffington's words of wisdom. Stood in front of a twitter wall facing an audience lit by the glow of laptop and tablet screens, she was asked by one of the multi-tasking onlookers, tapping away on their computers, what her prediction was for the future. She said that we would all need to disconnect.

I'm with Arianna – I think she's right. I'm fortunate to work in an industry that is full of creative people. But after careful

consideration and some extensive peer research, I've started to recognise that the most creative people I know, or am inspired by, have the ability to 'disconnect' more than most. They live and work in a field in Kent, they 'commute' to a studio at the end of the garden, and walk the dog in the woods when they want to find an idea. What binds them all is they know how to stand back and switch off – and they don't all live in the city. They don't work in a hub. They are not emulating anyone else or producing in an engineered environment.

Organisations such as DO (thedolectures. com) are leading the charge with this approach. The annual festival is hosted on a small farm in Wales and is focused on giving people the chance to talk, share ideas and

be inspired. From small beginnings in 2008 it has now grown into a global movement. New and original is increasingly coming from a world that finds inspiration online, but is processed via the offline time and space we all need to process and decode the connected world.

To hit the sweet spot of 'new' you need two phases of action to happen: analysis and research, studying your subject so you know it inside out. And resting: where you drop everything. This happens naturally when you have a bath or go for a walk – which is why people often have breakthrough ideas when they're doing something else. Isaac Newton's concept of gravity came from a brief stop under an apple tree. Would it happen now if he was checking his phone? Albert Einstein

was unable to determine why or how his best ideas came to him in periods of relaxed daydreaming (specifically shaving). But it's rare that we get to daydream now.

A freethinking approach is what helps make great ideas, concepts and brands stand out. They have learned how to step back from what the rest of the world is doing. Brilliant brands harness and collaborate with like-minded spirits and people who share a desire to create their own vision. They retain integrity in their ideas; they don't pander to what a perceived audience might want. The coolest brands show you what's going to happen next, but spend little time referencing what's going on now. That's why the likes of Google and Apple shine – they engage the artists and thinkers who exist in their own space, and that's what helps keep them fresh. Not every brand can do it but those that get it right shine through the fog of normality.

To create work that really delivers a deep connection, and really says something, we need the time to step away and reflect. Connected noise can inspire us, but might not be conducive to the creativity we crave

unless we get the opportunity to opt out of it too.

Banksy's Dismaland installation was a fantastic example of how to stand back and harness the power of observation. It was a work of genius created in collaboration with a roll call of incredible artists. But you won't find Banksy on Twitter, or be able to like him on Facebook; he's anonymous. He's an artist who understands the impact of distraction who knows that when you build in some space, inspiration rises and solutions reveal themselves.

Brands can and should be bolder and braver when it comes to developing new ideas. In an era of data and tracking, it's more challenging to do things differently, but go with your gut, be the first to innovate. That's what many of the brands we admire most do – they buck the trend, they go their own way and they maintain their integrity. It's important that more brands, like artists, do this. Because according to Wikipedia, magpies are some of the most intelligent animals in the world, so it's going to take a lot of effort to really impress us in the future.

Sam was previously Managing Partner at House PR.

Work with purpose

House PR is an independently owned PR agency in London who produce creative work that gets results. A public relations and communications consultancy.

housepr.com

The Data Dilemma

An issue that no brand or business can afford to ignore

David Day

President & Global CEO, Lightspeed GMI

I was recently browsing the internet for a thoughtful birthday present for a loved one. Having made a purchase on a site I moved on, only to be faced with an ad for the product I had just bought on the next site I visited. The same happened on the next website, and the next. For the following few weeks, I continued to be haunted by the images of the product I'd bought, wherever I went online. It was a virtual version of Groundhog Day.

Was someone with a zoom lens watching over my shoulder? Of course not, but for some the more routine explanation is just as spooky: our online actions are being tracked. Not by MI5 or GCHQ, but by marketers who want our money.

For a company that researches consumers, with more than five million people on online panels across the globe, protecting people's Personally Identifiable Information (PII) is extremely important and Lightspeed GMI invest a huge amount of resource into it. It's the same today for any brand or business – it is essential to strike a balance between using data to target people effectively while at the same time not crossing the line by being too personal.

I am sure you have also noticed something similar when searching online. Indeed, search engines and ad servers are becoming increasingly sophisticated. Using cookies and complex algorithms, they can record what you are searching for and are able to track searches across your devices through the sites you visit. By doing so, they can serve you adverts that, based on your search behaviour, are likely to be of interest to you. Similarly, they can avoid showing ads that are not likely to be relevant. At least that is the theory. The aim of doing this is, of course, to provide a better and more efficient browser or search experience, making it easier and quicker to find what you are looking for and to make a purchase.

With people using mobiles to access the internet, technology can be used to provide brands with a fuller picture of their customers because location is added to the mix. Not only can brands see when people shop online and the search phrases they use but, using geo-tracking, where they are too. This provides brands with the opportunity to target customers with specific ads or offers at the right time, when they're in the right place and frame of mind, i.e. when they are in-store.

Mobile phones are intensely personal devices. They are a key part of people's

everyday lives, travelling with them wherever they go. For this reason, they can offer the marketer incredible, real-time insight into consumer behaviour, enabling brands to track the consumer as they complete their journey from exposure to purchase. Given this intimacy, people are more likely to feel brands are intruding on their time and space by using this device to interact with them. So it's critical that each interaction is a valuable one to the consumer. In the case of targeted ads, for example, brands need to get better

at tracking data and using it to anticipate behaviour, rather than just reflect history. Currently, the anticipation is less effective after the fact. For example, if you search for and purchase a watch, do you really need to see ads for more watches?

Better-targeted ads have huge advantages for both consumers and brands, but there is an element of eeriness about companies tracking consumers' every move. People are becoming increasingly sensitized to the idea of data theft and, while many appear less concerned about their privacy by widely

sharing information about their lives on social media, many (often the same people) are becoming more protective of their personal data. Ultimately it is the perceived value to the consumer that influences whether data is shared or not and how secure that data is. Perception is reality in the minds of the consumer. So brands have to communicate successfully how and why data is being collected, the lengths taken to ensure it is secure, as well as the benefits to the sharer. A breach carries both financial and reputational risks and, as we all know, it is far easier to lose a reputation than to build one.

Ever-changing legislation means it is likely that the tracking and storing of information that makes these targeted ads possible may become difficult, or even illegal, in some countries in the future. Getting over the hurdle of what is deemed acceptable to consumers with regards to use of their data is the starting point, but brands must also be careful not to break the law. The recent European Courts of Justice ruling on the transferring of personal information between the EU and US – 'Safe Harbour' – is an example of this. As a result it is important that brands future-proof their approach to handling and storing customers' personal data to avoid potential upcoming issues to stay compliant.

The dilemma brands have about personal data and privacy is not new, but with the proliferation of new technologies and demands on people's personal information, it is important for a brand to ensure that it is at the leading edge of using data responsibly – and to ensure that consumers know this.

Here are some guidelines for brands – think of consumer data as you would your own data; always ask if the requested information is essential; protect the customers' trust; stay up-to-date on legislation; respect consumers requests, it's their data; communicate, communicate and communicate; if things go wrong, fix it quickly and refer to the previous point; do not leave it to others – focus on how you can drive consumer trust forwards; provide real value to reward your consumers for providing you with their data; and remember data is a luxury, not a commodity.

Brands will get better at this as the technology used in data collection, storage and management evolves, but only if consumers grant permission to use their data to drive campaigns. Such data is priceless as it allows us to build up a complete picture of the consumer and their purchase journey. The Superbrands of the future will be those that use this knowledge to guide their every action. They will be the ones leading from the front in terms of best practice in gathering data, and reaping the business benefits of consumer trust.

Lightspeed GMI is the market researchers' choice for digitally accessing and deriving insight from consumer opinions and behaviors whenever, wherever and in whatever segments needed.

lightspeedgmi.com

Appendix

Superbrands Selection Process

The annual Consumer Superbrands and Business Superbrands surveys aim to identify the UK's strongest business-to-consumer and business-to-business brands respectively.

Brands do not apply or pay to be considered for Superbrand status. For the past eleven years, both surveys have been independently managed by The Centre for Brand Analysis. The key details are:

Consumer Superbrands: Chosen by 3,000 British adults from a list of over 1,500 brands that has been ratified by the independent and voluntary Consumer Superbrands Council.

Business Superbrands: Jointly chosen by 2,500 British business professionals and the independent and voluntary Business Superbrands Council from a list of just under 1,200 brands.

Please visit Superbrands.uk.com for full details of the research methodology.

Definition of a Superbrand

All those involved in the voting process bear in mind the following definition:

'A Superbrand has established the finest reputation in its field. It offers customers significant emotional and/or tangible advantages over its competitors, which customers want and recognise.'

In addition, the voters are asked to judge brands against the following three factors:

- **Quality** – Does the brand provide quality products and services?

- **Reliability** – Can the brand be trusted to deliver consistently?

- **Distinction** – Is it well known in its sector and suitably different from its rivals?

Our Research Partners

As well as managing the overall research process, The Centre for Brand Analysis compiles the initial shortlists and appoints and surveys the Expert Councils. Lightspeed GMI informs the consumer stage of the voting by surveying the British public (for Consumer Superbrands) and business professionals (for Business Superbrands) through its online panels.

About The Centre for Brand Analysis

The Centre for Brand Analysis (TCBA) is a strategic brand consultancy that specialises in internal and external brand equity research and consumer, market and competitor analysis. It uses gathered evidence and insights to create potent brand and marketing strategies that drive competitive advantage.

tcba.co.uk

About Lightspeed GMI

Lightspeed GMI is an award-winning global digital data collection enterprise. Founded in 1996, Lightspeed GMI delivers unparalleled quality, capacity and targeted research, allowing clients to develop comprehensive strategies to help shape their business decisions. Lightspeed GMI is part of Kantar, the data investment management arm of WPP, the world leader in marketing communication services.

lightspeedgmi.com

Introducing
the Experts

The pages that follow give a brief introduction to the members of the Business Superbrands (B) and Consumer Superbrands (C) Expert Councils.

Business Superbrands Council

Uri Baruchin
Strategy Director, The Partners

Richard Bush
Founding Partner, AndPartners

Kirsty Dawe
Managing Director, Really B2B

Gail Dudleston
CEO & Digital Brand Evangelist, twentysix

Steve Dyer
Managing Director, Clockwork IMC

James Farmer
Publisher & Founder, B2B Marketing

Pamela Fieldhouse
CEO, EMA, PPR Worldwide

Helen Hourston
Managing Director, Gate Edinburgh

Kate Howe
Managing Director, Gyro

Jennifer Janson
Managing Director, Six Degrees

Nick Jefferson
Partner, Monticello Partnership LLP

Steve Kemish
Managing Partner, Junction

Mark Lethbridge
CEO, Gravity Global

Stephen Meade
Chief Executive and Founder, McCann Enterprise

Vikki Mitchell
Director, BPRI Group

Rob Morrice
CEO, Stein IAS

Michael Murphy
Senior Partner, Michael Murphy & Ltd

Domini Pettifar
Joint Managing Director, OglivyOne dnx

Amanda Pierce
CEO, Burson-Marsteller UK

Andrew Pinkess
Director of Business Innovation and Consulting, AMV BBDO

Rebecca Price
Partner, Frank, Bright & Abel

Louise Proddow
Founder, Tweak UK

Lucy Purdy
Owner & Director, Rainmakers CSI

Shane Redding
Managing Director, Think Direct

Susanna Simpson
Founder & Managing Director, Limelight

Paul Stallard
Managing Director, Berkeley PR

Matthew Stibbe
CEO, Articulate Marketing

Terry Tyrrell
Worldwide Chairman, The Brand Union

David Willan
Chairman, Circle Research

Alan Wilson PhD
Professor of Marketing, University of Strathclyde Business School

Peter Young
Marketing & Brand Development Specialist, B2B Marketing Awards

Consumer Superbrands Council

Ed Bolton
Creative Director, BrandCap

Emma Brock
Founding Partner, Design Collective London

Vicky Bullen
CEO, Coley Porter Bell

Colin Byrne
CEO, EMEA, Weber Shandwick

Jackie Cooper
Global Chair, Creative Strategy, Edelman

Lee Farrant
Partner, RPM

Cheryl Giovannoni
CEO, Ogilvy & Mather London

Emily Hare
Managing Editor, Contagious Communications

Lucy Hart
Head of Influence, Mischief PR

Lisa Hill
Managing Director Northern Europe, Lambie-Nairn

Jack Horner
Executive Creative Director, FRUKT

Vanella Jackson
Global CEO, Hall & Partners

Ben Kay
CEO, Rainey Kelly Campbell Roalfe Y&R

Debbie Klein
Chief Executive Engine, Chairman WRCS, ENGINE

Nick Liddell
Strategy Director, Dragon Rouge

Andrew Marsden
Master of the Worshipful Company of Marketors

John Mathers
Chief Executive Officer, Design Council

Richard Moss
Chief Executive, Good Relations Brand Communications

James Murphy
Founder & CEO, adam&eveDDB

Natasha Murray
Managing Director, Havas Media

Sam Oxley
PR and Communications Consultant

Jon Puleston
VP of Innovation, Lightspeed GMI

Julian Pullan
Vice Chairman & President International, Jack Morton Worldwide

Crispin Reed
Managing Director, JDO

Gary Robinson & Owen Lee
Executive Creative Directors, FCB Inferno

Nicolas Roope
Creative Partner & Co-Founder, Poke London

Emma Sant
Director, Mash Strategy

Lisa Thomas
CEO, M&C Saatchi Group

Chris Walmsley
Co-Founder & Head of Planning, Cubo

Mark Wickens
Founder, Brandhouse

Stephen Cheliotis

Chairman, Expert Councils,
Chief Executive, The Centre for
Brand Analysis (TCBA)

🐦 @TCBA_London

A leading global brand consultant, Stephen offers strategic business advice and undertakes comprehensive brand and market evaluations. He develops detailed research reports for brand owners and leading consultancies, while also providing consumer and marketing trends and insights. Stephen offers brand commentary for global media and is a Visiting Professor at the London Metropolitan University Business School.

Uri Baruchin Ⓑ

Strategy Director,
The Partners

Uri joined The Partners London in 2011. A senior strategist, he has extensive experience taking on a wide variety of marketing challenges with clients spanning the UK, Europe and the Middle East. His work covers strategy, customer experience and digital environments. At The Partners, Uri's clients include UBS, White & Case, PA Consulting, Deloitte and Kantar. Uri is an active writer on the topic of creative strategy and is also an Associate Lecturer at the London College of communication.

Ed Bolton Ⓒ

Creative Director,
BrandCap

Ed heads up all things creative at BrandCap. A relatively new player, BrandCap holds a unique position in the market – a business consultancy that combines commercial acumen with creative, entrepreneurial brand thinking to transform the performance of organisations everywhere.

Emma Brock Ⓒ

Founding Partner,
Design Collective London

🐦 @emmabrock

Emma specialises in elevating brands. With a background in leading global advertising agencies and brand design consultancies she understands how to build strong, award-winning brands. She talks globally about how to create brand desire. Her client experience includes Diageo, Coca-Cola, Nestlé, Unilever and McDonald's. In 2015 she became a Founding Partner of Design Collective London.

Vicky Bullen Ⓒ

CEO,
Coley Porter Bell

CEO of Coley Porter Bell since 2005, Vicky leads work for brands including Unilever, Tesco and Pernod Ricard, delivering brand strategy, brand architecture solutions, visual identities, naming and innovation. She has a particular interest in how learnings from neuroscience can be practically applied to create beautifully persuasive brands and has led the agency through the development of some guidelines for use by themselves and their clients to make this happen. Vicky also sits on the Ogilvy & Mather UK Group Board.

Richard Bush Ⓑ

Founding Partner,
AndPartners

AndPartners is a new B2B Strategic Consultancy that provides the expertise needed when tackling strategic projects, like rebrands, mergers, or product and proposition development projects, for the first time. Collaborating with agencies and clients they bring the experience needed, but in a way that transfers skills for future projects. Formerly Richard was the CEO of Base One where, for 18 years, he worked with global brands including Vodafone, PayPal, Facebook, Elsevier and Experian.

Colin Byrne Ⓒ

CEO, EMEA,
Weber Shandwick

🐦 @capbyrne

Colin is one of the UK's leading PR practitioners, with 35 years' experience spanning domestic and international communications campaigns for consumer and corporate brands, governments and NGOs. Colin joined Weber Shandwick in 1995 and is now CEO of the global agency's Europe and Africa network – Europe's most award-winning PR agency – and a member of its global management team.

Jackie Cooper Ⓒ

Global Chair, Creative Strategy,
Edelman

🐦 @JackiePRCooper

Jackie is one of the pre-eminent voices and influencers in UK brand marketing today. Jackie sold Jackie Cooper PR to Edelman in 2004 and now serves as Global Chair, Creative Strategy. Jackie oversees the firm's creative offering and the teams across the network, ensuring clients benefit from campaigns that make movements, change worlds and create fame.

Kirsty Dawe Ⓑ

Managing Director,
Really B2B

🐦 @kirstydawe1

Co-Founder and Director of award-winning B2B marketing agency Really B2B – whose work includes campaigns for clients including the BBC, Orange Business Services, Compass Group, Santander and HSBC – Kirsty is also Marketing Director for the MarketMakers group. With a particular interest in emerging B2B channels in the digital space, Kirsty is also a member of the IDM B2B Council.

Gail Dudleston Ⓑ

CEO & Digital Brand Evangelist,
twentysix

Gail is global CEO of twentysix, an award-winning full service digital agency with offices in the UK, Asia and the US. The agency has organically grown since it was started by Gail in 2005, from six to 130-plus talented digital specialists across every digital discipline from digital strategy, design and build, SEO, PPC and Performance Marketing, social and mobile services. One of The Sunday Times Top 100 Best Places to work, in 2015 twentysix's turnover was approximately £10 million.

Steve Dyer Ⓑ

Managing Director,
Clockwork IMC

Steve founded Clockwork IMC, a dedicated B2B integrated agency, in 1993. He has over 20 years' B2B agency experience, supporting various industrial, technology and professional service brands. A strategic communications marketer, he has helped to develop a number of industry initiatives while on the DMA's B2B Committee, and as a past Vice Chair of the Association of Business-to-Business Agencies.

James Farmer Ⓑ

Publisher & Founder,
B2B Marketing

🐦 @MarketingB2B

James Farmer is Founder of the information provider, B2B Marketing. Launched over 10 years ago James has led the business from a small start-up, UK magazine to a global media, with a portfolio of products from business data, news and reports, to events, awards and training. James is also one of the founding members of the marketing association, the Business Marketing Collective.

Lee Farrant ©
Partner,
RPM

Lee manages RPM Ventures, an entrepreneurial arm of the marketing agency RPM, set up to encourage, finance and provide expertise to new business start-ups. He is a sports, marketing and visual image specialist who works with several sports brands, rights holders and governing bodies. As an avid sports fan, he believes in encouraging participation and accessibility to varied sports, at all levels and all ages.

Pamela Fieldhouse ®
CEO, EMA,
PPR Worldwide

🐦 @pamelaf10

A senior communications consultant with more than 20 years' experience of international communications, Pamela specialises in corporate reputation, issues and crisis management, brand strategy and change management. She provides counsel to senior executives from the public and private sectors and advises clients across a range of industry sectors including technology, electronics, retail and financial services.

Cheryl Giovannoni ©
CEO,
Oglivy & Mather London

With a career spent working in the communications industry in both advertising and strategic branding roles, Cheryl is particularly interested in coaching and nurturing young talent, and has written several thought leadership pieces on the role of women in the communications industry. Cheryl has also worked with many multinational clients including Unilever, P&G, BP, M&S, Diageo and Nestlé.

Emily Hare ©
Managing Editor,
Contagious Communications

At Contagious Emily identifies and analyses the most important developments that are driving marketing, business, design, technology and creativity. She is currently a scholar in the 2015/16 Marketing Academy. She has judged at London Innovators Awards and D&AD New Blood Award. She is passionate about mentoring, and mentors at School of Communication Arts 2.0 and through Bloom, a group for women in advertising.

Lucy Hart ©
Head of Influence,
Mischief PR

Lucy heads up the Influencer team at Mischief, one of the country's top consumer PR agencies. She spends her time connecting brands to powerful influencers, creating content partnerships. She's worked in the PR industry for 12 years for a range of brands, from baby food to beer, energy drinks to energy companies.

Lisa Hill ©
Managing Director Northern
Europe, Lambie-Nairn

Lisa joined Lambie-Nairn in 2009 as Executive Client Director and was made Managing Director in London in late 2010 and Managing Director Northern Europe in 2015. Lisa is responsible for the London, Munich and Prague offices and plays a key role in pitching for business, developing key client relationships and mentoring the team. Her experience includes working with ITV, BBC, Pinewood Studios, NatWest, Telecom New Zealand, Panasonic, GroupM, MEC, Mindshare, Pure Radio and Airbus.

Jack Horner ©
Executive Creative Director,
FRUKT

Jack is Executive Creative Director of creative entertainment specialists FRUKT. Part of the IPG network, the company has offices in NYC, LA, Singapore, Milan and Rio and work on campaigns for Coca-Cola, Mastercard, Jagermeister and Sprint.

Helen Hourston ®
Managing Director,
Gate Edinburgh

Helen's passion for brands began back in 1990, when she quit university and accepted a 'Girl Friday' job in a four-strong agency start up. Now, having worked her way up through agencies in the UK and overseas, she is Managing Director of The Gate Worldwide, an award-winning, interactive communications agency, with offices in Edinburgh and London.

Kate Howe ®
Managing Director,
Gyro

🐦 @kateshowe

With agency and client-side experience, Kate has previously worked for DMB&B, Leo Burnett, AMV BBDO and FCB, with brands including Coca-Cola, Sony, McDonald's, Heinz, Post Office and NIVEA. Client-side, Kate worked for Burger King and Gala-Coral Group, serving on the board as Group Marketing Director running multi-channel campaigns across land-based and e-commerce estates of three brands.

Vanella Jackson ©
Global CEO,
Hall & Partners

🐦 @HallandPartners

Having spent 20 years in some of the best UK advertising agencies in the UK, including BBH, AMV and JWT, Vanella now provides inspiration, energy and direction for the team at Hall & Partners. Helping them advice clients on the new ways to build relationships with brands. Vanella has won a UK Woman of the Year award and is a Fellow of The Market Research Society.

Jennifer Janson ®
Managing Director,
Six Degrees

🐦 @JenJanson

Owner of Six Degrees, a specialist reputation management agency serving the science, engineering and technology fields, Jennifer lectures on reputation-related topics. She is author of The Reputation Playbook: a winning formula to help CEOs protect corporate reputation in the digital economy and Co-Founder of My Business Book Club, promoting positive businesses culture through reading.

Nick Jefferson ®
Partner,
Monticello Partnership LLP

🐦 @monticellollop

A partner with the advisory firm, Monticello LLP, Nick is a strategy consultant, with particular expertise in the space where brand meets culture. An Englishman who speaks Spanish and French, he works all over the world. Nick writes a weekly column for the Marketing Society, and is a regular contributor to both the Huffington Post and Campaign Magazine. He sits on the advisory boards of both the Design Council and Innovation Capital Advisors.

Ben Kay ©
CEO,
Rainey Kelly Campbell
Roalfe Y&R

Ben has been CEO of RKCR/Y&R since 2011. Prior to this he was Chief Strategy Officer from September 2009 after five years at the agency, two of which he spent as the agency's Head of Planning. RKCR/Y&R is home to brands as diverse as M&S, Emirates, BBC, TUI and Oxfam. Previously Ben has spent 15 years working within WPP since being hired as a graduate on the WPP Fellowship, demonstrating extraordinary loyalty or lack of imagination, depending who you talk to.

Steve Kemish ®
Managing Partner,
Junction

🐦 @skemmo

Past Chair of the IDM Digital Council and a member of the DMA future proofing group, Steve has nearly 20 years' experience in digital marketing. Having worked client-side in B2B and B2C, he offers considerable hands-on expertise and has worked on digital marketing strategy with global brands including Motorola, ITV, Skype, BBC, British Airways and Oracle.

Debbie Klein ©
Chief Executive Engine,
Chairman WRCS, ENGINE

🐦 @girlfromafrica

Starting out at Saatchi & Saatchi, Debbie became Head of Planning at WCRS in 1999 and Chief Executive in 2005. She has been Chief Executive of Engine – the UK's largest independent communications company – since 2010. Debbie is author of the influential study Women in Advertising: 10 Years On and was named The Drum's Woman of the Year in 2014.

Mark Lethbridge ®
CEO,
Gravity Global

Specialising in brand development, Mark is the founder and CEO of Gravity Global, a specialist B2B marketing and communications agency which represents global brands. Mark is also President of MAGNET which acts for more than 800 brands worldwide setting best practice in global marketing and communications across 42 agency locations. Prior to this, Mark founded and was CEO of the AGA Group – a communications group focused on B2B and brand development. Mark held this post for more than 20 years.

Nick Liddell ©
Strategy Director,
Dragon Rouge

🐦 @baronsauvage

In his current role, Nick is responsible for ensuring that creativity is underpinned by great ideas. Previously, Nick was Global Strategy Director at Clear and spent seven years at Interbrand, where he was Director of Brand Valuation. He's worked his way through an alphabet of the world's biggest brands, including Amex, BP, Durex, GE, Guinness, HTC, Nissan, Prada and Samsung.

Andrew Marsden ©
Master of the Worshipful
Company of Marketors

After 30 years in FMCG businesses, Andrew is now a brand consultant and also has a non-executive portfolio. He served on the Governmental Advisory Committee on Advertising, is former Chairman of the Institute of Promotional Marketing and past President of The Marketing Society. He was Chairman of The Advertising Standards Authority Code Review and is Master of the Worshipful Company of Marketors.

John Mathers ©
CEO,
Design Council

🐦 @johnmathers2

John is CEO of the Design Council, appointed to assist its transition from government body to enterprising charity. The Design Council exists to champion and promote the use of design, to transform the way people live their lives. His career has previously spanned marketing in the private sector as well as running a number of well known brand and design agencies.

Stephen Meade ®
Chief Executive and Founder,
McCann Enterprise

Stephen is Founder and CEO of McCann Enterprise, a corporate and B2B specialist agency with McCann Worldgroup, having previously been European and then UK Head of Planning for McCann. Prior to joining McCann, he was Managing Director of Springpoint and spent some 15 years at both Publicis and HHCL, which was named Campaign's Agency of the Decade in 2000.

Vikki Mitchell ®
Director,
BPRI Group

Vikki is a specialist in branding and positioning, corporate reputation and creative development research. She regularly partners with FTSE brands to align insight with corporate and communications strategies, delivering optimal impact for her clients. Vikki sits on the BIG Group board – representing B2B research and market intelligence services – is a frequent speaker at B2B events and writes articles for various business and research magazines.

Rob Morrice ®
Global CEO,
Stein IAS

Under Rob's guidance, Stein IAS has become a truly global B2B agency force. Named Business Marketing Association's B2B Agency of the Year four times, it has collected numerous global B2B awards since its inception in 2013. With locations across North America, EMEA and APAC, Stein IAS works with brands including Samsung, Chicago Board Options Exchange, Iron Mountain, Juniper Networks, Ricoh, Ingredion and Trelleborg.

Richard Moss ©
Chief Executive,
Good Relations Brand
Communications

Richard currently runs one of the UK's leading PR and content agencies. Starting his career in FMCG marketing, managing the Andrex, Carlsberg and Mr Kipling brands, he moved into Public Relations some 15 years ago. Today his agency's clients include Subway, Airbus and Samsung.

James Murphy ©
Founder & CEO,
adam&eveDDB

adam&eveDDB is one of the UK's leading creative agencies and was recently awarded the coveted Cannes Lions Agency of the Year title. Clients include John Lewis, Google, Foster's, Volkswagen, Harvey Nichols, YouTube and the FT, as well as numerous charities including Save the Children and Changing Faces.

Michael Murphy Ⓑ

Senior Partner,
Michael Murphy & Ltd

Following a long and distinguished career in public relations – latterly as global CEO of Grayling – Michael is now as Partner in his own advisory firm, Michael Murphy & Ltd, providing non-executive and advisory services around the world. Passionate about helping early-stage businesses to develop and prosper, Michael loves watching and participating in sport and is a fan of all things Scottish.

Natasha Murray Ⓒ

Managing Director,
Havas Media

🐦 @frickermurray

Natasha joined Havas Media in 2000. With Meaningful Brands™ at the heart of Havas Media, Natasha's passion is to provide solutions that truly make a difference to their clients' businesses. She also focuses on ensuring that meaningfulness applies to the agency and its people as much as it does to clients.

Sam Oxley Ⓒ

PR and Communications
Constulant

Sam Oxley is an independent PR and communications consultant with over 16 years' industry experience. Sam was previously Company Director at House PR in London, where she worked on a diverse client portfolio across consumer and entertainment brands including Sailor Jerry Rum (UK and global), Remy Cointreau UK, Absolut Vodka, Peugeot, MTV and the BBC.

Domini Pettifar Ⓑ

Joint Managing Director,
OglivyOne dnx

Domini is Joint Managing Director of OgilvyOne dnx, the UK's largest dedicated B2B Customer Engagement Agency. Clients include IBM, Barco, Cisco and EY. Prior to founding dnx, Domini's agency career was spent at Dorlands, DMB&B and Publicis, working on both B2B and B2C brands.

Amanda Pierce Ⓑ

CEO,
Burson-Marsteller UK

🐦 @BMUKNews

Having headed Burson-Marsteller's UK Corporate & Crisis team, Amanda was appointed UK CEO in June 2013. An award-winning corporate communications professional, she has worked with some of the world's leading companies including Shell, Amazon, Kimberly-Clark and GSK. Previously, she was Head of Media and Internal Communications at McDonald's UK.

Andrew Pinkess Ⓑ

Director of Business Innovation
and Consulting,
AMV BBDO

🐦 @apinkess

Andrew is responsible for helping the agency and its clients deal with the impact of technology disruption and the opportunities of new marketing. Previously he was Director of Strategy & Insight at marketing technology agency LBi, and has experience in advertising, brand consultancy, marketing and digital strategy.

Rebecca Price Ⓑ

Partner, Frank,
Bright & Abel

🐦 @FrankBrightAbel

Rebecca is a brand strategist and communications specialist. She has a knack for finding what matters and expressing it well, and knows that the right creative expression is about so much more than design alone. She is Co-Founder and Partner of creative consultancy Frank, Bright & Abel.

Louise Proddow Ⓑ

Founder,
Tweak UK

🐦 @tweakuk

A global business leader and entrepreneur, Louise founded Tweak Marketing in 2011. She has also held senior executive positions at Nokia, Dell, and Sun Microsystems. She is a passionate pioneer of branding and marketing and has launched successful technology start-ups. With a career that has embraced branding innovation and commercialism for more than 25 years, Louise is also the author of two books.

Jon Puleston Ⓒ

VP of Innovation,
Lightspeed GMI

Jon is VP of Innovation of Lightspeed GMI, a Kantar business, where he heads an international team called QuestionArts specialising in the copy writing and design of surveys. He acts as a consultant on survey design techniques for companies around the world. He and his team have won multiple awards for their ground-breaking work exploring survey design methodology and, in particular, for is work in the field of gamification of research.

Julian Pullan Ⓒ

Vice Chairman & President
International,
Jack Morton Worldwide

Julian is Vice Chairman and President International of brand experience agency Jack Morton Worldwide. Rated among the top global brand experience agencies, Jack Morton Worldwide integrates live and online experiences, digital and social media, as well as branded environments that engage consumers, business partners and employees for leading brands everywhere.

Lucy Purdy Ⓑ

Owner & Director,
Rainmakers CSI

As Director of Rainmakers CSI, a customer strategy consultancy, Lucy helps B2B clients define the next opportunity for business growth through the application of market and customer insights. She is an international customer and brand strategist and previously a Planning Director at JWT and Y&R in New York, as well as Publicis in the UK.

Shane Redding Ⓑ

Managing Director,
Think Direct

Shane is an independent consultant providing digital, direct and data-led marketing consultancy. Shane provides strategic advice and practical training to large corporates as well as SMEs looking to grow profitably. A successful serial entrepreneur, Shane is an honorary fellow of the IDM and holds multiple NEDs.

Crispin Reed ©
Managing Director,
JDO

🐦 @crispinreed

Crispin has worked in leading global advertising and design agencies, brand consultancy as well as client-side in the fragrance and beauty sectors. An associate of Ashridge Management College, Crispin sits on the Advisory Boards of the Global Marketing Network and the Branded Content Marketing Association and is co-author of The 7 Myths of Middle Age – Implications for Marketing and Brands.

Gary Robinson & Owen Lee ©
Executive Creative Directors,
FCB Inferno

Owen and Gary have spent their career creating advertising for household names as diverse as BMW and first direct to Tango and Oreo. They have worked at a number of high profile creative agencies from Chiat/Day in the US to HHCL when it was named agency of the decade in the in 1990s. They were founder members of St. Lukes, the first advertising agency co-operative and they ran their own agency, Farm Communications for over 10 years. They now oversee the creative department of FCB Inferno.

Nicolas Roope ©
Creative Partner & Co-Founder,
Poke London

🐦 @nikroope

Nicolas is an impassioned digital and design visionary. He is Founder and Creative Director at Poke. He also founded and creatively directs cult electronics brand, Hulger, maker of the world's first designer energy saving light bulb, The Plumen 001. He is also the Co-Founder of The Lovie Awards.

Emma Sant ©
Director,
Mash Strategy

🐦 @Mashsocial

Specialising in landing ideas within businesses to drive growth, Emma works across a wide variety of sectors from technology and services to pharma and FMCG. She has led innovation projects, segmentation studies, global training programmes, and strategic implication workshops. She has recently developed a cutting-edge behaviour change model, to identify trigger strategies for in-market activation.

Susanna Simpson Ⓑ
Founder & Managing Director,
Limelight

🐦 @SusannaSimpson

Susanna is Founder of Limelight, which exists to give talented and ambitious businesses the recognition they deserve. Limelight's major skill lies in building business thought leaders for corporately and privately owned companies. Working exclusively in the B2B sector, Limelight delivers reputation-driven growth for businesses including Saatchi & Saatchi, VW, Pinsent Masons, St Ives Group plc and Telefonica.

Paul Stallard Ⓑ
Managing Director,
Berkeley PR

🐦 @Paul_Stallard

Paul is Managing Director of Berkeley PR and a passionate believer in the power of story. The agency helps digital, technology and consumer companies get the recognition they deserve, both online and offline, by creating highly newsworthy ideas that grab attention and drive action.

Matthew Stibbe Ⓑ
CEO,
Articulate Marketing

🐦 @wearearticulate

Matthew is CEO of Articulate Marketing, a B2B inbound marketing agency that specialises in technology clients, including Microsoft, LinkedIn, Symantec and HP. He is also founder of TurbineHQ.com, a web application that simplifies purchase orders, expense claims and time off requests. He writes for the popular Bad Language blog at www.articulatemarketing.com/blog.

Lisa Thomas ©
CEO,
M&C Saatchi Group

Lisa was promoted to CEO of the M&C Saatchi UK Group in 2010 – under her leadership the group has enjoyed notable growth. Most recently, in 2014, she championed the acquisition of award-winning digital agency, Lean Mean Fighting Machine. Lisa joined M&C Saatchi to launch a direct marketing business – LIDA opened for business in 2000 and was awarded Customer Engagement Agency of the Year in both 2013 and 2014.

Terry Tyrrell Ⓑ
Worldwide Chairman,
The Brand Union

Terry co-founded The Brand Union in 1976 and today it employs more than 500 people in 23 offices across the world. Responsible for major corporate branding programmes, Terry leads teams across The Brand Union network. Recently these included UBS, Shell, HSBC, Credit Suisse, SABMiller, Qatar National Bank and Fidelity Investments. Terry is a trustee of the Design Council.

Chris Walmsley ©
Co-Founder & Head of Planning,
Cubo

Chris co-founded Cubo in the same year Superbrands was born – 1995. In the ensuing 21 years Chris and his team have developed a distinctive way to tackle the growing indifference to marketing communications. Cubo's approach centres around finding creative ways for brands to engage with people by making a contribution to their lives through their communications.

Mark Wickens ©
Founder,
Brandhouse

Mark founded Brandhouse in 1989 as the first Brand Agency, uniting brand consultancy and design agency skills under one roof. His work gave Tango iconic status. Mark has led projects for Britvic, GSK, Kellogg's, Mars and Unilever, and is currently helping a number of brands harness the power of emotion through branding. Brandhouse is now part of Hangar Seven, the UK's fastest growing content creation agency.

David Willan Ⓑ
Chairman,
Circle Research

A Co-Founder of BPRI (now part of WPP), David has worked in B2B marketing research for more years than he's prepared to admit to. A frequent contributor to the likes of B2B Marketing, David is also a guest speaker at Ashridge Business School. He is currently Chairman of B2B marketing research agency Circle Research and works as a practitioner in branding, development and customer relationship management.

Alan Wilson PhD Ⓑ

Professor of Marketing,
University of Strathclyde
Business School

🐦 @ProfAlanWilson

Alan is a Professor of Marketing at the University
of Strathclyde Business School. Before joining the
University, he was a Senior Consultant at a London-
based marketing consultancy. He has written numerous
articles on corporate reputation, customer experience
management and branding, and is a fellow of both
the Chartered Institute of Marketing and the Market
Research Society.

Peter Young ⒷB

Marketing & Brand
Development Specialist,
B2B Marketing Awards

Peter is Chairman of the B2B Marketing Awards,
Consultant and Non-Executive Director helping
businesses establish more effective supplier
relationships, and advising on marketing and
brand planning. Formerly a member of board level
management teams in Europe-wide consultancies,
he has helped grow brands in the service and
product categories ranging from major PLCs to
government departments.

Highlights of the 2016 Results

By Stephen Cheliotis

Chairman, Expert Councils and Chief Executive, The Centre for Brand Analysis (TCBA)

It's not unusual, when sitting down to write my annual review of the Superbrands results, to note the incredible consistency of many leading brands. It's also not uncommon to reference the difficultly other brands face breaking into the Top 20, especially younger brands who, despite garnering plenty of media attention and even shaking up established sectors, have yet to build enough brand value across the UK to challenge proven, reputable businesses. This year the stranglehold incumbent leading-brands enjoy has been particularly marked, reinforcing their reputational advantage and its role in protecting their businesses' market position.

Only one brand in the Business Superbrands Top 20 didn't feature last year, British pharmaceutical giant GlaxoSmithKline. It is no stranger to the top group having regularly featured recently, albeit not in the last two years. In the Consumer Superbrands Top 20, only four brands entered the top group afresh. Like GlaxoSmithKline in the business-to-business survey, these new entries are not challenger brands or rising stars but brands that have been in and out of the Top 20 over the last five years and are therefore no strangers to the elite placing.

Changes in many markets may be accelerating, the shift in attitudes and behaviours of consumer and business professionals may be hastening and new tools, platform and products speedily introduced, but ultimately the familiarity and track-record of major, established brands

has ensured they are often reverted to by those seeking options they can trust and rely on. Whether perceived brand leaders in a personal or professional capacity, brands that have clearly demonstrated their capabilities time and time again, throughout ours lives, are rewarded with considerable goodwill and belief.

Demonstrating this trend is the remarkable performance of our 'national airline' British Airways, which has managed to fend off all competitors to retain the number one position in both the Consumer and Business Superbrands rankings. The airline fended off 1,576 brands in the consumer survey and 1,429 brands in the business-to-business equivalent, proving that whether we are talking to ordinary Joes or leading business executives, British Airways continues to be deemed a perfect representation of a brand that embodies quality, reliability and distinction; the three facets inherent in a Superbrand that voters are asked to consider when judging the lists.

Inside the Consumer Superbrands Top 20 there was, of course, the usual jostling for position. For instance LEGO, still reaping the benefits of its first film and the launch of new ranges linked to Star Wars and Jurassic park, continues its remarkable renaissance

by taking third position, up eight places from last year. Dyson in fourth was, once again, also a fairly noteworthy mover within the Top 20, climbing 10 places. Heinz too recovered from its fall last year to 21st regaining its Top 20 berth, moving nine places back up the table.

Conversely the biggest faller within the Top 20 was US tech giant Microsoft, which dropped 16 places. There were four brands that dropped out of the Consumer Superbrands Top 20 altogether, with the biggest among these being the BBC. Only once in recent times has the British public broadcaster not been in the top five, let alone the Top 20, so its fall of 20 places to 23rd might be a worry. The attention on the broadcaster's funding, various 'attacks' by the Government and negative perceptions of its coverage of the Scottish independence debate might have taken a toll on its latest performance. Nevertheless, one suspects that the BBC could bounce back next year if these issues die down, rather than this fall representing the start of further decline. Much will depend on the political and funding situation over the next few years and what the BBC charter renewal looks like and how that is received at large.

The other brands dipping out of the Top 20 are those that I have described previously as yo-yo brands – rising and falling in and out of the top group. One can assume that for some of these the drop is just part of this continuous pattern, rather than a tipping point toward a consistent downward spiral. The fact that all three – Boots, Fairy and BMW – fell less than 10 places backs up this theory. Equally, the re-entry in to the Top 20 of brands, such as Marks & Spencer, that have perhaps not fundamentally updated their positioning or offering, suggests the erosion of goodwill is a very slow process indeed.

Nevertheless some iconic brands, such as Cadbury and Sony, that fell out of the Top 20 last year have not regained their positions, so recovery and a continuation of the pattern of dipping in and out of the elite group is certainly not guaranteed. In both these cases the brands have continued to fall quite meaningfully. Looking at the data over a longer period some established brands have struggled to regain momentum, re-engage with consumers or recapture their perceived leadership. In these cases the break in the bond between consumer and brand might be so severe as to represent a genuine fall that will not be short-lived or recovered. At least these genuine faders open up opportunities for the challengers, facing such headwinds in breaking into the top group.

Of the fallers in this year's Top 20, BMW might be especially disappointed that the gap between it and German rival Mercedes-Benz continues to grow. Having outperformed its peer two years ago, its rival overtook it last year before extending its lead this time out. Reinforcing that concern is the re-emergence of Jaguar, which jumped a very significant 22 places to drive into eighth.

In Business Superbrands only one brand

fell out the Top 20, the Rolls-Royce Group. Its reputation possibly suffered from profit warnings and bribery allegations in the last year. Still, lying just outside the Top 20 this British engineering icon, key manufacturer and exporter should, if it solves these short-term issues, regain its reputational strength. Only five brands shifted more than five ranking places year-on-year in the Business Superbrands top group. In the ascendancy the biggest mover was PayPal, which continues to rise up the table. Having climbed 13 places, it has overtaken older rivals Visa and MasterCard for the first time despite both competitors remaining in the top group, albeit marginally down on last year. BP too rose, moving up eight places to settle in ninth. Its rival Shell also moved back up six places to sit just behind BP in twelfth. Conversely descending more than five positions were FedEx, down nine, and Johnson & Johnson, down seven. The pharmaceutical and consumer healthcare titan had re-entered the Top 20 last time, having been absent for the last two years, but could not consolidate its revival. FedEx meanwhile risk falling out the top group like its competitor DHL, which dropped out of the Top 20 in 2015 and has not climbed back this time around. Despite the importance of the distribution sector in enabling the internet economy, the Royal Mail too risks falling outside the top group next year, it is currently just clinging on in 20th place.

As is the case every year, no brands submitted an entry to be included in the survey, instead the leading brands operating across key sectors in the UK are considered in the respective consumer and business-to-business programmes. A total of 2,500 consumers voted this year in the consumer

survey, while 31 leading business-to-business marketing experts and 2,500 business professionals voted on the business-to-business list, with the two audience views combined on an equal weighting.

With the votes tallied and the league tables created, it is clear that the leading brands

continue to maintain their power and position in the hearts and minds of voters. Can newer brands nevertheless challenge some of those established brands that are falling, rather than dipping temporarily? Which of the challenger brands will achieve this feat, and when? We will be back next year to discover.

RANK	CONSUMER SUPERBRANDS	BUSINESS SUPERBRANDS
1	British Airways	British Airways
2	Rolex	Apple
3	LEGO	PayPal
4	Dyson	Google
5	Gillette	Microsoft
6	Mercedes-Benz	Visa
7	Apple	Virgin Atlantic
8	Jaguar	MasterCard
9	Kellogg's	BP
10	Andrex	IBM
11	Nike	American Express
12	Heinz	Shell
13	Coca-Cola	Bosch
14	John Lewis	GlaxoSmithKline
15	Häagen-Dazs	Samsung
16	Google	BT
17	Virgin Atlantic	FedEx
18	Marks & Spencer	Johnson & Johnson
19	Amazon.co.uk	Boeing
20	Microsoft	Royal Mail

Qualifying Business Superbrands

3M
ABB
Abbott
ABI (Association of
  British Insurers)
ABPI (The Association
  of the British
  Pharmaceutical
  Industry)
ABTA
Acas (Advisory,
  Conciliation &
  Arbitration Service)
ACCA (The Association
  of Chartered
  Certified
  Accountants)
Accenture
Access Self Storage
Acer
Actavis
Addison Lee
Adecco
Adobe
ADT
Aegis
Aegon
Aggregate Industries
Aggreko
AgustaWestland
AIG
AIM
Air Liquide
Airbus
AkzoNobel
Alcatel-Lucent
Alcoa
Allen & Overy
Allianz
Alstom
Amcor
AMD
Amec Foster Wheeler
American Express
American Express
  Travel
Amey
Anglo American
AOL Advertising
Aon
A-Plant
Apple
ArcelorMittal
Arco
ARM
Arriva
Arup
Ashridge Business
  School
Associated British Ports
AstraZeneca
Atkins
Atlas Copco
Atos
Autodesk
Autoglass
Avanti Communications
Avery
AVEVA
Aviva
Avon Rubber plc
AXA
Babcock
BAE Systems
Bain & Company
Baker & McKenzie
Balfour Beatty
BAM Nuttall
Bank of America
  Merrill Lynch
Bank of Scotland

Barclaycard
Barclays
BASF
Baxi
Baxter
Bayer
BBA Aviation
BCG (Boston
  Consulting Group)
BDA (British Dental
  Association)
BDO
Belfast Waterfront
Bell Pottinger
Best Western
Bestway
BG Group
BHP Billiton
Bibby Line
Biffa
Big Yellow
Bird & Bird
Black & Decker
BlackBerry
Bloomberg
Bloomsbury Professional
Blue Arrow
BMA (British Medical
  Association)
BMC
BNP Paribas Real Estate
BOC
Boehringer Ingelheim
Boeing
Bombardier
Booker
Bosch
Bournemouth
  International
  Centre (BIC)
BP
BPP Professional
  Education
Braemar Shipping
  Services plc
Brakes Group
Brandon Hire
Brewers
Bristol-Myers Squibb
British Airways
British Chambers of
  Commerce (BCC)
British Council
British Gas
  Business Energy
British Gypsum
British Land
British Retail
  Consortium
Brook Street
Brother
Brunswick
Bruntwood
BSI
BT
Buildbase
Bunzl
Bupa
Bywaters
CA Technologies
Calor
Cambridge Judge
  Business School
Canary Wharf Group
Cannon Hygiene
Canon
Capco
Capgemini
Capita
Capital & Regional
Cargill

Carillion
Carlson Wagonlit
  Travel
Carr's Group
Carter Jonas
Casio
Cass Business School
Castrol
Caterpillar
CBI
CBRE
CEMEX
Centaur Live
Central Hall Westminster
Chartered Institute
  of Building (CIOB)
Chevron
Christie + Co
Chubb Fire & Security
Chubb Insurance
CIMA (Chartered
  Institute of
  Management
  Accountants)
CIPD
Cisco
Citi
City & Guilds
City Plumbing Supplies
CityJet
CitySprint
Clancy Docwra
Clear Channel
Clifford Chance
Clyde & Co
CMI (Chartered
  Management
  Institute)
Compass Group
Computacenter
ConocoPhillips UK
Co-operatives UK
Costain
Cosworth
Countrywide Waste
  Management Ltd
Cranfield School
  of Management
Credit Suisse
Crowdcube
Crowdfunder
Crown Trade Paints
Crowne Plaza
Cummins Inc.
Daikin
Datamonitor
Datanet
DCC Environmental
De La Rue
De Vere Venues
Dell
Deloitte
Deloitte Real Estate
Derwent London
Deutsche Bank
Devro
DeWALT
DHL
Digital Cinema
  Media (DCM)
Direct Line
DLA Piper
Dow
DPD
Draper Tools
Dropbox
DRS (Direct Rail Services)
DS Smith
Dulux Trade
Dun & Bradstreet
DuPont

Durham University
  Business School
E.ON
easyJet
Easynet
Ecolab
Eddie Stobart
Edelman
EDF Energy
Electricity North West
Elmwood
Elopak
Elsevier
EMAP
EMC
Engine
Epson
Equifax
Equinix
Ericsson
Euronext
Eurostar
Eurotunnel
EventCity
Eversheds
ExCeL London
Experian
ExxonMobil
EY
Fairtrade Foundation
FCC Environmental
Federation of Small
  Businesses (FSB)
FedEx
First
First Security
First Utility
Fisher Scientific
Fitch Group
Flybe
Forrester
Forth Ports
Fowler Welch
Freightliner Group
Freshfields Bruckhaus
  Deringer
FSC (Forest
  Stewardship
  Council)
FTSE Russell
Fujitsu
Funding Circle
G4S
Galliford Try
Gallup
Gartner
Gatwick Express
GE
General Dynamics UK
GfK
GKN
GlaxoSmithKline
Glencore
Goldman Sachs
Google
GRAHAM
Grant Thornton
Great Portland
  Estates
Green Energy UK
Greenergy
Grey London
Grosvenor
Groundforce
Hall & Partners
Halliburton
Hammerson
Hanson
Hapag-Lloyd
Harris
Harvey Nash

Hawker Siddeley
  Switchgear
Hay Group
Haymarket
Hays
Heathrow Express
Henley Business
  School
Henry Boot
  Developments
Heron International
Hewden
Hilti
Hilton Food Group
Hilton Hotels
  & Resorts
Hire Station
Hiscox
Hitachi
Hogan Lovells
Holiday Inn
Honeywell
Howden
Howdens Joinery
HP
HRG
HSBC
HSS Hire
Huawei
IBM
ICAEW
Icap Securities
  & Derivatives
  Exchange (ISDX)
ICM
Imagination
  Technologies
IMI
Imperial College
  London Business School
Inchcape Shipping
  Services
INEOS
Informa
Infosys
Initial
Inmarsat
Intel
Intelsat
Interlink Express
International Paper
Interserve
Intuit
Investec
Investors in People
Invista
IoD (Institute of
  Directors)
Ipsos MORI
Iridium
iris
Iron Mountain
Irwin Mitchell
ISS
J. Walter Thompson
  London
J.P. Morgan
JCB
JCDecaux
Jewson
JobServe
Jobsite
John Deere
John Dennis
  Coachbuilders
Johnson & Johnson
Johnson Matthey
Johnson Service Group
Johnstone's Trade
Juniper Networks
Kantar Media

Kaplan
Kaspersky Lab
Kelly Services
Keyline
Kickstarter
Kidde
Kier Group
KIMBERLY-CLARK
  PROFESSIONAL
Kingspan Group
Kingston Smith
Knight Frank
Komatsu
Kompass
KONE
KPMG
Kroll
Kuehne + Nagel
Lafarge Tarmac
Laing O'Rourke
Laird plc
Lambert Smith
  Hampton
Land Securities
learndirect
Lenovo
Leo Burnett London
LexisNexis
Lexmark
Leyland Trade
LG
Liebherr
Lilly
Linklaters
LINPAC Packaging
Lloyds Bank
Lloyd's
Lockheed Martin
Logitech
London Business School
London Business
  School
London Metal
  Exchange
London School
  of Economics and
  Political Science (LSE)
London Stock
  Exchange Group
Loomis
Lyreco
M&C Saatchi
Mace
Macfarlanes
Maersk Line
Magnet Trade
Makita
Manchester
  Business School
Manchester Central
Manpower
Marriott Hotels
  & Resorts
Marshalls
Martin-Baker
Massey Ferguson
MasterCard
McAfee
McCann London
McGee
McKinsey & Company
MEC
MediaCom
Medtronic
Menzies
Menzies Aviation
Menzies Distribution
Mercer
Mercure Hotels
Metro Radio Arena
  Newcastle
Michael Page

Micron Technology
Microsoft
Microsoft Advertising
Miller Developments
Millward Brown
Mindshare
Mintel
Misys
Mitie
Mitsubishi Electric
Mondi
Monsanto
Monster
Moody's
Morgan Sindall
Morgan Stanley
Mother London
Mott MacDonald
Munich Re
Murphy
National Express
National Grid
NATS
NatWest
NETGEAR
NetSuite
New Holland
NFU (National
  Farmers' Union)
NFU Mutual
Nielsen
Nokia Networks
Northern Gas
  Networks
Northern Powergrid
Northgate
Northrop Grumman
Norton
Nottingham University
  Business School
Novartis
Novo Nordisk
Novotel
npower
NVIDIA
Office Angels
Office Depot
Ogilvy & Mather
  Group
Olympus
OMD UK
Oracle
Orion Group
Osborne Clarke
Osram
Otis
OVO
Oxford BioMedica
P&O Ferrymasters
Panasonic
Parcelforce
  Worldwide
Park Inn by Radisson
Park Plaza
Parker Hannifin
PayPal
PayPoint
Pearl & Dean
Pertemps
Petrofac
Pfizer
PHD
Philips Healthcare
Philips Lighting
PHS Group
Pickfords
Pilkington
Pinsent Masons
Pipe Center
Pitman Training
Pitney Bowes

PKF International
Plumb Center
Plumbase
Plusnet
Polypipe
Portakabin
Portman Travel
Premier Farnell
Premier Inn
Premier Oil
Prudential
Publicis London
PwC
QA
QinetiQ
Qualcomm
Quintain
Rackspace
Radisson Blu
  Edwardian, London
Ramada
Randstad
RAPP
Raytheon
Razorfish
RBS (Royal Bank
  of Scotland)
Redbox
Reed
Reed Exhibitions
Regus
Rentokil
Research Now
Rexam
RIBA (The Royal
  Institute of British
  Architects)
Ricoh
Ricoh Arena
RICS (Royal Institution
  of Chartered Surveyors)
Rio Tinto
RM Education
Roche
Rockwell Collins
Rolls-Royce Group
Rothschild Group
Royal Mail
RS Components
RSA
Ryanair
Ryder
Ryman
Saatchi & Saatchi
Safestore
Sage
Said Business School,
  University of Oxford
Saint-Gobain
Salesforce.com
Samsung
SanDisk
Sandvik
Sanofi
Santander
SAP
SAS
Savills
Scania Group
Schillings
Schindler
Schneider Electric
Scottish & Southern
  Power Distribution
Scottish Exhibition
  and Conference
  Centre (SECC)
Scottish Hydro
ScottishPower
Screwfix
Seaco

Securitas
Seedrs
SEGRO
Selco
Select Appointments
Serco
Shanks Group
Sharp
Shell
Sheraton Hotels
  & Resorts
Shire
Shred-it
Siemens
SIG plc
Sikorsky
Simmons & Simmons
Simplyhealth
Sir Robert McAlpine
SITA UK
Sitel
Skanska
SKF
Slaughter & May
Smart Metering
  Systems
SmartWater
Smith & Nephew
Smith & Williamson
Smiths Group
Smiths News
Smurfit Kappa
Snap-on
Sodexo
Sofitel
Sony Professional
Sophos
Speedy
SSE Enterprise
Stagecoach
Standard & Poor's
Stanley
Staples
Starcom MediaVest
Stobart Group
Strutt & Parker
SunGard
Swiss Re
Swissport
Symantec
Syngenta
TalkTalk Business
Tata Consultancy
  Services (TCS)
Tata Steel
Tate & Lyle
Taylor Wessing
Telesat
Teradata
Tetra Pak
Texas Instruments
Thales Group
The Baltic Exchange
The Billington Group
The ICC Birmingham
The Institute
  of Financial
  Accountants (IFA)
The Law Society
The London Platinum
  and Palladium
  Market
The NEC
The Open University
  Business School
The Press
  Association (PA)
The Publishers
  Association
The Weir Group
Thistle Hotels

Thomson Local
Thomson Reuters
Thwaites
ThyssenKrupp
TNS
TNT
TomTom Telematics
Toolstation
Toshiba
Total
Totaljobs.com
Travelodge
Travis Perkins
Trend Micro
Triumph Group, Inc.
Tullow Oil
UK Mail
Unipart Group
Unisys
United Technologies
University of
  Bath School Of
  Management
University of
  Edinburgh
  Business School
University of
  Glasgow Adam
  Smith Business
  School
UPS
Vaillant
Vent-Axia
Venue Cymru
Veolia UK
Viking
Virgin Atlantic
Virgin Media Business
Virgin Trains
Viridor
Visa
VMware
Volvo Construction
  Equipment
Warwick Business
  School
Waterlogic
Wates
WCRS
Weber Shandwick
Western Power
  Distribution
Western Union
Westfield Group
WeTransfer
Wickes
Wieden+Kennedy
  London
Willis Towers Watson
Willmott Dixon
Wincanton
Wolff Olins
Wolseley
Wood Group
Woolmark
Workspace
Worldpay
Xchanging
Xerox
Yahoo Advertising
Yale
Yell
Yodel
YouGov
Zenith
ZenithOptimedia
Zimmer
Zurich

Please note that some brand names have been changed since the research was conducted. These lists reflect the brands as they are generally marketed (at the time of going to press) and may differ slightly from the name analysed in the survey.

Qualifying Consumer Superbrands

3
7-Up
AA
Absolut
Accurist
Actimel
Activia
adidas
AEG
After Eight
Airfix
Aldi
Alfa Romeo
Alka-Seltzer
Allinson
Alpen
Alton Towers
Always
Amazon.co.uk
Ambre Solaire
Ambrosia
American Express
Anadin
Anchor
Andrex
Ann Summers
Apple
Aptamil
Aquafresh
Argos
Ariel
Arm & Hammer
Arsenal FC
ASDA
Audi
Aunt Bessie's
Auto Trader
Autoglass
Avis
Aviva
AXA
B&Q
Bacardi
Baileys
Bakers
Barclaycard
Barclays
Barratt Homes
Bassett's
Batchelors
Baxters
BBC
BBC Children in Need
Beck's
Beechams
Ben & Jerry's
Benecol
Benylin
Berghaus
Bertolli
BIC
Birds Eye
Bisto
Black & Decker
Blue Dragon
BMW
Bob Martin
Bodyform
Bold
Bombay Sapphire
Bonjela
Boots
Bosch
Bose
Boursin
Bovril
BP
Branston
Braun
Bridgestone

Britax
British Airways
British Gas
British Heart
    Foundation
British Red Cross
Britvic
Brylcreem
BT
BT Sport
Budweiser
Bulmers
Bupa
Burger King
Buxton
Cadbury
Café Rouge
Caffè Nero
CALPOL
Campbell's
Cancer Research UK
Canon
Capital FM
Captain Morgan
Carling
Carlsberg
Carphone
    Warehouse
Carte D'Or
Carte Noire
Castrol
Cath Kidston
Cathedral City
Center Parcs
Centrum
Cesar
Channel 4
Charles
    Worthington
Chelsea FC
Chessington World
    of Adventures
Chivas Regal
Churchill
Cif
Cineworld
Clarks
Classic FM
Clearasil
Coca-Cola
Coca-Cola London Eye
Colgate
Colman's
Comfort
Comic Relief
comparethemarket.com
Continental
Converse
Corsodyl
Costa
Courvoisier
Cow & Gate
Cravendale
Crayola
Crown Paints
Crowne Plaza
Cunard
Cuprinol
Currys
Daddies
Daily Mail
Dairylea
Danone
David Lloyd
De Vere Hotels
Debenhams
Deep Heat
Del Monte
Dell
De'Longhi

Denby
Dettol
Direct Line
Discovery
Disney
Disney Channel
Dolmio
Domestos
Domino's Pizza
Doritos
Dorset Cereals
Douwe Egberts
Dove
Dr Pepper
Dr. Oetker
Dulux
Dunlop
Duracell
Durex
Dyson
E.ON
E45
Early Learning Centre
easyJet
eBay
Eden Project
EDF Energy
EE
Elastoplast
Electrolux
Energizer
Ernest Jones
Esso
Europcar
Eurostar
Eurotunnel
evian
Expedia
Facebook
Fairy
Fanta
Farley's
Febreze
Felix
Ferrero Rocher
Financial Times
Finish
First Choice
Fisher-Price
Flash
Flora
Flymo
Foot Locker
Ford
Foster's
Fox's Biscuits
Fred Perry
Freeview
French Connection
Galaxy
Gap
Garmin
Garnier
Gatwick Airport
Gaviscon
George Foreman
Gillette
Ginsters
Glenfiddich
Goodyear
Google
Gordon's
GOURMET
Gourmet Burger Kitchen
Great Ormond
    Street Hospital
Green & Black's Organic
Green Flag
Green Giant
Greggs

Grolsch
Guinness
Gumtree
H&M
Häagen-Dazs
Habitat
Halfords
Halfords Autocentre
Halifax
Hallmark
Halls
Hamleys
Hard Rock Cafe
Hardys
Haribo
Harpic
Head & Shoulders
Heart
Heathrow
Heineken
Heinz
Hellmann's
Helly Hansen
Help for Heroes
Herbal Essences
Hertz
Highland Spring
Hilton Hotels & Resorts
Holiday Inn
Holland & Barrett
Homebase
Homepride
Hoover
Hornby
Hotpoint
House of Fraser
Hovis
HP
HP Sauce
HSBC
HTC
Huggies
Iams
Iceland
IKEA
IMODIUM
Imperial Leather
innocent
Instagram
IRN-BRU
ITV
J2O
Jack Daniel's
Jacob's
Jacob's Creek
Jaeger
Jaguar
Jameson
JD Sports
Jessops
Jim Beam
John Lewis
John West
Johnnie Walker
JOHNSON's Baby
Jordans
Karen Millen
Kellogg's
Kenco
Kenwood
Kenwood (Kitchen
    Appliances)
KETTLE Chips
Kew Gardens
KFC
Kinder
Kindle
Kingsmill
KitKat
Kleenex

Knorr
KP
Kronenbourg 1664
Kuoni
Kwik Fit
Lacoste
Ladbrokes
Ladybird
Lakeland
Land Rover
lastminute.com
Lea & Perrins
LEGO
LEGOLAND
LEGOLAND
    Discovery Centre
Lemsip
Lenor
Lexus
LG
Lidl
Lil-Lets
Linda McCartney
Lindeman's
Lindt
Links Of London
Listerine
Liverpool FC
Lloyds Bank
LloydsPharmacy
Lockets
Longleat
L'Oréal Elvive
Loyd Grossman
Lucozade
Lurpak
Lynx
M&M's
Maclaren
Macleans
Macmillan
    Cancer Support
Madame Tussauds
Magic
Magners Irish Cider
Magnet
Magnum
Maltesers
Mamas & Papas
Manchester Airport
Manchester City FC
Manchester United
Maplin
Mappin & Webb
Marie Curie
    Cancer Care
Marks & Spencer
Marmite
Marriott Hotels
    & Resorts
Mars
Martini
MasterCard
McCain
McCoy's
McDonald's
McDougalls
McVitie's
Meccano
Mercedes-Benz
Michelin
Microsoft
Miele
Milkybar
Millets
MINI
Miracle-Gro
Miss Selfridge
Molton Brown
Moneysupermarket.com

Monsoon
Morphy Richards
Morrisons
Mothercare
Mr Kipling
Mr Muscle
Mr Sheen
Müller
Nando's
National Express
National Geographic
National Trust
Nationwide
Nature Valley
Nescafé
Nesquik
Netflix
Neutrogena
New Covent
    Garden Soup Co.
New Look
Next
Nicky Clarke
Nicorette
Night Nurse
Nike
Nikon
Nintendo
Nivea
NSPCC
Nurofen
Nutella
O2
Oasis
Ocado
Ocean Spray
Odeon
Olay
Old Spice
Olympus
Omega
Optrex
Oral-B
Oreo
Oxfam
OXO
P&O Cruises
P&O Ferries
Palmolive
Pampers
Panadol
Panasonic
Pandora
Pantene
Patak's
PAXO
PayPal
PC World
Pedigree
Pepsi
Peroni
Perrier
Persil
Pets at Home
PG Tips
Philadelphia
Philips
Philips AVENT
Pilgrims Choice
Pimm's
Pirelli
Piriton
Pizza Hut
Play-Doh
PLAYMOBIL
PlayStation
Pledge
Plenty
Post Office
Premier Inn

Pret A Manger
Princess Cruises
Pringles
Prudential
Puma
Purina
Pyrex
Quaker Oats
Quality Street
Quorn
RAC
Radisson Blu
Radisson Blu
    Edwardian, London
Radox
Raleigh
Red Bull
Reebok
Regatta
Rennie
Ribena
Rightmove
River Island
RNLI
Robertson's
Robinsons
Rolex
Ronseal
Rotary
Rowntree's
Royal Albert Hall
Royal British Legion
ROYAL CANIN
Royal Caribbean
    International
Royal Doulton
Royal Worcester
RSPCA
Russell & Bromley
Russell Hobbs
Ryvita
S.Pellegrino
Sainsbury's
Samsung
San Miguel
Sanatogen
Sandals Resorts
Santander
Sarson's
Save the Children
Savlon
Scalextric
schuh
Schwartz
Schwarzkopf
Schweppes
Scottish Widows
Scott's Porage Oats
Screwfix
SEA LIFE Centres
Seiko
Selfridges
Sensodyne
Seven Seas
Sharwood's
Sheba
Shell
Shredded Wheat
Siemens
Silentnight Beds
Silver Cross
Silver Spoon
Simple
Sky
Skype
Slazenger
Slumberland
SMA
Smeg
Smirnoff

Sony
Southern Comfort
Specsavers
Speedo
SportsDirect.com
Sprite
St John Ambulance
Standard Life
Starbucks
Stella Artois
Strepsils
Strongbow
Subway
Sudafed
Sudocrem
Superdrug
Superdry
Sure
Swarovski
Swatch
Tabasco
TAG Heuer
Tampax
Tango
Tassimo
Tate & Lyle Cane Sugar
Taylor Wimpey
Taylors of Harrogate
TCP
Ted Baker
Tefal
Tempur
Tesco
Tetley
Texaco
The Body Shop
The Co-operative
The Daily Telegraph
The Famous Grouse
The Guardian
The Independent
The National Lottery
The North Face
The Observer
The Salvation Army
The Times
The Warner Bros. Studio
    Tour London – The
    Making of Harry Potter
Thomas Cook
Thomson Holidays
Thorntons
Thorpe Park
Ticketmaster
Timex
Tissot
Toblerone
Tommee Tippee
TomTom
Tomy
TONI&GUY
Topman
Topshop
Toshiba
Toyota
Toys R Us
Trainline
Travelodge
TRESemmé
TripAdvisor
trivago
Tropicana
Turtle Wax
Twinings
Twitter
Twix
Typhoo
Umbro
Uncle Ben's
Vanish

Vaseline
Veet
Velvet
Vicks
Vidal Sassoon
Virgin Active
Virgin Atlantic
Virgin Holidays
Virgin Media
Virgin Mobile
Virgin Trains
Visa
Vision Express
Vodafone
Volkswagen
Voltarol
Volvic
Volvo
VTech
Waitrose
Walkers
Wall's
Wall's Ice Cream
Warburtons
Waterford
Waterstones
WD-40
Wedgwood
Weetabix
WhatsApp
Whirlpool
Whiskas
WHSmith
Wickes
Wikipedia
Wilkinson Sword
William Hill
Winalot
Wrigley's
Xbox
Yahoo!
Yakult
Yeo Valley
Yorkshire Tea
Young's
YouTube
Zanussi
Zara
Zoopla
ZSL London Zoo
Zurich